THE DISAPPEARANCES

A Story of Exploration, Murder, and Mystery in the American West

SCOTT THYBONY

THE UNIVERSITY OF UTAH PRESS

Salt Lake City

The Defiance House Man colophon is a registered trademark
of the University of Utah Press. It is based on a four-foot-tall
Ancient Puebloan pictograph (late PIII) near Glen Canyon, Utah.

20 19 18 17 16   1 2 3 4 5

LIBRARY OF CONGRESS CATALOGING-IN-PUBLICATION DATA
Name: Thybony, Scott.
Title: The disappearances : a story of exploration, murder, and mystery in the
American West / Scott Thybony.
Description: Salt Lake City : The University of Utah Press, 2016. | Includes
bibliographical references and index.
Identifiers: LCCN 2015045229| ISBN 9781607814832 (paperback : alkaline paper) |
ISBN 9781607814849 (ebook)
Subjects: LCSH: Missing persons—Utah—History—20th century. | Missing persons—
Utah—Biography. | Thrapp, Dan L. | Garrett, Lucy, 1920–1991—Kidnapping, 1935. |
Ruess, Everett, 1914- | Utah—Biography. | Utah—Description and travel. | Wilderness
areas—Utah—History—20th century. | Utah—History—20th century.
Classification: LCC HV6762.U5 T47 2016 | DDC 362.76—dc23
LC record available at http://lccn.loc.gov/2015045229

Cover photo © jphilipg, *My Shadow*. From Flickr.com creative commons.

Printed and bound by Sheridan Books, Inc., Ann Arbor, Michigan.

Contents

ILLUSTRATIONS

Acknowledgments

My account of Dan Thrapp's journey relies heavily on the journals he kept. His family generously allowed me to use them and the many photographs he took. His daughter, Linda Nicholl, deserves special acknowledgment for coordinating communication among family members and encouraging my efforts. The main Thrapp archive lies at the Haley Memorial Library and History Center, where archivist Jim Bradshaw provided not only assistance in navigating the collection but also encouragement for the project. I also had a lively visit in Lubbock with Dan's sister Bea Zeeck, whose wit and sense of humor gave me a better understanding of his early years. For Dan's later years, I relied on the insights of his Tucson friend Bruce Dinges.

By foot, four-wheel drive, and sometimes by rope, Chuck LaRue and Tony Williams joined me in a range of investigative travels. Michael Behrendt, owner of the Horsethief Ranch, generously invited me to spend the night at his place, and the ranch caretaker, Ben Johnson, showed true hospitality by opening his home to a stranger. Archaeologist Winston Hurst helped identify some of the places photographed by Thrapp.

My primary sources for the disappearance of Andy Delaney were his daughter, JoAnn McCosh, and historian Mike Rose. For many years Mike has pursued his passion for the history of Utah's canyon country, interviewing many of the old-timers. He was generous with his time and sources during the research for this book, and I am grateful for his help.

My primary sources for the ordeal of Lucy Garrett were witness statements given under oath prior to the trial of James Clinton Palmer. I also relied on a taped account by former sheriff Lawrence Palmer and the written statements and oral histories from men involved in the manhunt. Special thanks go to Clyde and Linda Sconce, Melvin Gaines, Helen Shumway, and Rigby Wright. They opened their homes and memories, tolerated my prying questions with grace, and gave me a greater understanding of the tragic events that unfolded so long ago. Without the help of Mike Rose, I would have been hard-pressed to locate the last camp of William Oliver and Norris Shumway. A number of leads came from Gene Foushee, Don Fowler, Ronny Glossup, Brandt Hart, Steve Lacy, John Sellers, and LaVerne Tate. And when it came down to the actual writing, Tom Bailey, Kip Stratton, and Jack Vernon offered useful suggestions.

My primary sources on Everett Ruess were his letters and diaries, augmented by a trove of material archived at the J. Willard Marriott Library, University of Utah. During my research I had useful exchanges with Philip Fradkin, David Roberts, and Bud Rusho—all biographers of Everett Ruess. And Roberts generously invited me to accompany him on a hunt for a "NEMO" inscription with Greg Funseth, the software engineer who located it. Although Roberts and I disagreed on the identity of the bones from Comb Ridge, our overlapping interests led to hours of wide-ranging conversations in the field. During the Comb Ridge Man controversy, I was in contact with a number of skeptics who shared their ideas with me. Paul Leatherbury was the most diligent in pursuing overlooked lines of evidence, and I appreciate his generosity in sharing his findings. Kevin Jones, Diane Orr, Chuck LaRue, Mike Rose, Ken Sanders, and Drifter Smith all weighed in on the identity of the burial. And Ken Sleight deserves a special mention for the years of research he has put into the Everett Ruess mystery. He's not shy about expressing his opinions, and we had a good conversation one day at the Pack Creek Ranch.

Also providing help on various aspects of the story were Rick Nelson, Bill Stone, Nate Thompson, Rigby Wright, and Merri McKee, daughter of Brad McKee from the Rainbow Bridge–Monument Valley Expedition. Navajos Leo Manheimer and Chester Salt added to my understanding of Everett's travels, while two Hopi, Delfred Leslie and Gary Tso, helped put into perspective the artist's claim of having participated in a Hopi ceremonial dance. Escalante residents Arnold Alvey, Roe Barney, and DeLane Griffin provided useful leads and good stories. To historian Jerry Roundy I owe special thanks for putting into context the events of 1934 and 1935. And I owe a debt to the many skilled archivists, especially Roy Webb and Liz Rogers, who helped me sort through both the obvious and the obscure. Finally, cowboy poet and mule packer E. T. Collinsworth provided his commentary on the feasibility of swimming a pack horse across a river at flood stage. "To attempt it," he said, "would be plumb-ass crazy."

A NOTE TO READERS

You will find this book divided into three parts, following natural fault lines. Each tells the story of a person who went missing in the canyons of the American Southwest at the same moment in time. Searchers scoured the three-rivers country, where the Green, Colorado, and San Juan Rivers join, for two of them. A posse chased after the third. My fascination with the girl, who was kidnapped and taken far from home, and two young men, who set off on adventures of their own, grew stronger the more I learned about them. And as I wrote, their longings and struggles drew me deeper into their lives. I found myself traveling with Dan Thrapp, Lucy Garrett, and Everett Ruess into what for them was the unknown, a journey we all take in different ways.

Although set in the 1930s, this book includes sections called "field-notes," first-person accounts taken mostly from the research phase of my writing. For some readers, including my wife, history comes alive only when the past connects with the present. So the fieldnotes open a way into the story and show how the canyon country still has its resident characters and adventures for the choosing. In the epilogue I carry the story forward, letting readers know what became of the key individuals.

Because this is a work of nonfiction, all people in it are real, and their quoted statements come from the most reliable sources available. These include court documents and oral histories, letters and telegrams, magazine and newspaper accounts, journal entries, and interviews I've conducted. During the course of writing this book, many people have generously given their time and their advice, and some have opened their lives to me. My thanks cannot be expressed properly, but I've made an attempt to acknowledge their help.

Thrapp, Garrett, and Ruess journeyed into the Four Corners region before legendary film director John Ford discovered it. Soon after the events of 1934 and 1935, he would transform the landscape into an American icon familiar throughout the world. Their stories let you return to one of the most remarkable regions of America when much of it was still wild country, still parts unknown.

PROLOGUE

Missing, Feared Lost

A stack of old newspaper articles sat on my desk in the under-the-stairs office where I work. My plan was to write an extended essay on the exploration of ruins, and I was going through research material dating back seventy-five years. Most accounts of archaeological discovery have focused on the scientific expeditions, the professional excavators, and sometimes the pothunters. I needed an example of exploration in its purest form. I wanted to find the spark behind these endeavors, the impulse driving such a deep fascination with the past. I was searching for someone who had undertaken an expedition for the sheer adventure of it.

Among the books and files crowding my office were remnants of travels I had taken. On a shelf lay a moose-hide pouch, beaded and bloodstained, from the far reaches of Canada next to a shard of meteoric glass from deep in the Sahara Desert. And nearby hung an early map of North America, showing a mythical river lying beyond the Spanish settlements and Pueblo Indian villages of the Southwest. The rest was left blank, an immense territory spreading westward, still unexplored and unnamed. To fill up the empty space the cartographer had labeled it "Parts Unknown" and left it at that.

These blank spots have a gravitational pull for some of us, and at that moment I was being drawn into a story set in one of the most remote corners of America. Working through the articles, I came across one from the *Salt Lake Tribune* dated February 27, 1935. The headline caught my eye:

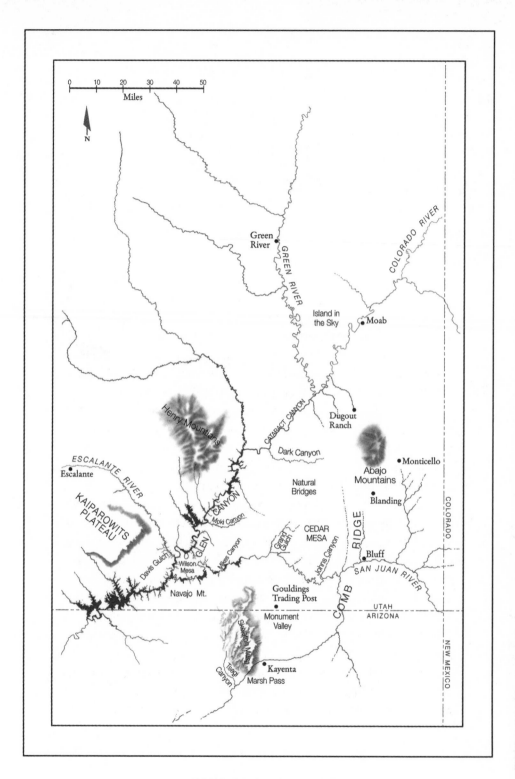

FOUR CORNERS COUNTRY

Southern Utah Wastes
Veil Fate of Scientist
Missing Three Months

Young Explorer Believed Dead or Fighting for Life in Mysterious Dark Canyon;
Indian Legends Lured Lost Man

And I began to read.

In the trackless wastes of southern Utah in which he disappeared last November, Daniel L. Thrapp, 21-year-old scientist on leave from the American Museum of Natural History, Tuesday was believed to be either dead or fighting for life in a land where the chances of natural sustenance are exceedingly slim. . . .

He accompanied a party of scientists on a fossil hunt in Wyoming last summer, following which he entered the Dark canyon, near Hanksville, alone in a search for undiscovered cliff dwellings. At that time he carried provisions for only two weeks. Leaving a ranch 60 miles west of Greenriver, Utah, on November 28, he entered the canyon. Since then there has been no word as to his fate. . . . Young Thrapp was regarded in scientific circles as one of the most promising of the young explorers now seeking to learn secrets of unknown sections of the country.

That was what I needed. In the fall of 1934, I learned, Dan Thrapp wrapped up a field season spent excavating dinosaur bones. Instead of returning to New York City, he gave in to the pull of the unknown and undertook a long solo journey across southeastern Utah. The young scientist had heard rumors of undisturbed prehistoric cliff houses in Dark Canyon and set out to find them. He rode south on horseback from Island in the Sky, traveling without a map across one of the most broken and barren landscapes on the face of the earth. Somewhere in the maze of canyons the twenty-one-year-old went missing, and when he was long overdue a ground and air search began.

My own investigation started on a snow-covered road beyond a landmark known as the Bears Ears, a pair of high-elevation mesas. A friend and I were heading toward a branch of Dark Canyon, the place Dan had wanted to reach. What had drawn him, rumors of pristine ruins, drew us.

As navigator, Tony Williams directed me down increasingly obscure roads, difficult to find under a foot of snow. As a classics scholar turned Colorado River boatman, he had a taste for the remote. We had made trips together for years into big, empty spaces, having found our abilities and interests closely matched.

Where the last track ended, I parked the truck and scouted for a way below the rim cliff. At a break I descended a talus slope, slippery with snow and ice, while Tony found his own way. I kicked footholds downward as a gust of wind blew a load of snow from a tree limb, creating a momentary whiteout. When it cleared I glanced below into a lost world. Snow-heavy branches framed a perfect stone house illuminated by sunlight. It was set inside a half-dome pocket on the cliff face, an ancient storehouse standing unruined for 750 years.

Reaching it, we found a row of vigas supporting an intact roof, each beam jutting out four feet and casting an even longer shadow. The two of us explored the site, moving carefully to avoid damaging the masonry walls still standing true. The structure was divided into a pair of granaries with a drift of thumb-length corncobs remaining in one and the interior walls holding the prints of fingers pressed into the plaster when wet. Even in a region known for well-preserved archaeological sites, this place was exceptional. The cliff house showed no signs of having aged over the centuries, conveying the sense of a past still present but largely undetected, the way stars continue to shine even at midday.

As the light angled low from the Southwest, Tony and I returned to the truck and headed to warmer elevations for a place to camp. We retraced our route by threading between the Bears Ears and switchbacking down to Cedar Mesa, down from the fir and ponderosa forest to the piñon-juniper tablelands and sagebrush flats. The two of us had previously explored the surrounding archaeological wilderness and knew each fold of rock held the possibility of a cliff house or wall of ancient pictographs. Paralleling the rim of Johns Canyon, the paved road ended at the Mokee Dugway, where the land itself seemed to end, and a gravel road whipped back and forth down the cliff side.

At the foot of the mesa we skirted the Valley of the Gods and turned west onto a dirt road leading to Johns Canyon, a branch of the San Juan River. Considered a good back road by local standards, it had enough rough and ragged cuts to discourage the casual visitor. We continued on across a gaunt land worn to tendon and bone, a cliff-bound stretch of country new to both of us. And what we found at the end of the road came as a surprise. It entered a box canyon sheltering a grove of spring-fed cottonwoods, and the place was deserted. We hadn't seen a single truck on the way in, and even more puzzling was the lack of any ranch buildings. Water in the desert draws life from all points of the compass, but for some reason no one lived here.

Next day we headed back and stopped for lunch at a café in Mexican Hat on the San Juan. As we waited for our order, an old-timer walked in with white hair spiking out like rime frost from under a ball cap. Taking a seat at the next table, he gave his name as "Gaines" and left it at that. His blue eyes had been bleached pale by years in the open, and he spoke with a western accent that hollowed out the vowels. Still curious about Johns Canyon, Tony asked Gaines why no one had homesteaded it. The seventy-eight year old paused a moment before settling in to tell us about events in the late winter of 1935.

"Well," he began, "it's a hell of a long story. This young girl, Johnnie Ray, she was thirteen years old when she come into this country, just a girl."[1] Gaines told us about the woodcutter's daughter from Texas who had been tricked into heading west by a man who had murdered her father. Lawmen had traced them to New Mexico, where the trail went cold. Taking her west into Utah, the fugitive ended up in an isolated canyon along the San Juan River.

The girl caught my interest, and I learned her real name was Lucile Garrett. She had been held captive at the same time Dan Thrapp was reported missing. A front-page account in the March 4, 1935, edition of the *Deseret News* updated readers on the fate of Dan Thrapp. It was posted by a reporter who had searched for the young scientist by flying over the canyons in a biplane. Beneath it was a story about the manhunt for Lucy and her kidnapper:

Posse Trails
Slayer in War
Over Grazing

Two Dead, Bodies Hidden in Wasteland of San Juan

The article began:

Two Blanding men are dead and their slain bodies hidden somewhere in the trackless wastes of San Juan county, while more than 40 possemen, balked by heavy snows, trail the killer, alleged to be Jim Palmer, reputed outlaw and desperado, who is believed heading for Old Mexico.

And a shorter article appeared on the same front page under the head-line "Missing Artist Feared Dead." It described the search for Everett Ruess, a young wanderer from Los Angeles who had vanished in the Hole-in-the-Rock country. His story is well known and often told. On each new trek, the artist traveled into more distant country with his sketchbook, diary, and a knack for turning his travels into aesthetic adventures. Pushing deeper into the canyons, he sought to live more intensely, wanting to be swallowed by the beauty of rock and sky. And then he disappeared.

All three incidents played out in the tangle of canyons and slickrock expanses of southeastern Utah. All three people were missing and feared lost; all were young. This unusual convergence of events was intriguing, and an idea began to take shape. I would find out what had happened to the scientist, the woodcutter's daughter, and the artist. Investigating the murders and even the madness, I would learn what had been left untold. And I would try to understand the wonder and dread they had experienced in a place so different from any they had known before. Knowing that the terrain might still hold some trace of their travels, I began gathering clues.

PART 1

THE BONE HUNTER

Dan Thrapp

THE EXPEDITION

Each trip has a starting point, a milepost 0, and only later as the distance unfolds does the real beginning become apparent. For Dan Thrapp, the journey began below the Big Horn Mountains with the first shovel of dirt he dug from the ground.

He found himself moving deeper back in time, descending into worlds so old the mud had turned to stone and the river gravels to solid rock. Under a vast Wyoming sky, the young paleontologist shoveled away the fill from an earlier investigation, slowly uncovering ancient bones turned to dark fossils. At first glance the skeletal remains appeared to be a random scattering, and then a certain order emerged as his eye picked out a column of fourteen linked vertebrae. And then another nearby. On his first excavation, Dan L. Thrapp was facing the massive tailbones of two dinosaurs disappearing into the claystone. He began to follow the bones below the surface.

JUNE 1934

It was a new field season, and the crew from the American Museum of Natural History continued to expose dinosaur fossils on a day in late spring. Many of the surrounding hilltops were capped with the striking blues and reds of claystone. Behind them, jagged flatirons angled upward at the foot of the Big Horn Mountains, cresting into summits still snowcapped. And to the west lay the basin country under a high plains sky so expansive that the horizons stretched beyond the chance of ever reaching them. Each day the excavation team of ten men worked deeper into the hillside to level the site and expose a growing jumble of interlocked fossils.

As they stripped back one layer after another, they uncovered bones so immense that all sense of human scale collapsed. Vertebrae as thick as the trunk of a palm tree emerged, and they uncovered a femur nearly as large as the person kneeling next to it. The crew faced a mass of tangled bone as they worked the fossil quarry. With the excitement building, twenty-year-old Dan Thrapp kept shoveling. An expedition-grade fedora shaded the paleontologist's gray eyes and long, narrow face. Nearly six feet tall, he wore a pair of jeans and a chambray shirt hanging on a lean frame. His passion for the West had grown only stronger during his time in New York City, and now all the pieces of his dream were falling into place.

His travels had begun several years before by going against the wishes of his parents, the way adventures often begin. Unable to settle down to the academic routine at the University of Wisconsin, his grades had suffered and school became a struggle. He spent days facing a blackboard, longing to get outside the classroom and engage the world firsthand. Increasingly restless, Dan dropped out of college at the end of his freshman year and headed west without telling his parents. After working as a cowboy on a ranch in Lordsburg, New Mexico, he took to the open road when the job ended.

Hordes of young men were hitchhiking and riding the rails by necessity during the 1930s. Dan did it by choice, wanting to see the western states firsthand. As he crisscrossed the land, new experiences poured in. He drank his first shot of whiskey and in Las Vegas witnessed a fight between a drunk and a madman at Mac and Bob's gambling joint. In a Montana town Dan complained about "the crummy jail and a lousy police force."[1] At times he went hungry and had to knock on the doors of strangers, offering to mop floors or split firewood for meals. Sometimes he slept in flophouses or worked as a handyman for room and board. With little money, he spent his evenings in libraries, pouring through books of faraway travels and exploration. Despite the hard times, his sense of humor remained intact. "Doggone!" he wrote in his journal. "The other night I dreamt of Sally. If I could have a dream like that every time I went to sleep—I'd sleep all the time."[2]

Arriving in New York City in the summer of 1933, Dan began looking for work and didn't take long to find it. Not only did he manage to land a job at the prestigious American Museum of Natural History, but he did so in the middle of the Great Depression, without a college degree, and with no formal training. In July he began work as a volunteer "bone duster," a position that brought him into contact with some of the finest scientists and explorers of the day. Dan would wander through the museum halls, watching one crew mount an African lion and another assemble a dinosaur skeleton from twenty thousand pieces of fossil bone. Everywhere he turned he found something unexpected to feed his curiosity.

A world of possibilities opened up, and he pursued his interest in exploration by regularly attending lectures at the Explorers Club. And one night he pushed through a crowd of fifty thousand spectators at Roosevelt Field to watch Wiley Post land his plane to complete the first solo flight around the world. By January Dan had worked his way into a paying position as a fossil preparator, cleaning and sorting specimens for curator Barnum Brown. One of the greatest American paleontologists, Barnum had traveled the world collecting tons of fossil bones for the museum, including the first specimen of *Tyrannosaurus rex*. "Old Barnum Brown is the big shot," Dan wrote in a letter home. "He's the curator of fossil vertebrates and has an egg shaped head that is just as bald as an egg...but he's a good egg."[3]

The young paleontologist soon learned that his boss was planning an expedition to excavate dinosaur fossils during the coming field season. Dan wanted to be part of the action and was determined to land a slot on the excavation team. Normally quiet and self-contained, he let nothing stop him once he made up his mind.

Reporters had caught wind of the expedition, and the publicity generated hundreds of applications from young men wanting to sign on. But Dan had the jump on them and went directly to Barnum with a proposition. If the paleontologist would agree to take him along, he would work for nothing and furnish his own transportation to the site if necessary. Being a field scientist, Barnum understood the young man's enthusiasm but delayed making a decision. When Dan didn't hear from him for several days, he confronted the curator and threatened to quit unless he got a raise and a position on the expedition. To his surprise, Barnum agreed in principle, and a few weeks later the young scientist received official word of his acceptance. He was offered fifty dollars a month, a pay cut, but the bone duster was elated by the opportunity.

On May 21, 1934, Dan left the city with other expedition members as a Paramount cameraman shot newsreel footage of their departure. They drove cross-country in a Buick touring car and made a brief stop at Dan's home in West Chicago, Illinois—not the west side of Chicago but a railroad town of four thousand inhabitants on its outskirts. After six days of driving they reached the National Hotel in Billings, Montana, the staging point for the expedition, where additional crew members joined them. Barnum would come out later in the season, once the work got rolling.

The night before leaving for the dinosaur site in northern Wyoming, Dan had a date with a waitress at the hotel and didn't make it back to his room until two thirty in the morning. Less than three hours later he was behind the wheel of a Ford truck heading south on his first scientific expedition. He had never driven a truck before but soon got the hang of it. After covering 175 miles he reached the Howe Ranch, at the foot of the Big Horn Mountains, and that night in camp he lay awake listening to the cry of a coyote in the distance, content to have found his way west again.

Over the weekend the excavation team focused on setting up a camp below the fossil quarry. They pitched their canvas-wall tents out of sight of the ranch house and its scatter of outbuildings. The place belonged to Barker Howe, an eighty-four-year-old homesteader who had guided Barnum Brown to the first bones several years before. "A windstorm was carrying plenty of dust," Dan wrote in his journal, "since this country had had no rain to speak of since last summer and no moisture since the last snow."[4] Dust storms had ravaged the plains states, laying waste to vast areas and impacting a much greater region. Another dust storm swept across the Big Horn Basin the next day, and no one gave it much thought. A hard drought had gripped the region for so long that dealing with it had become second nature for the local ranchers.

With the digging set to begin, Dan needed to drive into the town of Greybull to have an abscessed tooth pulled. Most of the roads were little more than improved wagon tracks, and many were washed out. On his way back to camp he took a wrong turn among the branching two-tracks. When he realized his mistake he turned around instead of taking a shortcut, unwilling to admit he had gotten lost. "I'll be damned," he wrote, "if I'd let these guys think I couldn't find my way home."[5]

Below the Bighorns

Rain followed the dust storms, slowing work at the dig. When the weather improved, the excavators put in full days at the quarry, going strong from the cool of morning through the heat and glare of the afternoons. They were digging in the Morrison Formation, a deposit dating to the Late Jurassic period, about 150 million years ago. The bones lay in a bed of claystone two feet thick, sandwiched between layers of sandstone. To open a new section of the quarry, a team of horses was brought in. Dan volunteered to assist, since he knew how to handle a plow and Fresno scraper. "It was my job," he wrote, "to shake the plow and handle the Fresno—a devil-invented bit of machinery that runs on runners and is so hooked up to the horses that it whips the man on the handle around according to the way the horses pull."[1]

June to November 1934

When the crew had uncovered enough of the site to realize its extent, Dan recognized they had discovered a Jurassic graveyard. "So far have found at least 6 all twisted up & so many bones matted together probably a dozen more," he noted, "and we've just begun. It's the greatest find since the last century and probably the greatest dinosaur bed ever discovered. It may fizzle out, but we don't see how it can. It gets bigger and more complicated every day."[2]

They had uncovered remains of several types of sauropod, including *Camarasaurus*, *Diplodocus*, and *Apatosaurus*. Standing about fourteen feet tall and ranging up to forty feet in length, these were huge creatures weighing several tons with whiplike tails and improbably small heads set on the end of long necks. They bore a striking resemblance to Dino the Dinosaur, the popular mascot of Sinclair Oil, the expedition sponsor.

Barnum Brown arrived in early July and told a reporter from the *New York Times* that the site was one of the most important dinosaur deposits ever discovered in this country. "In more than thirty years of fossil-hunting," he said, "I have never found a more intriguing or difficult problem of excavation.... This welter of bones, the biggest and most complex I have ever seen, is so mixed up that we cannot take them out of the ground until the entire site has been excavated and charts and photographs made showing the position of the skeletons.... Instead of having two sauropods by the tail, we have at least twelve, with more threatening to crop up at any moment."[3] The complexity was nearly overwhelming.

As Barnum inspected the Howe Quarry, he was viewing the dinosaur remains through a lifetime of field experience. With his practiced eye, he could stand before a rock exposure and watch the epochs pass like time-lapse photography, seeing a dune field sink below the sea or a mountain rise from the plains. A single glance was enough to compress an immense accumulation of time, and in this dinosaur graveyard he saw something intriguing. The crew had uncovered a dozen immense leg bones standing upright on attached feet, showing no signs of having been water worn or scattered by scavengers. This indicated the animals had become mired in the mud along a riverbank or stuck in quicksand. The dinosaurs were still standing in place exactly where they had died millions of years before.

At the end of each day, Barnum would gather the crew around him. They set folding chairs next to a campfire and tuned in a cumbersome battery-operated radio or listened to Barnum recount one of his far-flung adventures. The fossil hunter had fallen into the crater of an extinct volcano in New Mexico on one expedition, had crossed the deserts of Ethiopia by camel, and had once been shipwrecked south of Tierra del Fuego. And no matter how remote the expedition, he managed to dress impeccably while in the field. At the Howe Quarry he wore khakis, a pressed white shirt, and a bow tie. His round glasses and pith helmet enhanced the image of a fastidious scientist-explorer, but despite his appearance no one doubted who was in charge. "Brown is plenty tough when he has to be," Dan noted. "He's the type of adventurer you read about. Instead of running guns or prospecting for gold, bones are his field. He's a tough man to cross."[4]

With Barnum now directing operations, the national media increased their coverage, and visitors soon overran the site. A constant stream of cars snaked along the hogback ridge leading to the dinosaur graveyard. So many curiosity seekers got lost on the way that the crew had to place road signs to direct them to the bone quarry. One souvenir hunter managed to slip away with a fossil rib, only to return it later with an apologetic note, while the more conscientious visitors snatched only the hand-painted road signs. The excavating continued, and by early August the quarry appeared to have been worked out. Barnum talked about shifting his efforts to Dinosaur National Monument the next year and wanted Dan to return with him. But the young excavator, who had turned twenty-one years old, longed for a more distant country, perhaps a trip to the wilds of Labrador. So he delayed giving Barnum a firm commitment.

Once the quarry had been mapped, the difficult process began of removing the individual bones from the chaotic mass. The diggers applied two coats of shellac to each specimen, followed by a layer of rice paper and a final coat of burlap soaked in plaster. After the reverse side was treated, the bone was packed in a straw-padded box for shipment back to the museum. Collecting the fossils now became a race against time, since many rested on pedestals of crumbly claystone, vulnerable to erosion. If rain threatened, the crew had to cover the site to protect it from damage. When a rainstorm caught them by surprise one night, Barnum dragged Dan and the others out of bed and had them scurry around with lanterns, pulling canvas tarps over the diggings.

By now Dan had traded in his fedora for a cowboy hat. After work he often climbed on Smoky, a black horse he had bought for thirty dollars on the promise of a twenty-dollar buyback at the end of the season. "I think it will be a valuable experience for me in view of my proposed Utah trip this fall," he wrote. "The horse needs a lot of hard riding, and so do I."[5] Participating in a dinosaur dig would have satisfied most adventurous young men, but Dan was already preparing his next move.

When the American Museum–Sinclair Expedition ended, he planned to undertake a solo exploration through southern Utah to search for traces of the human past. History fascinated him, and he had heard a rumor of pristine cliff dwellings hidden deep in the canyons. To reach them he would need horses, one to ride and the other to pack his gear. As a little boy in West Chicago, he used to wait by the window for the trash collector to drive

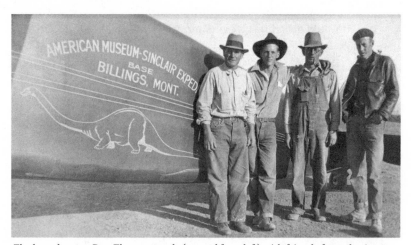

The bone hunter. Dan Thrapp stands (*second from left*) with friends from the American Museum of Natural History expedition. During the 1934 field season, he excavated dinosaur fossils at a site in Wyoming. Courtesy of the Haley Memorial Library and History Center.

by with a horse-drawn wagon. When it came into view, he would shout, "Hoss!"[6] It was his first spoken word, and he never lost his love of animals.

At times Dan joined the neighboring ranchers to round up cattle or chase wild horses, and one occasion turned into an ordeal when he helped a cowboy retrieve some horses. Riding back, the two of them left the trail and took a shortcut across a canyon. "Sounds easy," Dan wrote in his journal, "but have you ever tried to lead a horse down a sixty or seventy degree slope with high-heeled boots on your feet and the slope slippery and shaley to boot?"[7] Reaching the bottom, they were forced to cut steps up the opposite side with their pocket knives to give their horses enough traction to climb out. "Anyway, it was a great experience—and not particularly dangerous, providing you hang on to the reins so you don't fall too far and too fast and always travel fast enough and zigzaggy enough so your horse doesn't fall on you. All the time, however, you must pick your trail and not fall into a blind alley."

Toward the end of summer he found a new interest besides horses. A cowgirl named Lola Walker, staying at a ranch on Beaver Creek, caught his eye. "She's the best woman rider I've ever seen. She can ride anything and isn't afraid of anything."[8] He made a point of seeing her again, and as their relationship deepened he learned about her past. Lola told him that her father had died when she was young and that her stepfather had spent ten years in prison for horse stealing. From the age of nine, she was forced to make her own way in the world. Dan was impressed.

The first snow of the season fell on September 19, coating the ground with four inches. That evening Dan showed up at the Ben Allen ranch and was alarmed to learn that a strange man had stalked Lola when she drove in the cows. She was still frightened, and after supper Dan accompanied her to the sheep wagon where she slept. They returned to the main house at midnight, and she accepted Mrs. Allen's offer to spend the night. When Lola went back to the wagon to get her things, Dan headed to the corral to check his horse.

Suddenly, he heard screams and ran to help as Ben came charging out of the house buck naked, firing his pistol. The rancher got tangled in the clothesline, and Dan found Lola kneeling on the ground a moment before she passed out. Ben fired another wild shot into the night and then returned to get his pants so he could help carry the girl inside. She had a lump on her head, scratches on her side, and a torn shirt. She soon revived and described being choked by the same man who had followed her earlier. He was trying to drag her away, she said, when the first shot scared him off. Dan sat up with her the rest of the night and in the morning rode back to the expedition camp for help. He returned with Dallas Hurst, a local ranch hand, and they searched the area. Unable to find any sign of the stranger, their suspicions turned toward Ben, but they lacked enough proof to accuse him. Lola soon moved out.

The Wyoming cowboy and the bone digger from Illinois became friends following the incident. The two of them briefly worked together at the dig and made a horseback trip high into the Big Horns to visit the Medicine Wheel, a prehistoric ceremonial site. But they usually spent their free time with Lola. One evening Dan rode over to the ranch where she was now staying. Dallas was already there, and they made popcorn and played cards until one in the morning. The three of them got along so well that Dan didn't consider the cowboy to be a rival. In the saddle a few hours later, he rode back to the quarry in time for work, nearly freezing his feet on the way. "That's real love," he noted in his journal. "Or something."[9]

With winter closing in, the expedition leaders hurried to shut down the dig. The crew had recovered bones from at least twenty dinosaurs, and Brown planned to mount three complete skeletons for display. The rest would be traded to other museums or used for research. On November 17 they loaded the last crate of fossil bones onto the train, filling an entire boxcar with 144 cases. Weighing thirty-two tons, it was the final collection of large sauropod fossils the American Museum would ever excavate.

On his last night, Dan drove into Greybull with Lola and Dallas to have a few beers and say good-bye. He was leaving Wyoming; they were staying. It was a sad parting since he had fallen in love with the cowgirl and considered the cowboy one of the finest people he had ever met. The following day Dan headed to Cheyenne, where he caught the train to Denver and points west. With the field season at an end, he now crossed the Rockies on the Denver, Rio Grande, and Western Railroad into a more distant land.

WEST OF SOLITUDE

The young explorer left the train at Green River, Utah, and checked into the Midland Hotel. He planned to spend a few days in town buying supplies before continuing south. In that direction lay the edge of the unknown, a vast labyrinth of canyon rifts and plateaus cut off by barrier cliffs. Wild rivers divided it, and drifts of snow covered the higher reaches. The terrain presented a bewildering complexity, and crossing it without maps would be a test of his determination, and luck. Dan Thrapp had no real idea of the dangers he faced or the time it would take him to cross the canyons.

LATE NOVEMBER 1934

A thin haze scattered the light and softened the lines of the far cliffs as Dan stepped out of the hotel to get his bearings. He walked up Broadway and down Main, passing a dozen or so brick buildings facing the unpaved streets of Green River. Frame houses stood widely spaced along the side lanes, built by residents who felt no need to press tightly together in the presence of such raw and open country. As he looked things over, Dan came upon a man with a stubble beard and beat-up fedora, bundled in a heavy coat against the cold. His appearance was not unusual in those hard-hit days, but what set him apart was his companion. The man was out for a stroll with a coyote fastened on the end of a long chain leash.

Tree branches stood bare, and with winter closing in the air had a bite to it. Dan continued through town until he reached the river's edge. The Green River descends from headwaters in the Wind River Mountains of Wyoming, running strong and turbulent for hundreds of miles through a string of can-yons. One of the great rivers of the West, it breaks from Desolation and Gray Canyons to flow through a stretch of open country, passing the town that took its name, before threading down Labyrinth and Stillwater Canyons.

In 1883 the town was laid out where the rails crossed the river, east of a siding called Sphinx and west of Solitude. The railroad withdrew most of its operations several years later, leaving behind a scaled-down settlement where trains paused only long enough to take on coal and water. When Dan arrived it was a trade center for local farmers, miners, and a few ranchers in from the San Rafael Desert and the Book Cliffs. Far from any city, Green River was an outlier on the fringe of a vast cauldron of slickrock and sunken rivers to the south. Scientific expeditions used it as a staging area for inves-tigating the archaeology of the region and the much deeper geological past. For Dan, it became a gateway to an older West.

The region south of town was so isolated that the currents of change had bypassed it, leaving in place a relict frontier where people maintained an ethic of tough individualism, hard work, and indifference, if not outright hostility, to government authority. The immense blank spot on the map drew not only the adventurous but the outcast as well. Beyond the normal reach of the law and conventions of the wider society, it harbored both saint and sinner, renegade and recluse. At the time, no reliable maps existed of the region, spreading out for thousands of square miles beyond the converging lines of the Green, Colorado, and San Juan Rivers. Only a handful of trails entered it. A National Geographic Society expedition had crossed this cor-ner of Utah in the 1920s and found the early government maps to be "erro-neous and misleading."[1] The entire region, it reported, "must be regarded as unknown to the men of science and still unexplored." Dan's plan was to head south into the heart of the last great wilderness outside of Alaska. And then find his way back out.

He would need to thread a labyrinth of canyons and cross the Colorado to reach Dark Canyon, where he planned to follow up on rumors of undis-turbed cliff dwellings. He next had to ride across the immense cliff-broken topography and find a place to ford the San Juan River. His journey would end far to the south at the railroad town of Winslow, Arizona. Traversing a country unknown to him, he would need to negotiate more than four hun-dred hard miles. To carry enough supplies, he needed a saddle horse for himself and a packhorse for his food and gear. And to succeed, he would have to quickly hone his skills in route finding and horse handling, while tapping into a resourcefulness rarely needed growing up in Illinois. The trip would be physically demanding and dangerous, since even a minor injury so far from help could turn life-threatening. A mistake in judgment might strand him days away from anyone close enough to hear his cries for help.

Despite the cold, travel in this season had its advantages. Dan could avoid the intense heat of summer, have a better chance of finding water in potholes, and make river crossings at lower flows. On the other hand, he faced deep snow in the higher reaches, ice-thickened rivers, and long winter storms. Dan estimated it would take five or six weeks to complete the trip along an uncertain route, and he was anxious to leave town as soon as he could arrange the necessary logistics. As luck would have it, he made a key contact on his first day.

A local named Harry Tasker had worked for a US Geological Survey expedition on a run down the Green and Colorado Rivers. During the survey he had spent time at the mouth of Dark Canyon, so he was able to fill Dan in on the terrain. But more important, Tasker introduced him to Art Murry, who had a ranch sixty miles south of town. It straddled the Horsethief Trail, near Island in the Sky, an ideal location to launch his one-man expedition.

Murry was a cattleman who had managed to survive in an uncompromising land. He began breaking horses when he was eight years old and had a reputation for standing up to anyone trying to push onto his range. Rather than carry a gun, he relied on his own ingrained toughness. While Murry had made his share of enemies, the chief of police once came to his defense when an accusation of rustling surfaced. "Now I have no doubt but Murry," T. S. Brown said, "along with most of the other cattlemen, have branded calves belonging to the other fellow. Most of them have a fast horse and a long rope, but as I have said Murry has been on the up with me."[2] As a young man, Murry had been arrested for selling Indian ponies he didn't own and broke out of jail before standing trial. He never admitted to stealing horses, only to having been chased for stealing them. "He has offered to sell me two horses for $55," wrote Dan, "which he says will do the trick."[3]

The young explorer couldn't find anyone in town willing to cash his paychecks from the American Museum, so he wired his father in West Chicago for thirty dollars. It was the first time he had ever asked his dad for money, and while the amount appears small, it was a time when a pair of Levis sold for less than a dollar. That evening he returned to the Midland Hotel and sat in room 115, trying to untangle a knot of emotions. Before he could focus on his upcoming adventure, Dan had to come to terms with the girl he had left behind in Wyoming. He opened his journal and began to write.

"Lola is going to marry Dallas, and I'm glad in a way," he said, trying to convince himself it was for the best. "She's one of the dandiest girls I ever met. If I'd been in a position to, I'd have married her myself—if she'd have had me."[4] Dan went on to describe Dallas Hurst as one of the finest people he had ever met. Before proposing to Lola Walker, Dallas had asked him if he had any objections, and he admitted his feelings for her but didn't try to stand in the way. While Dan had made many friends, the cowboy stood out. "Dallas is the only guy out here that I think is good enough for her— and that's saying a lot for Dallas." And it said even more for the girl.

"That's one thing I loved about Lola," he continued. "She was as game as they come; she was always square—as square as she knew how to be, and she had a heart. . . . She always played the game square and she's the first girl I've met in a long, long time that I had any respect for—any at all. I'd do anything in the world for her and I hope she realizes it—as I think she does." Alone in his room he then backfilled, covering this episode of his life the way he had closed the bone quarry. With a difficult journey ahead of him, the explorer had no time for regrets. He would soon be traveling into a country empty of memories.

Over the next few days, Dan was busy working out the logistics of his expedition. He bought supplies at the W. F. Animus Hardware and Grocery and made his final arrangements with Murry. Dan mailed his last letter home without divulging his full plans to avoid causing his parents undue worry. Murry picked up Dan at the hotel in his Hudson coupe, and the two of them crossed the river and headed south. It was the last day of November 1934.

Dan was leaving behind a country of straight lines where the streets were laid out in an orderly grid, the railroad tracks ran true, and the telegraph line stretched to the horizon. By leaving Green River, he was cutting his tether to the outer world and entering a landscape weathered into interlocking pieces as intricate as a puzzle. The first twenty miles followed a bladed road, and then the rancher took a desert track so rough he could rarely go faster than ten miles per hour. A grader had never passed over it.

Cut by numerous washes, it climbed toward the high mesas over stretches of broken rock and deep sand. Sometimes the locals referred to these two-tracks as roads, and being the only routes of travel a few of them appeared on maps. But the true roads detoured around this outback country, not through it. The two travelers skirted massed cliffs and domes of pale Navajo sandstone, forerunners of the dramatic canyons ahead.

In a day of hard driving they gained one thousand feet in elevation. As the grade began to level off, the landscape spread out on all sides in an ocean of space. They had entered a place where everything came on a large scale—horizons stretching wider and canyons cutting deeper. No half measures, no scaling back to fit expectations. It was an immense, undivided country easy to lose yourself in. The rock and sand, the scatter of prickly brush and juniper, gave it a unique texture. Even the colors had a tactile quality, with the sky a glazed blue and the tracks left in the sand behind them a gritty red. Off to the south a narrow promontory formed a sky island above the confluence of the Green and Colorado Rivers hidden two thousand feet below. Cowboys called this wedge of high country "Between the Rivers."

The young scientist from the American Museum was entering the northern margin of a vast, empty quarter. The crest of Comb Ridge bounded it on the east, the spires of distant Monument Valley stood to the south, and far to the west stood the Aquarius Plateau. On maps it was left blank, but the Navajo Indians who crossed it knew the lay of the land, together with the Paiute who periodically took refuge in its rock fastness and the Ute who wintered in the canyons along its eastern edge. And it wasn't a complete blank to the handful of prospectors and trappers who barely ruffled the surface as they passed through the region. The few cowboys working within it followed a nomadic pattern of moving from camp to camp as the sparse grass and water dictated. They took shelter below overhanging ledges much like archaic hunters had done thousands of years before them. Anthropologist Edward T. Hall traveled through the region in 1932 and said it was "like traveling on another planet."[5]

The road approached the Horsethief Ranch, named for the trail running nearby. Cattle rustlers and other assorted outlaws had regularly camped at the lower spring, giving the country a lawless reputation long before Murry appeared on the scene. Turning up a draw into a box canyon, he drove to the ranch house folded between low sandstone cliffs. The cowboy introduced his wife, Muriel, who was only a few years older than Dan. She had grown up in the Robbers Roost country across the Green River at the far end of the Horsethief Trail, and her parents had often rubbed shoulders with Butch Cassidy and the Wild Bunch. As kids, Muriel and her brothers played a variation of cops-and-robbers where the outlaws always managed to outwit the marshal.

A low doorway led into the kitchen, and juniper beams, unusually long and straight, supported a low-pitched roof. Murry had quarried the local sandstone a few years before and laid it in thick walls with red-clay mortar, building the house solid enough to withstand a siege. To put together a workable ranch, he had bought the grazing rights to Grays Pasture on Island in the Sky, the lower benchlands along the White Rim, and the Green River bottoms. It was a handshake deal with no government officials involved or permits filed. That's the way they liked doing business. Neighbors generally respected each other's territory, but being open range anyone could crowd onto grasslands claimed by Murry if they had the nerve. And some tried. Disputes over grass and water often led to threats, intimidation, and the scattering of the other man's herd, but they rarely involved guns. When another rancher drove a herd of sheep onto lands claimed by Murry, push came to shove. He used his fists to intimidate the herders, and as events escalated some accused him of running his enemy's horses off the rim of Island in the Sky. After several years of conflict, aggravated by drought, the others pulled out for greener pastures. Murry had outlasted them, and by the time Dan arrived the range war had run its course.

HORSETHIEF RANCH

A row of buttes staked the bottom of the sky as I entered Utah through Monument Valley. Beyond it, the road continued north and took me through towns strung like knots on a cord between the San Juan and Colorado Rivers. The highway continued past Moab and cut through high desert toward the town of Green River. At Seven Mile Canyon I turned west and climbed in tight curves to the upper grasslands where slickrock outcropped in bare knuckles of sandstone. Before reaching Island in the Sky, I took an unpaved road leading to Hell Roaring Canyon on the Green River.

My destination was the Horsethief Ranch, not shown on the map, so I turned onto a narrow track leading toward a spring by the same name. It didn't look promising until I saw a hand-painted sign advising me to turn around, now. I kept going and before long found a ranch house tucked out of sight in a pocket of slickrock cliffs. It was the third week of March, and Ben Johnson sat on the porch waiting for his first visitor of the year.

The ranch caretaker wore a black T-shirt and jeans with his hair pulled back in a short ponytail. The effort to stand and shake hands forced a groan out of him. A few days ago he had broken a couple of ribs and hadn't seen a doctor or taken any medication. "You need to keep moving," he said, "and you don't want to mask the pain."

As Ben showed me around the place, he sketched in the details of his injury. He was riding one horse and had the lead rope of a second horse dallied around the saddle horn. When the trailing horse began to buck, the rope twisted behind his back and wrenched him off the saddle. The impact of hitting the ground broke his ribs and knocked him out. Surprised by the

25

intensity of the pain, he mounted his horse with difficulty and made the long ride back.

The pole corral behind the ranch house, I noticed, hadn't changed much from the photos taken by Dan Thrapp in 1934. But the bunkhouse had been salvaged from a World War II internment camp for Japanese Americans. A friend of the caretaker, an old cowboy, was resting inside. "He's missing one lung," Ben said, "one kidney, a gallbladder, and assorted other parts."

Later I spotted the cowboy sitting outside and walked over to say hello. His clothes hung from a thin frame, and he wore a thin mustache. I quickly showed my lack of manners by asking his last name. "K. C. will do," he said, and then told me about his twenty-one years of cowboying, working herds as large as eight thousand head of cattle. Since I needed to sort out a number of incidents having to do with horses, mentioned in Thrapp's journal, I tapped his expertise.

"Have you ever swum a horse?" I asked.

The old cowboy smiled and said, "Plenty. A horse will swim naturally. All you got to do is hang onto the tail." And when I mentioned Thrapp having trouble getting one of his horses into the river, he said, "Yes, sometimes you get one like that. But it's not being mean; it's not angry at you. They're thinking about theirselves." Trying to come up with the right way to say it, he repeated, "They're thinking about theirselves; they're thinking about their fear." When I described the condition of Thrapp's horses after weeks on the trail, K. C. wasn't surprised. "That country's hard on a man," he said, "and harder on a horse."

The two of us sat without speaking for a while before he asked, "Do you want to know the only thing I believe in?"

"Sure," I told him.

"The only thing I believe in is horses," he said. "I never get mad at a horse."

With that said, we moved over to an outside fire pit where Ben had a cook fire going. K. C. wobbled dangerously close to the flames, so Ben shifted into a position to spot him. Despite the pain whenever he moved, Ben insisted on cooking "taters and onions" in the Dutch oven.

As darkness settled in, I walked beyond the ranch house to view the night sky. To the east a scrim of clouds filtered the new moon, floating sharp-prowed over Island in the Sky. Tomorrow I would head into the canyons below to locate where Thrapp had crossed the Colorado River. I had brought along the key photographs and his journal to help in the search. For him, the Horsethief Ranch was the jumping-off point for his chance at real exploration. For me, it was a chance to piece together more of the puzzle.

Back at the cook fire Ben grimaced as he bent over to check the food, and K. C. stood up to teach me the secret Cherokee handshake of friendship. He claimed to be part Indian, and before eating he had the three of us hold hands while giving a blessing in Cherokee. To my ear the words sounded like a Pentecostal Navajo talking in tongues, but his sincerity was genuine. While I was scooping out a plateful of food, Ben and K. C. went at each other in a good-natured way. Ben made a crack, and K. C. said, "I'll get you for that."

"Remember," Ben told him, "I can run scared faster than you can run mad."

After dinner they sat by the fire rolling cigarettes from their own cans of Tops tobacco. Ben and the cowboy lived twenty miles from their nearest neighbor in a place so remote they could give free rein to their eccentricities. But when an outsider like me showed up, they had to check those impulses. It's not hard to recognize someone trying to act normal, and K. C. was having more of a struggle with it than Ben. A peculiar expression skewed his features when he recalled an incident that occurred in Tombstone, Arizona. He rambled on in a disconnected manner, talking about a fight where he had to take a pistol away from a man. It was unclear from his account whether the guy was beating up his girlfriend or threatening K. C.— probably both. Soon the police arrived and arrested him. "The law was after me," he admitted. "I'm not saying I'm perfect. They had a warrant on me."

Later Ben told me K. C. was still dealing with a few demons from Vietnam and mentioned the multiple sides that emerged when he was "in his cups." The old cowboy was probably the kind of guy wired with an on-off switch. One drink too many, and click, the rational world goes out like a light. I decided not to retrieve the bottle of wine I had brought for dinner.

When a doctor informed K. C. he had only two months to live, he gave Ben his hat in a gesture of friendship, thinking his end was near. Several months later Ben was surprised to find him on the streets of Moab still alive. "The doctor talked me out of it," K. C. said, and Ben returned the hat. With nowhere to go and no family, K. C. accepted the invitation to spend time at the Horsethief, and Ben put him in charge of the horses and cats so he would feel useful. The old cowboy would sit in the corral for hours read-ing Mark Twain to the horses.

Years ago Ben quit his job in San Francisco and headed for the desert. Traveling north of Moab, he saw a sign at the Island in the Sky turnoff read-ing, "No gas, no lodging, no food, no water." He told his friend, "Whoa, let me off here." He grabbed his backpack and headed up the road, intending to walk across the canyonlands. Following the unpaved road, he reached the Green River at Mineral Bottom. His next problem was how to cross the river. Ben stowed his gear in trash bags, wrapped everything in a tarp, and pushed off into the current. The improvised raft gave him enough flotation to drift downriver five miles to Barrier Creek. Starting up the canyon, he intended to reach a rock-art panel known as the Great Gallery and continue to Robbers Roost. It turned into a rougher traverse than anticipated, and while making a jump he landed wrong and snapped a bone. All he could do was splint the broken foot and keep walking. After a painful ordeal he reached the Great Gallery trail and followed it to the rim, catching a ride by standing in the middle of the road and forcing a car driven by tourists to stop. Over time, and to Ben's surprise, he had become a cowboy by hav-ing to take care of the horse herd and helping nearby ranchers during cat-tle roundups.

As we talked, he began looking for a pair of work gloves needed to remove the Dutch oven from the coals. Suddenly realizing they were miss-ing, he exploded. Ben was certain a shady friend of his had taken them, and he was expecting him to show up later that night. His anger got K. C. riled up, and they started making plans to confront the glove thief. The old cowboy tottered to his feet, ready for a fight, with Ben wincing as he tried to keep him from falling into the fire. Ben warned me not to get involved. "No matter what happens, stay out of it—okay?" But soon the crisis ran its course, and things returned to as normal as they were likely to get.

With dinner over K. C. turned in, and the two of us washed dishes to wrap things up. Next we worked out sleeping arrangements, with Ben insist-ing on giving me the bedroom and taking the couch for himself. Because of his injury he couldn't lie down flat. "It doesn't matter because I don't sleep anyway," he said. "Maybe three hours a night." Early next morn-ing as I slipped past him in the dark, he said hello in a wide-awake voice and joined me in the kitchen while I made coffee. As I measured out the grounds, he mentioned living in the middle of the desert and the center of the sky. I liked the image and told him it was going in the notebook. But he refused to take credit and recited the full line: "We all live in a capital *I*, in the middle of the desert, in the center of the sky." "*Sesame Street*," he told me. "Early *Sesame Street*."

LABYRINTH,
A WAY IN

Next day Dan left the bachelor quarters at the Horsethief, a log cabin he shared with one of the cowboys. On the first day of December, he crossed a skiff of snow, leaving behind dark tracks with each step. Cliffs behind the house rounded into a shoulder of slickrock, the pale stone warming in the morning light. He headed to the juniper pole corral to join Art Murry and one of the ranch hands, both wearing Stetsons and Levis with the cuffs turned up. They were shoeing a pair of horses brought in for Dan.

DECEMBER 1934

The explorer packed his supplies into canvas panniers, making sure the loads were balanced as he hefted them onto the mare's back. He finished by lashing his bedroll on top using a simple squaw hitch rather than trying to throw a diamond hitch, preferred by more experienced packers. The 150-pound load was heavy for a small horse, but he knew it would get steadily lighter as the days passed. After saddling the buckskin, he rode with a cow-puncher named Vas down the draw and turned west on the Horsethief Trail, first used by rustlers around 1890. Running for 140 difficult miles, the trail began at Moab and crossed the Colorado more than 30 miles below town. It stayed as hidden as possible, climbing out of the gorge near Island in the Sky, over the flats, and descending to the Green River at Horsethief Point. Once across, it snaked through blind canyons and broken cliffs into the Robbers Roost country.

The two horsemen rode under a sky pulled tight to the horizons. Five miles from the ranch house, they reached the edge of Labyrinth Canyon, where the land snapped off in a perpendicular drop of 850 feet. While a mountain anchors the skyline and might be visible for a hundred miles, a canyon lies below the surface. It appears suddenly to someone approaching at ground level, and even knowing what to expect the first view triggers a moment of surprise. Dan and the cowboy peered into the rock corridor below, a deeper and greener place, river swept and cliff bound. The two riders descended the sharply zigzagging trail, which led them down a cliff side of narrow ledges and sheer drops. Once below the rim they were enclosed in solid masses of rock carved into deep and sinuous curves by the Green River, now carrying a slurry of ice.

After a rest, Dan helped Vas drive a herd of cattle downriver, a skill he had picked up while working on the ranch in New Mexico. During those months he was intrigued by the tales of an old-timer named Ben Black, who had witnessed the close of the frontier. At first Dan had trouble getting him to open up unless he was drunk. But once he gained his trust, the stories rolled out, and Dan never doubted a word he heard. "Ben was apt to shrink the truth," he wrote, "rather than stretch it."[1]

The old hand took it upon himself to teach Dan the habits of a cowpuncher. In addition to handling cows, he learned to butcher beef and stretch fence. It was an open-air school where he took his share of hard knocks, once getting kicked in the face while flanking a calf during branding. And because a cowboy was expected to fend for himself, he learned to cook simple fare such as sourdough bread and beans they called "free holies," after the Spanish frijoles. His recipe for son-of-a-gun stew, a traditional standby, was straightforward: you skin a steer, stir him up, and cook him. Since the old cowboy had always packed a pistol, Dan followed his lead by wearing a Colt .32-20 revolver.

Nearly ten miles downriver, the horsemen stopped at Fort Bottom, where Murry had a cow camp. Every expedition needs a shakedown period where the kinks get worked out, and this one was no different. From his base of operations, Dan began working with the horses to learn their quirks and limitations, to get a handle on their capabilities. He found the buckskin to be a smooth rider and named him Buck, and the gentle roan mare was called Queen. When not wrangling horses, Dan and Vas rode the bogs to check for cows caught in the quicksand along the river bottoms. Both went unshaven, letting their beards grow. The days spent at Fort Bottom gave Dan a chance to adjust to living out of a bedroll and to get in sync with the rhythms of weather.

At a bend to the south, bluffs deflected the river on one side and looped around the half-moon flats on the other. Colorful badlands spread above the channel, and broken talus angled below the Wingate cliffs. Whenever he had the chance, Dan explored the surroundings on foot, hunting for Indian ruins. Knowledge of the past is always fragmentary, built from the chance recovery of things lost and abandoned—artifacts, ruins, and shards of human memory. He found granaries tucked under ledges and came upon scatters of broken pottery and arrow points. The human past was rooted deeply in this particular landscape, each pile of masonry rubble and handful of potsherds a clue to the people who once inhabited the canyons. Dan called the ruins "Moquis," having picked up the local term for prehistoric sites, derived from the Spanish name for the Hopi.

Not far from camp the remains of a round tower stood on the end of a spur ridge where the river made a sweeping 230-degree bend. The stone walls of the main structure were ten feet high and connected to the ruins of a second tower. The site provided long views upstream and down, and could be approached from only one direction, giving it a defensive advantage. Earlier travelers had named it Aztec Fort, despite having no connection to the Aztec and no direct evidence of warfare. The two-story tower was built by early Pueblo people who periodically occupied this section of canyon until the late 1200s. These prehistoric farmers stayed in the river bottoms long enough to plant and harvest their crops, long enough to experience whatever loves and sorrows held them together as a people, and then moved on.

Dan's interest in the past came directly from his father, Frank Thrapp, who never attended college. Each evening at the dinner table in the house he had built, Frank discussed what he had been reading, often a book on frontier history or the Indian wars. He made his living as a railway mail clerk, but held forth in the evenings when teachers would stop by to discuss the past. Of his five brothers and sisters, Dan was the one who ended up sharing his father's passion for history.

On December 9, Dan and Vas went upriver to retrieve a deer the cowboy had shot the day before. If they could get it back to camp, Dan would have venison for his trip. The buck had fallen on the ice eighty feet from shore, and they had spent the previous afternoon trying unsuccessfully to rope it. To compound their troubles, a dog owned by Vas slipped back to camp and ate the mulligan stew Dan had cooked. Now they were ready for a second round with the ice still churning downstream. They found the river frozen next to shore, so Vas took a chance and worked across the dangerous ice jam to tie a rope around the antlers. After a struggle they managed to drag the deer to the bank and pack it back to camp. An hour before sundown, Art Murry rode in from the Horsethief Ranch.

The rancher tried to convince Dan not to make the trip alone, only to realize the young explorer was determined to proceed no matter what advice he offered. "Dan didn't bend for anybody," recalled his younger sister years later. "He was always very pleasant, but you couldn't budge him. He was going to do it his way. Agreeable but stubborn if he'd made up his mind about something."[2]

Next morning Murry escorted Dan along the trail to get him started on his way. They rode to the head of Stillwater Canyon where the White Rim Sandstone outcrops at river level. Dan would come to know the geological formation well. A thin layer of windblown coastal sand, deposited 225 million years ago, forms a resistant caprock known as the White Rim. Lying above the Green and Colorado Rivers, the rock formation appears on a map as a great chevron angling around the end of Island in the Sky. Headward erosion from the lower gorges has gnawed into the bench, forcing a traveler to make long detours to go from point to point. Ravines have to be headed and crossed, ridges climbed. Still, the White Rim provided the best possible route for Dan to take.

The two horsemen followed the trail along the broad bench as Murry pointed out key landmarks. He warned Dan about the difficulties of finding a route no one had used since the Robbers Roost outlaws drove cattle along it years before. He continued to guide Dan for a couple more miles until they reached what the rancher called "the edge of the unknown country."[3] Before turning back to camp, Murry gave Dan a few final directions, which he quickly forgot. It was all so new that the various pieces of the complex terrain hadn't begun to fit together in any meaningful whole.

The explorer began his solo traverse across the esplanade, skirting below the unbroken scarp of the sky island and above the river gorge. Dan traveled through the angling light of late fall, riding into distances so great they swallowed any normal sense of scale. A stone spire miles away might appear close enough to reach out and touch, and a moment later with a shift of light it receded into blank space. The unreal quality of the scene had a liberating effect on the senses by upturning the old rules of perception. Space kept stretching to the horizon and then beyond its visible limits into a distance only imagined. Dan stopped for a moment and grabbed his camera tied to the saddle horn. Through the viewfinder he framed a scene of detached buttes and a river canyon, a scene too big to fit onto a negative. He snapped a shot and made a note reading simply, "It starts."[4]

Having left the river behind, Dan no longer had a dependable source of water. An hour before sundown, he found a shallow pothole with enough for himself and his horses, so he called it camp. Before seeing to his own needs, he grained the tired horses with corn, hobbled them, and turned them loose to graze on clumps of Indian ricegrass. Overhead the evening sky darkened as the weighted blue shifted west, dissolving into a yellow band on the rim of the horizon. Left to his own thoughts, he spent more time with his journal than usual. "Well, I'm on my own again," he wrote. "I left Art about 1:30 P.M. today and so far have seen no sign of anyone else. And don't expect to, until I get across the Grand and into the Indian Creek cattle outfit's territory where some of their cowhands may run across my tracks and trail me to find out what in hell I'm doing over there."[5]

Dan was following local custom by referring to the Colorado River as the Grand. Originally, the Colorado began at the junction of the two main branches, the Green and the Grand, which had its headwaters in the Colorado Rockies. But a congressman from the state of Colorado thought it only proper to have the Colorado River run through the state named for it. He lobbied hard, and in 1921 the Grand was officially renamed the Colorado. Many in Utah, considering it merely the whim of a politician, refused to recognize the change.

"Right now," Dan continued, "I'm camped on the White Rim—about fifty feet from the edge of one of the innumerable box canyons that run off from the Green, Grand, and Colorado Rivers. This White Rim is found in the shape of cliffs, or 'bald' or 'slick' rocks. In the horizontally bedded slick rocks are tanks, or natural wells, that never run dry—some of them. That is what I have to depend on for water until I get down to the Grand. There is no running water in this country."[6] And there were no roads, and only a hint of trail soon lost in the shifting sands and bare rock.

DESOLATION CAMP

Next morning the young scientist got a late start as he worked out his routine of breaking camp. From cooking breakfast to wrangling horses, he was still having to think through the simple tasks that would later become second nature. Once all was ready, he rode south across the stark terrain of Soda Springs Basin. Most of the place-names at the time were unofficial, and Dan was familiar with only a few. He mentioned the rivers and the White Rim by name, but little else. As the morning lengthened, he encountered a crested ridge barring his way, and even without knowing its name he knew it would be a challenge. A trail ran somewhere closer to the escarpment, he remembered being told, but decided to take a shortcut straight across. "There is no straight across in this country," he noted, "and the guy that said that a straight line is the shortest distance between two points, never saw south-eastern Utah!"[1]

It took him most of the day to work out a way over the hogback ridge. Rising six hundred feet, it was steep and ledgy with enough obstacles to stop a horse. Dan dismounted and climbed to the top, searching for the right combination of breaks. After finding nothing practical, he descended and moved farther along its foot. Twice more he climbed to the rim with growing uncertainty. All of his plans depended on solving this problem, and he was worried. Adding to the difficulty of the terrain was the absence of water holes, forcing the animals to eat patches of snow as they went. Toward sundown he finally spotted the only route through the caprock possible for horses. After a struggle, he got to the top where a ripped and scarred landscape spread out below in a land of standing rocks and sandstone barrens.

He found himself on the rim of a canyon within the hold of an even greater canyon, but had little time to take in the dramatic setting. Dan pushed on, needing to locate a water source before dark.

Being a high desert, everything depended on finding water. Springs were scarce and chancy, potholes ephemeral, and streams often ran at the bottom of defiles too deep to reach. The far side of the hogback was not as steep as the ascent, and he led his horses down to the White Rim in the failing light. To his relief, Dan found a pair of water pockets and enough wood washed down from the upper reaches for a campfire. Later that evening he opened the journal and recorded his thoughts. "Today was a day of trials, errors, and cuss words," he began.[2] And then he recounted his attempts to find a route over the barrier ridge. "There was only one way—and that was sure a man and horse-killer. But we made it and finally got down on this side."

By morning heavy clouds had moved in, filling the sky and carrying with them the scent of winter. A storm was on its way. Dan began packing, and before he finished the snow started to fall. Riding one horse and leading the other, he followed the sandstone bench along a staggered course. The cloud cover had obscured the sun, and the lack of shadows made it hard to stay oriented. The terrain itself presented few difficulties without the dangerous climbs and descents encountered yesterday. As the morning wore on, the snow changed to rain, with one or the other continuing to fall for the rest of the day. He crossed a cold and wet desert, and as always had to deal with the aggravations of leading a packhorse. At one point Queen lay down on a patch of sand and tried to roll, forcing Dan to repack the load. Soaked through and cold, he made an early camp not knowing where he was.

He had crossed the divide between the Green and Colorado Rivers, that much he knew. But he was uncertain how far he was from the river and didn't know where to find a trail leading to it. Without realizing it, Dan had rounded the extreme end of Island in the Sky above the hidden confluence of the two rivers. His camp was on the edge of Monument Basin, a bewildering scrabble of converging drainages. He faced red cliffs at every turn, cliffs shattered into angular boulders and decomposing into rubble and red sand. Deep-red fins of shale, topped by white sandstone, had eroded from the rim in freestanding walls. And monoliths, hundreds of feet tall, clustered like ancient columns supporting an empty sky. Dan had reached one of the most spectacular sections of the White Rim, but aesthetics were put on hold while he focused on essentials. Of these, water was an absolute necessity, and a lot hinged on the weather, so he paid close attention to it. And everything depended on his finding a way through the canyon maze.

The following morning he stayed in camp and waited for the weather to break. A bank of clouds had come to ground and stalled, closing his field of view and muting all but the nearest sounds. Fog shrouded the cliffs and settled over the bedrock surface as thick as a geologic deposit, filling the rough contours. It buried the land in a deep stillness, leaving a moment so weighted, the hours stalled. When the desert fog finally lifted in early afternoon, Dan saddled up. He rode the buckskin to a point on the rim overlooking what appeared to be the river gorge, but couldn't confirm it. He was caught in a confusion of canyons as clouds continued to smolder on the highest points. Riding back along the rim, he searched for a way across the mile-wide basin, but finding nothing returned to camp for a second night. Despite the miserable conditions, his journal entries lacked any hint of self pity. Indifferent to his own comfort, he was out in the elements by choice, taking satisfaction in pushing hard against the resistance of weather and terrain.

The dank weather continued to compound his troubles the following day. Rain was falling by the time Dan woke and was still falling when he brought in his horses. He mounted and rode on, finding a route at the head of the basin where the bench was pinched between cliff and canyon. Continuing on, he swung north across a blackbrush flat with the rain continuing and storm clouds gathering behind him. To his surprise, he came upon the trace of an old trail leading straight toward the rim of the inner canyon, but he kept going, not wanting to stop until he found a source of firewood. The trail could wait. In late afternoon he bivouacked at a place he called Desolation Camp, a reflection of his mood. He was now above Gooseberry Canyon, which for him was another nameless canyon in a succession of dry and unknown clefts. After the clouds cleared off that evening, the temperature dropped, and Dan spent a cold night under a stiff canvas cover.

Conditions remained unsettled, and at daybreak the fog moved in again, blocking the warmth of the sun. Dan dragged breakfast out as long as possible before wrangling his horses and feeding them. Mounting Buck, he rode back to inspect the trail he had passed the previous day. From what he had been told, Dan expected to find a route leading down to the river, but this wasn't it. What had looked promising yesterday led only to the rim and an abandoned camp. He followed the canyon edge back to his camp-site, taking in several views of the river along the way. Studying the sand-bars, he was able to tell the direction of flow and finally confirm it was the Colorado. Even this key topographic feature had been uncertain until now.

"There were one or two places where I think a horse might get down," he wrote, "but I think it better to continue on up the river tomorrow and look for a better place. Queen is young and a bit clumsy with her pack, and I don't want to risk losing her. There might be a trail off of here up the river someplace."[3] Unable to find a way down the cliffs, he was rimrocked. So he settled into Desolation Camp for a second night, alone in a broken expanse of canyon, unable to find a way through.

His reasons for being in the three-rivers country set him apart from those trying to make a living from the land. He hadn't come to punch cows, to trap, or prospect. His journey reflected a shift in thinking about wilder-ness that was beginning to take hold in the wider society. He was here for the adventure of it, to experience a pristine wilderness and uncover the clues to the past it held. And he was here for something more fundamen-tal, for the qualities a place like this drew out of him. Certain traits tend to atrophy when left unused, remaining dormant in the course of daily life. Dan had placed himself in a situation requiring a rough grace, a resilience, and a compassion for the animals who depended on him. That was satis-fying in itself, and going alone heightened both the risk and the sense of accomplishment. But it had its trade-offs. That evening as Dan watched the fire die down, his thoughts turned inward to old friends and lost loves. Unable to do more, he listed their names in his journal and left it at that.

Waking up the following day, he lifted the canvas cover enough to peer out. Seeing more fog and dark rain, he burrowed back under the blanket, trying to convince himself it wasn't time to get up. When he couldn't post-pone it any longer, he threw the tarp off and sat up. His cowboy hat went on first, and then his shirt. Before standing on the cold ground, he put on his shoes and socks, then pulled his pants on over them. He finished with a roll-collar sweater of such dark red that it was almost maroon. The can-yonlands weather swings from one extreme to the next, heating up in sum-mer to more than one hundred degrees and sometimes dropping below zero in winter. The conditions Dan was experiencing, with temperatures hovering around freezing, were ideal for hypothermia. His wool sweater gave some insulation even when wet, but a warming fire was essential and he wisely limited his travels until the weather improved.

He shuffled over to the fire and stirred up the coals, adding a few twigs. After getting breakfast started, he wrangled the horses and fed them. His routine was to eat only two meals a day, so he cooked a full breakfast of coffee, bread, and venison with rice. On other mornings he would fix cornmeal mush or pancakes. The fog showed no sign of lifting, so he stayed put for another night.

Waiting for Daylight

Clouds snagged on the cliff rock above camp, and as daylight strengthened they spilled down the face of the vertical sandstone. Leaving the horses behind, Dan walked the rim to look for any sign of the missing trail. The rain-washed morning left the sand firm under foot, and he soon surprised a bighorn ram with a three-quarter curl to its horns. It disappeared over the rim while he watched. While growing up in Illinois, Dan had spent days in the woods tracking animals and now steadily scanned the ground for traces of wildlife, excited by the profusion of bighorn tracks. He reached a point overlooking Buck Canyon after covering five miles and turned back. Despite not having found the route to the river, he reached camp encouraged by the wind now kicking up on the trailing edge of the storm. The sky was clearing.

Cliffs circled the horizon the following dawn, their black silhouettes angular and flat topped. In the far distance stood the outline of a mountain peak, dark and solid against the strengthening light. Dan got an early start under a sky turning blue and a landscape growing red. Snow on the Abajo Mountains to the south indicated winter was moving down from the higher elevations, and nearby stood immense redrock sentinels detached from Island in the Sky. Climbing hundreds of feet from footings of talus-covered bedrock, they ended in spired summits and buttes shaved flat. And everywhere stretched open country where stacked layers of rock spread into wide benchlands, all jigsawed into complex shapes and incised by cleft and chasm. The lone traveler moved steadily along the White Rim, riding one horse and leading the other.

Dan had covered a dozen miles by early afternoon and rode onto a point between two lateral canyons. Peering over the edge, he could make out a trail threading down the bed of Lathrop Canyon below. By chance he had hit the right spot to see the long-sought river trail. Working his horses close to the head of the side canyon, he found where it left the White Rim. He descended a breach in the caprock, down a steeply pitched slope to the bottom of the drainage. This was it. He had finally picked the lock, finding the right combination of ledges and crumbled cliffs to continue his journey. A trickle of water surfaced from the gravel as he rode, leading the packhorse along the streambed for several miles. Then without warning, the cliffs opened onto the main canyon to reveal the river. Sheathed within rock walls, the great Colorado carved a sweeping bend through the plateau country at a point twenty-four miles from the confluence with the Green. It formed the moving floor of the canyon, a powerful, kinetic presence.

Knobby cliffs flanked the river along the outer curve of a meander where Dan studied the situation. The turbid waters appeared too deep to ford. Unknown to him, the outlaw trail crossed three miles upstream, and few traces of it remained in the sand and slickrock along the river margin. A terrace widened above the mouth of the side canyon, and Dan scouted for a place to spend the coming night, finding remnants of old camps. He reversed the morning routine by unpacking Queen and unsaddling Buck, always taking care of his animals first. The horses fed while he dug deep into the food bag to celebrate his success. "I sure cooked a real feed tonight," he wrote in his journal. "Rice, apricots, corn bread, white bread, gravy and meat. It sure went down good."[1]

Shadows filled the hollows of the river gorge as the water caught the last light and brightened for a long, glimmering moment. After the horses had finished eating, he hobbled them and returned to the fire to drink tea and think things over. He had solved one part of the puzzle and now faced the hazards of a solo crossing without a clear idea of how to get himself, two horses, and all of his gear over to the far side. At this moment, Dan remembered his father and wished he were here to show him how to do things. When the young explorer turned in, he was still working on the problem.

His first chore in the morning was to track his horses and bring them back. Since the packhorse would be too heavily loaded to swim, he settled on a plan to first raft his gear across and then return for the animals. Dan found them up the side canyon and led them to camp, where he put Buck to work, snaking three large cottonwood logs to the bank. He tied cross pieces on each end with the thirty-foot lash rope to make a crude platform. After securing his gear in the middle with the bedroll on top, he placed his saddle and waterproof duffel on one end. The cold river spread a hundred yards wide in front of him and moved with a deceptively tranquil flow, hiding its vagrant currents and contrary eddies. He removed his shoes, climbed on board the raft, and pushed off.

Poling his way to a sandbar, he jumped into the icy shallows to land it. His feet ached from the sharp cold and then quickly numbed. He pulled the raft to the upstream end of the bar and launched it into a wider and deeper channel. Difficult to maneuver, the raft barely held together for the crossing. He again dropped into the water as he reached the south side and walked it in. The work wasn't over. It took multiple carries up the cut bank to unload his gear. The riparian thicket was nearly impenetrable, so he searched until finding a way through to the open ground beyond and began exploring the river bottom to keep warm. The fringe of heavy vegetation screened a terrace, which curved for more than two miles between the water and a line of set-back cliffs. At both the upper and the lower ends, sheer walls blocked all passage.

In the dimming light he returned to the raft and spent the rest of the evening hacking a path through the brush and moving his outfit to higher ground. The floor of the canyon trench was still four thousand feet in elevation, and the air temperature plunged without a lid of clouds to hold in the heat. Deep in the desert, Dan faced a cold night. The canyon grew colder, and his woodpile thinned. The embers drew the last heat inward, turning ashy gray, and the young explorer fell asleep listening to water sluice coldly along the shore.

After a fitful night, he inspected the river bottom for another place to land his horses. The activity warmed him, but he was unable to find a better landing. By noon the air had heated enough to try another crossing. This time he had more trouble, and there were moments when he was uncertain he would make it. "Only after some very ticklish work and some narrow escapes" was he able to reach the north side again.[2] He immediately set out to round up his horses. "They had strayed," he wrote, "and I had a five mile chase to find them." Bringing them in used up critical time, and already late in the day he was anxious to begin the return crossing. Dan quickly dismantled the raft to retrieve his rope. He climbed bareback on Buck and held Queen by the lead rope. "All aboard," he shouted. "Let's go!"[3]

Into the dark water they stepped, each animal tensing at the unsure footing and the pull of unseen currents. The river deepened. When it reached the buckskin's shoulder, the horse suddenly panicked, releasing the tremendous forces contained within its mass and triggering a moment of terror in the other horse. Scrambling and splashing, the two horses lunged back to dry land, eyes bulging. They were no longer reacting to the river or the rider but to their own fears. Dan made another attempt, ending in another wreck, and a third try worked no better. Exhausted, he had to cut his losses before conditions turned deadly. Wearing only long johns and pants, he was soaked through and dangerously cold. Shivering, he led the horses back to his first river camp and with stiff fingers improvised hobbles using the bridle reins. Letting them graze, he quickly set about making a fire with the matches he had prudently carried in a waterproof match safe. What he didn't have were warm clothes, bedding, and food—all had been left on the other side of the icy river.

On the edge of winter, the air held the cold. Before he could sort things out, Dan had to get warm. If hypothermia gained the upper hand, his judgment would unravel, so he kept moving by gathering firewood for what he knew would be a long night ahead. The temperature dropped below freezing with the onset of darkness, and the cold drained down each cut in the cliffs to settle in the lowest contours along the river. Without a shirt to wear, he could only sit hunched by the campfire, unsheltered.

All attempts to cross his animals had failed, and lacking experience he was unsure what to do next. To retreat back to the Horsethief Ranch would require rebuilding the raft and risking another round-trip crossing to retrieve his outfit. Then he would have to retrace the difficult route that had taken him so many hard days to complete. And the worst part would be having to face Murry and the cowboys, admitting he had failed. On his own and days from any help, he had to figure out a way to cross the river. Until then, all Dan could do was stoke the fire and wait for daylight, confined by a dark river on one side and darker cliffs on the other.

WINTER CROSSING

He reached the far side of a night so long that dawn brought only a momentary reprieve. "It was one miserable night," Dan noted in his journal.[1] As the darkness thinned above the gorge, the cold continued to deepen. Needing to bring in his horses, he got moving under an opening sky and followed their tracks. They had not strayed far. Leading them back to the water's edge, he faced a dark river running cold. Dan mounted the buckskin and urged him into the water.

"We thought it over," Dan wrote, "and then backed off."[2] In below-freezing weather, he was still wearing only long johns and pants. Everything depended on getting to the south side, where he'd left his warm clothes and food. Using a switch to persuade the horses, he started again and finally got them to swim. The next stretch beyond the sand bar was even more difficult. "The widest and the deepest was before us," he wrote, "and it was a bad five minutes. Queen swam around us and got tangled up; I tried stepping off Buck and grabbing his tail, but Queen came up behind, so I climbed back in the saddle again." Despite the impromptu rodeo, they made it across the icy river.

DECEMBER 1934

Dan quickly got the coffee going, changed clothes, and ate a long-deferred dinner and breakfast combined. As the day warmed, he grew curious about his surroundings and set out to explore the cliffs for Indian ruins. Remnants of prehistoric masonry walls turned up as he checked the overhanging ledges. Some sites appeared undisturbed, while others showed signs of digging. He found corncobs and the bones of fish and rabbits in one overhang and the fragments of a basket in another. Nearby a fine rock-art panel contained the pictograph of a bighorn topped by a multicolored arc with human figures and handprints. As Dan moved along the river bottom, he came upon fresh beaver cuttings and, most important, horse tracks. If other horses had found a way in, he was confident his horses could get out.

His landing had placed him on a strip of bottomlands at the apex of a great bend in the river, isolated by riverside cliffs both upstream and down. His only chance of escape from the gorge was finding a way to reach the benchlands high above. Next day he rode along the river terrace, searching for the outlaw trail, dismounting each time he needed to check out one of the side canyons. When nothing turned up, he concluded it must have been washed out. Unknown to Dan, he had picked the wrong place to cross the Colorado. The old trail descended from the White Rim and followed the river upstream before reaching the actual crossing. Cut off in an isolated pocket, he now had to find a route up the south side of the gorge to escape.

On the following day he took off on foot and after a difficult search found a way through the cliffs. He climbed six hundred vertical feet at the far end of the river bottom along a route he thought might be passable for a horse. Once he reached the top, a faint trail pointed south toward the Indian Creek cattle ranch; at least he thought it lay in that direction. Not knowing where he was, he couldn't be sure. He faced the uncertainties ahead without wavering, knowing he had little choice. The following morning Dan broke camp and rode to the start of the route. With difficulty he led the horses up a series of ledges and finally above the cliffs. It proved to be "one long, hard pull to the top—but we made it O.K."[3] It had taken Dan nearly a week to complete the dangerous crossing of the Colorado River and break out of the inner gorge.

He had climbed out between Horsethief and Rustler Canyons. The trail on top grew plainer as he followed it across terraces deeply incised by a vascular network of canyons and ravines, branching and twisting downward to the main river stem. Cliffs of Wingate Sandstone to the east pushed the horizon upward another fourteen hundred feet, with benchlands spreading out below them. He rode slowly southward. A lone traveler in such country is left to his own thoughts until the last of them are worn smooth, and he finds himself in space so vast it absorbs all sense of motion.

Stone cairns marked the trail where it crossed patches of slickrock, but Dan still managed to miss it. Forced to continue cross-country, he became rimrocked on the edge of a canyon until he was able to work out a route through the cliffs. The sand along the bottom held tracks of cattle and horses, indicating he was now within range of the Indian Creek outfit, and he settled into camp for another night alone. Christmas Eve came and went unnoticed, since Dan had not only lost the trail but lost track of the days as well.

The following morning he continued his journey, climbing out of the canyon and angling toward the cliffs to intersect the trail. He encountered fresh horse tracks and followed them along the main bench, which widened into a broad basin drained by Indian Creek. To the south rose the Needles, a dramatic stand of monoliths, banded in river reds and dune whites, and mesas worn down to pinnacled buttes. Dan reached the perennial stream before dark, and while he knew the ranch headquarters must be near he laid over the next day to let his horses rest. The spire-topped Six-Shooter Peaks stood high above the creek, pointing skyward, and whenever lightning flashes, the locals say, the rock formation appears to be firing shots. After a daylong buffeting by the wind, the explorer finally arrived at the Dugout Ranch, headquarters for what he referred to as the Indian Creek Cattle Company. The official name had changed in 1919 when the Scorup and Somerville brothers bought the holdings and called it the Scorup-Somerville Cattle Company. After a month of hard traveling alone, Dan was ready to celebrate Christmas with the ranch cowboys.

THE NEEDLES

Miles fell away as I left pavement where the road climbed Elk Ridge and threaded between the Bears Ears. At Kigalia Point I met up with friends, and for the next several days we caravanned north, skirting Dark Canyon and exploring Ruin Park. Our itinerary was fluid, and we decided to cross into Canyonlands National Park, entering the Needles through the back door.

Roads, some so rough they're better suited to a horse, have opened much of the backcountry since Dan Thrapp traversed these canyons in the winter of 1934–35. It now takes only hours to cover what it took him days to cross. The ratio between wild and tame has shifted, but some of us still find ways of getting into trouble. Our two vehicles dropped into Bobbys Hole along a plunging descent, too loose and washed out to provide much traction going uphill. Returning the same way in my four-cylinder pickup was not an option.

When I could take my eyes off the road long enough to look around, the scenery was stunning. Wild, rough country. Ridges of Cedar Mesa Sandstone had eroded into banded spires above narrow cliff-sided valleys called grabens. We camped at the head of one called Devils Lane, which should have been a clue to the difficulties ahead. Preferring the pure physicality of walking, I usually avoid serious four-by-four tracks except as a practical way to go from one point to another. So I had only a vague idea of the conditions I might encounter. Next morning I parted ways with my friends, needing to get back to Flagstaff a day early.

My limited knowledge of this section of the park had come from a backpack trip across Canyonlands, starting in the Maze and working our way down to the Colorado River. After crossing with pack rafts, we hiked through the Needles and exited by way of Elephant Hill, a notorious stretch of jeep trail. The details of the route had slipped away, but I remembered being glad I was walking and not driving.

After leaving camp, my first obstacle was a steep climb ending with a tight turn in a place called SOB Hill. I took a run at it, reaching the top where I lost momentum and stalled in a right-angle cut. I found myself walled in on both sides by cliff rock and stuck among the tank-trap rocks. Stepping out to survey the situation, I heard air hissing from a sidewall puncture. I had three inches of wiggle room behind, which might be enough, but I needed to move fast before the tire went flat. So I shifted a few rocks, got back in, and straightened the wheels. Sometimes you have to give it all you've got, barreling through whatever hazards lie in the way. I revved it up, popped the clutch, and lurched out of there with the tires smoking. This was just the beginning of the obstacle course.

Stopping at the first level spot to fix the flat, I discovered a slight over-sight. In my haste to leave town, I had left behind the full-size spare I nor-mally carry on back roads. All I had was an undersize tire designed to get you a few miles down the highway to the next gas station. And it was about ten pounds too soft. I had two choices: wait a day for my friends to show up, or take my chances. After changing the tire, I threw the tools in the back with the flat and kept going. The road took me down a descending series of stair-step ledges where I was forced to stop and scout the way ahead, much like running a rapid. It was essential to pick the right line through it to avoid breaking, bending, or puncturing some vital part of the vehicle. I kept the truck in first gear and still had to ride the brakes, bucking and tossing all the way down.

The road next twisted through washes and along sandstone benches until eventually it angled sharply upward at the base of a canyon wall. I stopped the truck, knowing this must be the Elephant. Walking it out, I care-fully studied each climbing zigzag and noticed where spinning tires had blackened the rock surface and the bedrock had been scored and dinged. If I ever lost momentum, it appeared nearly impossible to back down with-out slipping off one sheer side or the other. I finished inspecting the route without finding a graceful way of doing it. It would be necessary to hit each climb at the right angle with all the power I could squeeze out of an underpowered pickup.

I climbed in the truck without hesitation, knowing any delay would only make it harder. Pushing the accelerator, I punched up the first ramp. From then on it was a blur of racing engine, gear flying around at spin cycle in the back, and the steering wheel jerking me left and right with each concussion. Going full tilt up one pitch, I had to pull into the corner of a switchback, put it in reverse, and back uphill to the next corner. This counterintuitive move set me up to make the next turn, too sharp to negotiate if I had approached it straight on. In places the rock angled too steeply in front to see the ground, forcing me to rely on memory and luck. Any holding back, and the truck would stall. To my surprise the sky began to widen overhead, and suddenly it was over. Reaching the top, I stopped on the level and left the engine running to let it cool. With hands still gripping the wheel, I sat unmoving, stunned to have made it with everything still in one piece. I checked my watch and found it had taken two hours to go the last eight miles.

At Squaw Flat I stopped at the visitor center to ask where to get a tire fixed. The ranger smiled and said, "Nowhere. It's Sunday, and everything in southern Utah is closed." So another decision—camp here and find an open garage in the morning, or take my chances. Glancing at the visitor log on the way out, I read an entry, "Please move the park closer to Kansas." I'd settle for moving it closer to an open garage. I climbed back in the truck and headed for home.

The road followed Indian Creek where Thrapp had camped after his monthlong struggle across the canyons. At the sign for the Dugout Ranch, I considered turning in to see if Heidi Redd could patch a tire, but decided against dumping my problem on someone else. Heidi had first come to the ranch in 1964 before the national park was established and long before rock climbers had discovered the smooth, vertically jointed cliffs along the creek. At the time only a dirt road linked her with the outer world, and it was so rough and remote she would see only one car a week. Heidi had a strong connection to the land. She once showed me a row of red pinnacles on top of South Six-Shooter Peak, rising above the ranch. "Those are supposed to be a Moqui family turned to stone," she said. "One of these days I'm going to be up there with them."[1]

Where the road made a sweeping curve through Photograph Gap, I reached the Home of Truth. Or what was left of it. In the winter of 1935, a crisis engulfed an isolated religious colony set in the sagebrush plains above Indian Creek. Founded by Marie Ogden, a socialite turned desert oracle, the Home of Truth was located on what she believed was the original site of the Garden of Eden. It proved to be a dry and desolate paradise. Lacking water for irrigation, and lying at an elevation where temperatures ranged from twenty below in winter to more than a hundred degrees in summer, they were unable to farm. Sustained by faith, the inhabitants lived communally, using oil lamps for light and surviving the bitter cold huddled around woodstoves in raw frame buildings without insulation. At first no one outside the region took much interest in the community, and then word got out that Marie Ogden was trying to raise the dead.

The high desert was a long way from her old home in New Jersey. The cult leader had once filled her days attending charity functions and social clubs with little concern for the spiritual world until her husband died of cancer. The shock of his death changed her life. In her grief Ogden turned to astrology and numerology for answers, beginning a long journey into the world of the occult. Along the way she discovered a talent for communicating with the spirit world through her divine typewriter. Messages revealing God's will poured onto the page whenever she sat down to type. Traveling around the country as the Great Depression took hold, she inspired a growing body of believers through her lectures and newsletter. She claimed the Last Days were upon them and led her followers to a refuge near Church Rock in southern Utah. They built her a house at Photograph Gap, the place revealed to her as the axis of the earth.

"The days of tribulation are at hand," Ogden announced to the press. "The coming few years will see collapse of our economic systems, great natural catastrophes, such as floods, and human catastrophe in the form of revolution and war. Civilization as we know it will be destroyed, but from the wreckage will come a realization of the all importance of spiritual peace in life. It is for that day that the Home of Truth is preparing."[2] During her first year in Utah, she filled reams of typing paper with revelations and continued to have faith she would be granted the power to heal. Edith Peshak staked her life on it.

Having been diagnosed with terminal cancer, Edith joined the group and turned over all her worldly possessions to the community in hopes of finding a cure. When Edith's condition worsened, Ogden blamed it on a lack of faith. And then on February 11, 1935, Edith died. On hearing the news, the spiritual leader was shocked. "It cannot be!" she said.[3] Rushing to the bedside of the deceased, Ogden was determined to raise Edith from the dead. She instructed her followers to leave the corpse unburied, and each day they washed the body in a saline solution and gave it a "rectal feeding." The leader performed a daily laying on of hands and claimed to be receiving messages from the dead woman. Using her sixth sense, Ogden managed to detect a pulse, which convinced her their efforts at sustaining life were working.

Media savvy, Ogden owned the only newspaper in San Juan County and now gave readers updates on the attempted resurrection. The locals, mainly Mormons, were tolerant of unconventional religious beliefs, but reports from the Home of Truth caused concern and fed rumors of strange rites being performed. The national press ran with the story of a desert cult attempting to revive a dead woman. After seeing the newspaper accounts, the daughter of the deceased requested an investigation. County attorney Donald Adams drove to the scene and asked to see the body, but Marie Ogden refused.

"She told me the woman wasn't dead," Adams wrote. "She said there is a cord that connects the hereafter and the present life and this cord had never been severed."[4] When members of the cult blocked him from entering the "resurrection house," his only option was to return with Sheriff Lawrence Palmer and force the issue. Since no law required the burial of a body, the lawman's power to intervene was limited. Finally, a compromise was worked out, allowing a doctor to examine the body and determine if it presented a health hazard. He was unable to find any pulse, but reported the remains were so well preserved he had no grounds to demand a burial. The skin had turned to parchment, the body having mummified in the dry air. So the young sheriff took a pragmatic approach. Because many of the local families kept mummified remains of prehistoric Indians in their homes, he thought Ogden should be treated no differently.

An apostate from the Home of Truth later swore under oath he was instructed by Ogden to cremate the remains two months after the initial confrontation with the county attorney. But she insisted the body had only been hidden from curiosity seekers, and a reporter claimed to have tracked down the cave crypt and actually seen the mummified remains. So the final disposition remains a mystery. At its peak the community had around seventy members, but many left after the bungled resurrection. By 1937, when

Ogden signed a death certificate under pressure from the authorities, the group had dwindled to a dozen true believers.

Crossing the sagebrush flat, I turned south on Highway 191 and headed back to Flagstaff, uncertain if the spare would last another 280 miles. The next day a mechanic at the tire shop looked at it and shook his head. "I hope you didn't have to drive far on this doughnut."[5]

CIRCLING THE BLUES

Arriving at the Dugout Ranch, Dan Thrapp was surprised to learn it was the afternoon of December 27 instead of Christmas Day. The cowpunchers had left for the holidays, and the only inhabitants of the Dugout Ranch were two hay cutters and a trapper, Roy Musselman. Wearing faded Levis and a ten-gallon hat, he welcomed the young scientist by serving him a full spread. Dan took a seat and dug into a skillet of fried meat and a pan full of biscuits with a huge dish of applesauce on the side. After wolfing these down, he topped off the meal with two pieces of cake and three glasses of milk. "Ate enough for two men," he noted, "or ten, I guess."[1]

The trapper's knowledge of the surrounding country was detailed and accurate, having crossed much of it in pursuit of a legendary wolf known as Big Foot. The elusive predator outwitted his pursuers for years until Roy was finally able to collect the one-thousand-dollar bounty offered by local ranchers. Dan questioned him about the way to Dark Canyon, before finding a spot among the leafless cottonwoods to camp. The next morning he set out with a map drawn by the trapper in the back of his journal.

The slickrock desert gave way to piñon-juniper woodland as he proceeded, and then it transitioned into stands of ponderosa pine mixed with spruce and aspen. This was the first forest Dan had entered since arriving in Utah, and the weather began to turn cold as he reached the higher elevations. "The last two miles," he wrote, "we were traveling in snow—the last mile of which was up to the horses' knees."[2] The animals struggled as they kept breaking through the icy crust. "Sure was mean going," he added.

After ascending steadily for twenty-eight miles, he reached Mormon Pasture and stopped at a log cabin used by the Indian Creek cowboys in

Dugout Ranch, Utah. A month into his journey, Dan Thrapp prepares a meal along Indian Creek. He made a dangerous winter crossing of the Colorado River a few days before. Courtesy of the Haley Memorial Library and History Center.

summer. It sat in the La Sal National Forest at an elevation of more than seven thousand feet, only fourteen miles from Dark Canyon. So close. That night a snowstorm swept in and lasted through the next morning, forcing a layover. On December 30, Dan pushed through the deep snow for a mile or two until it reached the bellies of his floundering horses. He knew it would only get harder if he kept going. "I sure hated to turn back," he said, "but it seemed the only sensible thing to do."[3] And good sense was needed to stay alive in the mountains.

At key moments on his journey, Dan made the right decisions, and not by accident. It was as if he had been preparing for this expedition since his childhood in West Chicago. Whenever he had the chance, he would slip into the woods near his home to learn about the natural world. He spent his time tracking animals and making casts of their prints, and when not in the woods he read a lot of Zane Grey. "He had a real love of the West from day one," his sister later recounted.[4] Early on Dan displayed a tenacity that paid off in the difficulties he faced in southern Utah. "When he was sixteen," she said, "he decided to hitchhike to the West Coast. Of course, my parents were appalled." But if they had tried to stop him, he would have gone anyway. "Mother packed a lunch and took him out to the Lincoln Highway. He wore his Boy Scout uniform. He took a maroon sweater they'd gotten for him at Sears & Roebuck. That was his good-luck sweater." Dan's mother watched him standing next to the westbound lane with his thumb out and wouldn't see him again until high school started in the fall.

He had a thirst for knowledge and a passion for history encouraged by his father, who would sit at the dinner table discussing the campaigns of Caesar or the tactics of Crazy Horse. And Dan had a longing for wild and distant places. In South Dakota he walked across the Badlands by moonlight and fought forest fires in Washington State. He hopped a freight train down the coast to San Diego, hitched a ride to the Grand Canyon, and proceeded to hike across it. It was "26 miles," he wrote a friend, "and I am so stiff I can hardly move."[5]

His summer out west only whetted his appetite for more adventure, and he read everything on exploration he could get his hands on. During his last year of high school, Dan tried to join a Norwegian whaling expedition but had to settle for college when the captain politely turned him down. While at the University of Wisconsin, he learned Admiral Richard Byrd was scheduled to talk in a town one hundred miles away. So Dan hitchhiked to the home of Governor Walter Kohler, where the great polar explorer was staying, and knocked on the door. Before long he managed to secure an invitation to stay for dinner. Dan told Admiral Byrd he wanted to be an explorer himself someday and asked what had given him the greatest thrill on his Antarctic expedition. "The discovery of new land," he answered.[6] The governor must have realized Dan would stay until they threw him out, so he invited the enthusiastic student to ride with them to the lecture hall. After his talk Byrd told him, "Good luck to you, lad, I'm backing you."

Now off on his own adventure, the young explorer made his way back to the Dugout Ranch after failing to reach Dark Canyon. The new year had come and gone unrecorded. Again the trapper drew a map, advising Dan to circle Blue Mountain by way of Monticello and Blanding, outlying towns to the east. On official maps the Blues are known as the Abajo Mountains, but locals prefer their own name for them. So the explorer headed off on the next leg of his journey, hoping to avoid the deep snows of the high country.

He followed the Indian Creek road below sheer cliffs of sandstone cut into angular facets, warming red in the morning light. After climbing out

On the trail. Horses stand alert at the top of the Posey Trail, waiting for Dan Thrapp to descend Comb Ridge into the wilder country farther west. Courtesy of the Haley Memorial Library and History Center.

of the canyon, he spent the night at the Seeps, a water source only a couple of miles from the religious colony founded by Marie Ogden. The following day he passed through Photograph Gap and turned south at the main road leading to Monticello. At this point his journal went blank for several days, and he left his impressions of the Home of Truth unrecorded. He may have been unaware that truth had a home.

The return to civilization came as a jolt after more than a month in the wilderness, especially for the horses. "They had neither of them ever seen an automobile or a road or anything like it before," Dan wrote, "so we had a high old time on the highway and in town."[7] He was forced to spend forty-five cents on hay to feed his horses, using the last of his money, and that night camped in a Monticello lumberyard. In the morning he continued toward the next town, riding into the face of a blizzard.

Once past Blanding, Dan struck west on a trail weaving through the junipers and sagebrush. Again he was leaving the density of towns behind and entering a land filled with canyons and mesas stretching toward the confluence of the San Juan and Colorado Rivers. The trapper had given him a rough idea of what lay ahead, but he would have to navigate it without maps and few trails. A Ute rode into camp that evening while he was cooking supper. The man wore a high crown hat with a flat brim, and the tips of his horseshoe mustache nearly reached his jawline. "An Indian sheepherder stopped to talk," Dan wrote, "although he couldn't speak much English and I don't know any Ute."[8] Wary of the stranger, he added, "Hope the ponies don't stray too far tonight."

As late as 1923, when the only Indian wars still being fought were those on the big screen, a band of Ute engaged the local cowboys and townsmen in a running gunfight along the trail Dan was now following. The incident, known as the Posey War, began when a pair of Ute were taken into custody by Sheriff William Oliver and found guilty of robbery and bridge burning. Before sentencing, they broke free from the sheriff and jumped on waiting horses to make their escape. Oliver swung into the saddle and pursued the one who had grabbed his revolver in the scuffle. Riding neck and neck down the street, the fugitive tried shooting the sheriff, but the weapon kept misfiring. Finally, he got one shot off, wounding Oliver's horse. The loud report startled the residents of Blanding, and fearing a general uprising they began rounding up every Indian they could find. Those not held as prisoners fled westward under the leadership of Posey, a Paiute married into the Ute band.

As the sheriff formed a posse, he declared, "We're not going to let old Posey and a handful of renegade braves run this country any longer!"[9] The pursuit turned deadly along Comb Ridge, where the Ute fought a delaying action, giving their families time to slip away. Some of the unmounted pursuers had packed into a Model T Ford, and when it came under fire they scattered like quail. In the running fight a horse was killed and one of the fugitives shot dead. Posey was wounded in the hip when he escaped from the posse riding Indian fashion by clinging with one leg to the side of his horse. After fleeing farther west, the band finally surrendered, but their leader refused to give up the fight. Mortally wounded, Posey died alone while hiding in the broken country where Dan was now heading.

Entering Butler Wash, Dan had no idea where he was, the sense of disorientation having become familiar by now. He kept to the trail on the following day and rode up a steep slope to where the land abruptly broke away in a drop of 750 feet. "Just as we came through the last grove of cedars," he wrote, "we stepped out onto a great cliff with the valley below us and another ridge to the west."[10] He had reached the spine of Comb Ridge where a trail zigzagged down the sheer western flank, a "good, though perilous-looking trail." The valley of Comb Wash opened below, and in a land of twisting canyons it was set apart by running nearly straight south to the San Juan River, twenty-three miles below. Descending to the dry streambed, he made camp next to "the most beautiful spring I believe I've ever seen. The water runs along for a couple of hundred yards before it disappears and in places there are pools three or four feet deep—perfectly clear and cold. It sure is a dandy and the first clear water in days."[11]

He was now below the snow line and able to do without his coat for the first time in many days. And since the valley provided good grazing, he decided to rest his horses. For the next two weeks Dan explored the prehistoric ruins tucked into the surrounding cliffs. What he had hoped to find in Dark Canyon, undisturbed cliff houses, he found here. He climbed into ancient granaries, built with stone masonry to enclose overhanging ledges, and wandered through the mounds of rubble marking old villages. He came upon potsherds strewn everywhere and even complete pots lying in fragments. "I found enough pieces of pottery," he noted, "to fill a box car and there's lots more."[12]

After moving his camp up the wash to a line shack, he met a cowpuncher who was running a trapline in the winter season. Walt Stevens was heading to town and suggested they team up when he returned. He wore a stubble beard, and after weeks on the trail his pants were torn and patched. Soon another traveler leading a pack mule reached the cabin from the other direction and introduced himself as Andy Delaney. He normally worked for the TY Cattle Company and despite limited schooling was known to read good books. He had shaped the brim of his cowboy hat in right angles, and his pants were tucked into a pair of tall boots. "He was one of the wildest cowmen that I knew," recalled DeReese Nielson, a cowboy himself. "He was the only man that I have ever known in my life that never had any fear of anything, anytime. He had no superstitions and wasn't scared of anything. He didn't believe in anything, and he wasn't afraid of anything, man or beast."[13]

Around the campfire that evening, Delaney entertained Dan with stories about local characters and mentioned he ran a few dozen head of his own cattle across the Colorado River. The three of them settled in for the night, and at dawn Delaney discovered one of his mules had jumped the gate and headed back to town. "Walt and I sure kidded him about losing that mule," Dan noted.[14] The cowpuncher was forced to turn back to Blanding in hopes of overtaking the stray. Before Delaney left, Dan took a photo of him standing next to the pack mule holding his Winchester rifle. "I tried to get Andy to wear his chaps," he said, "but he thought it would hurt his dignity."

Later that year Andy Delaney disappeared. He had gone to check his cattle on the west side of the Colorado River and stopped at a miners camp in Red Canyon. After lunch the cowboy headed down to his regular crossing and never returned. The miners mounted a search, following Andy's tracks to the river's edge, where they found he had crossed to an island in midstream before entering the deepest channel. The miners rowed their boat across and inspected the opposite side without seeing any indication the cowboy had left the river. After determining he had gone in and not come out, they hurried to town to report his disappearance. Sheriff Lawrence Palmer gathered a search party and worked downriver for twelve miles without locating a body or more tracks. He concluded that the missing man had died by drowning, but rumors of foul play persisted.

Without a body, Delaney's fate was left unresolved, and his widow refused to accept the sheriff's findings. Lila knew the river was low that year due to drought, and Delaney had made the crossing without incident many times before. She came to believe her husband had been killed by Bud Vinger, a part-time bootlegger and full-time brawler with a knack for avoiding long periods of incarceration by breaking out of jail. Lila twice confronted Vinger in later years, accusing him of having murdered her husband, but he denied having any involvement in his death. She never accepted his denial and continued to believe he was behind the disappearance. Within a few days Dan would team up with Bud Vinger, unaware of his past.

FAR REACHES

The young scientist waited for Stevens to return, as unsettled weather brought rain and snow to Comb Wash. On some mornings heavy clouds filled the trough between the folded side of Cedar Mesa and the cliffs across the valley. Storms moved through in pulses, forcing Dan to postpone his journey since the trail might be impassable with snow covering the bare sandstone. Living close to the elements was forcing him to come to terms with the slower rhythms of winter. This gave him time to explore, and when he wasn't searching for ruins he sketched.

EARLY JANUARY 1935

Several pages of his journal contain drawings of broken pottery, which accurately depict the bold geometric designs painted on angular sherds. And he kept returning to a place he had discovered beyond the cabin. A knob of pale sandstone, forming a fine lookout, rose above a scatter of juniper growing from cracks in the slickrock. The landmark had attracted early Pueblo people, as indicated by the stubs of masonry walls breaching the sand at its base, and Dan found petroglyphs pecked into the smoother faces of the cliff above. He carefully drew the arcane images, having learned the need for accurate records from his excavations in Wyoming.

Most of the rock art dates to historic times. A mounted warrior dominates the main panel, indicating it came after the Spanish introduced the horse and before the Ute artist had mastered how to draw one. The image shows a horseman, with bow in hand, sitting upright on a wide-bodied animal appearing more bovine than equine. The rest of the panel displays a chaotic scene with men on horseback and foot hunting antlered animals thronging around an immense shield filled with other images. The meaning of these symbols has been lost, and what is left stands as a reminder of how even the core memories of a people can fade. After a blizzard swept through, Dan revisited the site to continue his sketching. "It was so doggone cold," he wrote, "and my hands got so stiff I couldn't draw any more."[1]

In mid-January two men rode up the wash from the river town of Bluff, intending to trap farther west. They spent the next few days hunting and waiting out the weather, during which time a friendship developed between the young explorer and the sixty-four-year-old trapper. With a brushy mustache, Bob Wise was as lean and tight grained as a Utah juniper. The two of them explored ruins together for the next few days, and they visited the site where a posse had buried Posey's body. A few renegades and outlaws from his band were still riding, Wise told Dan. The trapper scratched out a living on a farm near Bluff, having arrived from Texas years before with rumors of an outlaw past trailing behind him. His reputation as a kindhearted loner was offset by the trouble he caused whenever he went on a drunk. He once shot up a trading post in Cottonwood Wash, leaving behind bullet-riddled cans oozing their contents. Others like him had gravitated to southeastern Utah, finding a place to leave behind ruined lives and broken laws. When Dan met him, Wise had a warrant out for his arrest, but the sheriff would later drop the charges for his aid in the search for his young friend. Wise would continue to clash with the law into his eighties, when he pleaded guilty to selling liquor to the Indians.

The identity of the younger trapper remained a mystery to Dan. Using the alias "Bill Jones," Bud Vinger kept quiet about being on the run from the authorities. Unknown to Dan, he had escaped from the San Juan County jail in Monticello a couple of weeks earlier. The same age as the explorer, he had been in repeated scrapes with the law and had already served time in federal prison. His most recent troubles stemmed from having sold bootleg whiskey to the Ute, resulting in the death of an Indian who made the mistake of drinking the hooch.

The jailbreak happened before federal agents could escort him back to prison for parole violations. After escaping from "the local calaboose," as a reporter put it, he robbed two stores and secured a pack outfit.[2] The fugitive was spotted riding down Montezuma Creek, and upon reaching Bluff he teamed up with Bob Wise. An extended trip in the backcountry would give him a chance to let his back trail grow cold, a chance to lie low and breathe easy. And since there wasn't much trouble he could get into out there, the sheriff didn't push too hard to find him. The rough country and long distances were better barriers than jailhouse walls. Dan knew little about Vinger other than his toughness and desire for anonymity. Whenever Dan pulled out the camera, the young trapper would turn his back.

Having received no word from Walt Stevens, Dan decided to join the new arrivals. Wise claimed to know the territory beyond Grand Gulch, an asset for a party traveling without maps. Based on his accounts, Dan figured it would take only five days to cross the San Juan River and reach the outpost of Kayenta in Arizona. Once again, he seriously misjudged the difficulties ahead. He easily could have descended Comb Wash to a river crossing or used the bridge at Mexican Hat. Instead, he let the wilder country to the west draw him in. A few trails branched across it like veins on a hand, but these had been found and forgotten so often, it was as if they were entering it for the first time.

On the day of their departure, the three men were up before dawn, wrangling horses and making breakfast. As they loaded the packhorses, a string of riders with pack mules descended the mesa on their way to Blanding. Leading the cowboys was Harve Williams, the barrel-chested foreman for Al Scorup's outfit. They had started at Halls Crossing on the Colorado River, leaving a line of fresh tracks in the snow for Dan and his companions to follow. "The trail was a hard one," he noted. "We'd never have made it but for those tracks."[3]

The trappers got off to a rough start by having to return for gear inadvertently left behind, and they found themselves repacking the loads repeatedly. Dan and Vinger walked, and when they hit foot-deep snow in the uplands it turned into a cold, hard slog. Then it took a serious turn. Wise's dog began acting strangely, and soon it went into convulsions. Unable to help, all they could do was watch him die. The old trapper was outraged when he realized the dog had eaten poison bait left by a government trapper to kill predators. "Poor Old Bob felt pretty bad about it," Dan wrote. "He thought more of that dog than most people think of their kids and he raved and cursed around here most of the evening. He said: 'The dirty, God

Damned Bastard that would spread that stuff ought to be gutshot.'"⁴ With Dan's love of animals, the loss also hit him hard. They had to make camp that evening in deep snow with no feed for the horses. "Mr., this has been a hell of a day," he wrote, "all the way through."

The next leg of the trip took them to Grand Gulch, branching across Cedar Mesa in deep entrenchments. They were uncertain where they were until finding a dirt road, untraveled at that time of year, leading to Natural Bridges National Monument. Dan now made the only sightseeing excursion of his journey by visiting Owachomo Bridge, one of three natural bridges formed by White Creek. The dramatic sandstone span, only 9 feet thick, stretched 180 feet across Tuwa Canyon. He returned to camp, and at sunup the next morning the three of them began following the route taken by the Hole-in-the-Rock Expedition. In the long unfolding of western settlement, it has to rank as the best-executed worst idea on record.

In 1880 more than eighty covered wagons took a shortcut across one of the most rugged landscapes on the continent. For more than three hundred miles the Mormon settlers forced their way across the Colorado River gorge and through a vast torn-apart land on little more than black powder and a prayer. Suffering extreme hardships, they came to know each sand hollow and rock chute, each blizzard-swept headland and harrowing climb, along the divide between the Colorado River and the San Juan. Nearing their intended destination at Montezuma Creek, they could go no farther. The animals were exhausted and the people drained by all they had endured. Remarkably, they completed their epic passage without a single death and set about founding the town of Bluff. What they originally thought would take six weeks had ended up taking them six grueling months.

As the three travelers dropped below the snow line, the land opened to the south, and they entered what Dan called "a beautiful piece of country."⁵ The horses were kicking up dust on the road by afternoon, and that night they camped at the foot of the Red House Cliffs, an escarpment running from north to south. Next day the road swung west and began to climb through badlands composed of "brilliantly colored clays in vermillion, blue, whites and grey," Dan noted. Far to the southeast stood the stone columns of Monument Valley, drained of mass and color by the distance. They crossed the steep pass at the Clay Hills Divide and reaching the head of Castle Creek had no idea what drainage they were following. The presence of good water and grass was enough for now, but in the days ahead it became increasingly apparent they were lost.

Initially, they wanted to find "the Lakes," a reference to Lake Pagahrit. Surrounded by desert, it had formed thousands of years earlier when a falling sand dune created a dam, backing up waters sixty feet deep and nearly a mile long. It was such an unexpected oasis, the Hole-in-the-Rockers considered its discovery providential. What Wise didn't know was the lake had disappeared twenty years before. Days of steady rain had fallen on an overgrazed range, causing heavy runoff to funnel into Lake Canyon and breach the dam. A tremendous flood had torn down the canyon to the Colorado River, draining the lake waters and scouring everything in its path.

Somewhere in the drifting sands and washouts, Dan and his companions missed the trail taken by the Hole-in-the-Rockers. It had been abandoned within a year or two of the crossing and left to be absorbed back into the matrix of rock and sand. Dan was relying on Wise, who professed to know this country, but it turned out he was just as disoriented as his companions. Angry at the trapper's inability to guide them through the sandy plains and bare-rock mesas, Dan vented his frustrations in his journal. "He said he knew this country, but I don't think he has the slightest notion of where he is or which way he's going, or why."[6] Dan blamed the trapper's poor route-finding skills on his being distracted by thoughts of booze and a woman he had left behind. Among the Indians he was known as "Hoot Owl," a nickname referencing his covert visits to a Navajo woman. To let her know of his arrival, Wise would call out, "Hoo—hoooo." Dan ended his journal entry by tempering his criticism. "But you can't help liking the old boy," he added. "He'll do anything for you and he means to help you out. He's a kind hearted old guy and a good fellow to have along."

The two trappers and their young companion came upon a trail leaving the far side of the Castle Creek wash. It veered off in the wrong direction, but right now they were in the middle of nowhere and a trail had to lead somewhere. So they took it and began climbing the side of a mesa, again losing their way while crossing stretches of slickrock. Continuing into the sand hills, they found plenty of grass and water for the horses and made an early camp. Dan took in the beauty of the landscape opening to the north.

"Just after sunset," he wrote, "there was the light green of Brigham Tea and the darker green mixed with smokey grey of the cedars; the blue-grey of the black brush and the light yellow of the curley grass on the light orange-brown of the sand and near rocks; and in the far distance, the canyon of the Colorado and beyond it loomed the Henrys looking very high and wild—a light lavender turning to a deep purple with buttes and mesas and canyons all of a shade of blue or purple."[7] After scouting the surrounding country, Bud Vinger returned to camp with a report of having found the gorge of the San Juan River. "He said she was a mile deep," Dan noted, "and impossible to cross on account of rimrocks."

The young explorer decided to see for himself and the next morning rode to where the river had branched back into the uplands. From the rim he estimated the depth of the canyon at no more than two thousand feet, and he continued working along the edge of the cliff. Wise had told him these canyons held many ruins that had not been "essplured," so a pot-sherd lying in a sandy pocket caught his eye. And suddenly he came upon a pair of cairns marking a hidden trail and possibly a way to reach the river. Dan headed back to camp to tell the others.

THE BACKBONE

West of Clay Hills Pass, I pulled off the road at Castle House, an Anasazi (now known as the Ancestral Pueblo) cliff dwelling first noted by scouts from the Hole-in-the-Rock Expedition. It lies sunk within the face of a low cliff, half screened by junipers. To reach it, the three of us crossed a dry wash and climbed into the alcove where centuries of wood smoke had darkened the ceiling. The standing walls of the ruin, facing different directions, glowed red or tan depending on which angle caught the light. Each wall consisted of a row of stones set in mud mortar and stacked in layers, resembling a cliff composed of sedimentary rock.

We searched the cliff house for an inscription I'd heard was left here in the 1930s. Having retained its coat of red plaster for seven centuries, the outermost wall was so crowded with names and dates scratched in the surface that we had difficulty picking out any one inscription. After a close inspection we found a string of letters reading, "DAN THRAPP NYC FEB 20 1935." The young explorer was on a leave of absence from the American Museum of Natural History, so claimed New York City as home. The inscription was the only on-site evidence of his journey I had seen.

This was my third attempt to retrace the route taken by Thrapp. With me were photographer Shane McDermott and Krzysztof Arciszewski, a young traveler from Poland who went by Chris for our benefit. The twenty-three-year-old was undertaking a solo journey around the world and had joined us for his first encounter with the American Southwest. I knew Thrapp had ridden west of Clay Hills Pass, intending to cross the San Juan River and continue south. If he managed to stay on the Hole-in-the-Rock trail he was following, it would have intersected a trail leading to a known river crossing near the confluence with the Colorado. That would have been the logical place for him to head, assuming logic was part of the equation. Nothing was certain since the young scientist had teamed up with two trappers and relied on their knowledge of the topography. They soon found themselves bewildered by the ephemeral trails and unfamiliar landscape.

My initial investigations, taken with other companions, had followed the Hole-in-the-Rock road along a divide between the San Juan and Colorado known historically as "the Backbone." The region remains a wild land chopped into gorges and broken by swells of slickrock, a place so isolated we came across a wheel and wagon box from the original expedition. On my first trip Tony Williams and I camped west of Lake Canyon, and taking day packs we set out toward Grey Mesa. The track skirted a sandy basin known as Death Valley, and within a couple of hours we encountered a caravan of off-road vehicles led by a man with a full gray beard, driving a Jeep Cherokee. He had it fitted out for the backcountry with beefed-up suspension, a winch for getting unstuck, and even a welder for serious repairs. The driver eased to a stop, and as we talked he handed me a business card reading, "Frenchie La Chance, 4 x 4 Driving School & Guide Service." Frenchie told me he had made a hundred trips along the old trail and gave us critical information on water holes farther west.

Tony and I continued walking to the foot of Grey Mesa, cut off by a sea of churning sandstone. The route climbed a narrow stair-stepping dugway built in the 1950s to bypass the older, and even rougher, wagon trail. Extreme off-roaders had left evidence of their efforts to climb it with gouges scraped in bedrock, drips from punctured oil pans, and black rubber laid down on the steepest pitches where tires had spun and smoked until gaining traction. On the trail we encountered an average of two parties a day, and about half were descendants of the original pioneers who were undertaking a pilgrimage to reconnect with their heritage. At one point we met several generations of a Mormon family riding a string of quads with a support truck. They stopped to talk, and one of the women mentioned how inspirational it was following the historic trail and how faith must have brought the pioneers through such hard times. Her husband, a more practical sort, thought a little arm-twisting by the leadership might have been involved. "Brigham Young," he added with a smile, "must have scared them into going."

Having walked more than a dozen miles from camp, Tony and I sat overlooking the Great Bend of the San Juan arm of Lake Powell, visually broken into segments by the deep and twisting canyon. With binoculars we scanned the face of Navajo Mountain beyond it, an igneous mass rounding into a summit more than ten thousand feet high. Upthrust layers of sandstone circled the base, and an incredibly rugged country of slot canyons and slickrock domes spread out from it. The two of us had reached our turn-around point and now faced a long trek back to camp. Twin tracks, following the route laid down by iron-rim wheels, emerged from a vanishing point to the west, crossed the mesa top behind us, and disappeared over a rise to the east.

A month later I returned with field biologist Chuck LaRue to spend several days going farther west. Chuck always wears a pair of binoculars hanging from his neck, the black coating worn to silver by years of use. From the start he began identifying birds and by the time we finished had checked off thirty-three species, mostly migrants. Spring had come to the high desert, filling the air with the heavy scent of cliffrose and peppergrass. Navajo Sandstone formed the caprock along our route, rounding into bald heads and weathering into sand fill.

Where the old wagon road met the jeep trail at the base of Grey Mesa, a narrow dugway scarred the face of the cliff rock. This was the bottom of the trail engineered by the Hole-in-the-Rockers through what they called "the Slick Rocks," perhaps the first use of that term. Coming from the west, the Mormon scouts who found the route were on the verge of turning back in defeat until a herd of bighorn sheep showed them the way. And it's still better suited for bighorns than wagons. Climbing it, we found a hidden pocket and made camp under an old juniper, whose lower branches had been hacked off by ax 130 years before. That night we stretched out in the wagon tracks of the Hole-in-the-Rock Expedition. A landscape can shape a person by the qualities it draws out, and their epic trek drew out the best in those 230 pioneers.

Next morning we climbed what some maps call the Emigrant Trail, amazed by the skill and effort required to bring a train of covered wagons off the mesa. To force a way through the barrier cliffs, they blasted narrow ramps down sandstone faces, cut grooves to hold the uphill wheels on the steeper traverses, and hacked steps in the bare rock to give the horses better footing. We crossed sandstone worn by iron wagon wheels and stippled with pick marks where they had contoured along the cliff side. Starburst shatter patterns in the bedrock showed where the trail builders had detonated black powder packed into hand-cut drill holes. It took four days of determined effort for a crew of sixty men and boys to complete. And their journals recorded the relief at having put this stretch of road behind them.

We continued across Wilson Mesa and descended the Chute, where furrows funnel runoff into deep water pockets between slickrock domes. All around us the rock curved into shoulders and tongues of smooth sandstone. Laid down in a vast sand sea, the dunal layers fingered together in fine cross-bedding. Despite the heat, we stashed our packs and kept following the road to the west.

The route we followed headed Wilson Creek Canyon, passing the place where a trail once branched off to a crossing of the San Juan. I initially thought Thrapp might have gone this way, but his journal lacked any mention of several key landmarks here. The road we followed ended at the top of Cottonwood Canyon, where now only a foot trail continued down to Lake Powell, a distant patch of blue water. And above the lake stood a sheer cliff notched at the top. That was the actual Hole-in-the-Rock, where the wagon train had stalled on the brink of Glen Canyon until crews were able to cut a slot through the rimrock to reach the river. Chuck and I now turned back to camp, and as the light faded the first bat appeared. "It's the day shift heading home," he said, "and the night shift coming out."

Before continuing my search, I needed to rethink my approach. The attempt to force the route described in Dan's journal to fit the Wilson Mesa country hadn't worked. I was unable to tie his descriptions to the terrain or match his photos of the area with any certainty. Dan's journal becomes increasingly difficult to follow the longer he was away from civilization. He could recognize the landmarks of Navajo Mountain and the Henry Mountains, but most of the time he was lost. With little else to go on, I went back and studied his entries, focusing on each clue until I realized my mistake. They had been heading to points west, so when Dan said they rode down Castle Creek and left the wash, I assumed they had turned west. In fact, they had headed east.

The best clue to their location was a photo looking down a side canyon at the San Juan. Two landmarks stood out, a sharp prow of rock jutting from the rim and a lone knob on a prominent bench below it. I checked the topographic map and found a point that appeared to match. Next, I flew Google Earth to the right spot and tilted the perspective to almost ground level. Everything fit. It had to be the place where Dan first saw the river. Nearby he found a trail leading into the canyon where he attempted a crossing. Faint segments of a trail also appeared on the satellite view, and I marked these on the topo. To be sure, I needed to ground-truth it. So with Shane and Chris I had set out again.

Leaving Castle House after viewing the inscription, the three of us explored the shallow amphitheater where Dan's party had camped. Petroglyphs appeared on facets of cliff showing men holding immense atlatls, a stylized birth scene, and even a dancing flute player. Dan left no description of these images in his writings. Rock art occurs so often in this country that it forms a glyphic backdrop that soon goes unremarked. Returning to the truck, we headed down the highway, threading through a shallow canyon.

Soon I turned south onto a dirt track leading into Castle Creek wash itself. With a solid bottom I was able to drive down the gravelly bed for miles, dodging rocks and sand traps in a broad valley flanked by cliffs. Just as I was thinking it was too wide for a serious flood, I noticed the upstream side of a tree matted with more than six feet of debris. A huge flash flood had torn down here within the past couple of weeks. A deep mud hole soon forced us to detour, and then a sheer pouroff stopped us completely. Shifting into 4-low, I gunned it up the side of the wash to a bench above where the route continued.

Castle Creek soon began downcutting to form a canyon, making it impossible to proceed. I pulled out the binoculars and found where the road crossed the wash and climbed the far side. An exploration crew ran a blade through here in the 1950s, searching for either oil or uranium, and it appeared to follow close to the horse route taken by Dan and friends. We pushed on. While it was a rough ascent with one pitch requiring a little road building, it took us where we wanted to go. At the top of the first band of cliffs, I recognized a lenticular outcrop of Navajo Sandstone. I pulled out one of Dan's photos and matched it to the scene spreading out toward the blue haze of the Henry Mountains beyond. This confirmed we were on the right track.

The road ascended the high ridge between Castle Creek and Mikes Canyon, veering away from the logical route for someone on horseback. Dan's party had continued across the sands to a saddle and camped in a grassy basin. We stayed on the road, skirting the canyon rim where a spectacular view opened. Stopping where I figured Dan first saw the river, we got out on foot. The land was ribbed with sandstone, and sand filled the hollows between.

What we saw from the rim lined up with the black-and-white photograph I held from 1935. I could recognize the sharp prow, the solitary knob, and the creek snaking down to join the green bottomlands of the San Juan. Since the waters of Lake Powell had receded, the river had reclaimed its own and appeared much the way it did in the old photo. I even noticed a stretch of low cliffs opposite the mouth of Mikes Canyon that had forced Dan to go downstream before trying to cross. We kept moving along the rim, letting the crumbled expanse of cliffs and canyon reveal itself with each bend.

Back in the truck, I drove another half mile, searching for a level place to camp. I pulled onto an old drill pad marked by a stub of metal casing. To the southwest Nokai Dome rose above the horizon, partially obscuring the humped profile of Navajo Mountain. Below us the earth was cut to the bone, exposing the dermal layers of sand, mud, and clay turned to stone. And between mesas, I saw the distant spire of El Capitan on the edge of Monument Valley, casting a long gnomonic shadow. We settled into camp, where scrub juniper and prickly pear cactus mixed with ungrazed grasses.

Next morning Shane grabbed his camera and slipped out of camp at the first hint of light, while I took off to find Dan's trail. On each side the cliffs dropped sheer without a break in sight, so I worked back toward the first overlook and finally saw a possibility. Talus angled upward nearly to the top, and using binoculars I spotted the ruins of a trail. The route was so steep and improbable, I was excited by the prospect of trying to piece it together. Back at camp the three of us packed up for the day, not knowing if the route still remained passable.

Skirting the rim, we found an old camp tucked among the rocks. A rough shelter of juniper logs resembled a hogan, and a typical Navajo sweat lodge stood nearby. In this region, archaeologists had found strong influences from both the Mesa Verde and the Kayenta branches of the Ancestral Pueblo. At one site they also excavated the remains of a historic camp with a buggy, Navajo sweat hogan, Hopi pottery, and an early polychrome bowl from Zia Pueblo. It represented a frontier mix in a region long used as a refuge, a place beyond the reach of army patrols, lawmen, and irate husbands. As San Juan County sheriff Rigby Wright told me, "This has always been hideout country."[1]

We crossed a high point and located the break marked by two cairns. As Dan noted in his journal, you need to be right on top of the trailhead to see it. A set of tight switchbacks, with steps pickaxed from the bedrock, led to a plunging traverse across a cone of talus. Washouts and rock slides had nearly obliterated the trail, forcing us to pay close attention to route finding. Whenever it disappeared I stopped and carefully checked for any traces before proceeding. At times we spread out until one of us spotted enough of a lead to continue. Steep and loose, the route took us down to a bench below the bleached red of the Kayenta cliffs. At this point I lost the trail again.

We scouted for a way through the rimrock, working too far east. Finally, I pulled out one of Dan's photos, and we took turns studying it. Backtracking, we found where the landmarks aligned and soon came upon signs of a built trail. The cliff ledges had been widened with pick and powder, but little remained of the juniper limbs and rubble used for fill. The forces of erosion keep working on remnants of the trail to restore the profile of the cliff to its natural fall line. Even in 1935 the route had deteriorated to the point where Dan's companions refused to take their horses down it.

At first I kept an eye on Chris during our descent. Not long ago he was sitting in an office in New York City, and now he was scrambling through broken terrain a mile higher in elevation than his recent surroundings. But being fit and with plenty of mountaineering experience, he took it all in stride with the same self-confidence I had noted in Dan's journal.

Once below the orange Wingate cliffs, we entered the banded blues and purples of the Chinle badlands, and a sawtooth ridge bristled red against a blue sky. As we negotiated a steep slope, an abandoned Navajo camp came into view. It lay outside the reservation on the wrong side of the river, but families who had traditionally used these canyons often ignored the surveyed boundaries. The hogan sat on a terrace, hidden by a ridge from anyone riding along the canyon bottom, and a kerosene lamp still hung from a log wall weathered gray. We reached the wash below and turned downstream, winding between high banks studded with chunks of petrified wood. Taking a water break, the three of us decided to turn back just short of the river instead of thrashing through the tamarisk thickets.

Back on the rim we decamped. Days were long this time of year, and with the sun still hanging above the cliffs, we pushed on to Muley Point at the end of Cedar Mesa. Upon reaching it, I watched Shane dash from one vantage point to another with his camera, chasing the diminishing light. Below us the river carved through the heart of the land in great serpentine loops, exposing an inner gorge countersunk in a wider canyon reaching a depth of twenty-two hundred feet. Monument Valley, far to the south, broke the skyline with sharp-cut monoliths more ethereal, more mysterious than when standing next to their solid masses.

Back Trail

Blown sand had collected in the hollows where slickrock rolled and swelled. Each curve of sandstone flowed into the next until abruptly shearing into angular cliffs along the canyon edge. Dan Thrapp and his companions stood on the rim studying an old trail zigzagging through a hidden break below. The young explorer, confident after having traveled for weeks across hard country with no trails, was ready to give it a try. Bob Wise, however, took one look and backed off. His horse would never make it, he told Dan, so he would have to accompany him to the river on foot. Bud Vinger agreed with his partner, and the trappers unpacked their horses, leaving the saddles on since they expected to be back by dark.

Late January 1935

The three men edged over the rim and picked their way down the switch-backs, following a trail ripped by washouts and buried under cliff rubble. Unknown to them, they were descending into Mikes Canyon, a branch of the entrenched San Juan River named for a Paiute Indian. They made good time, despite having to work Dan's horses down two-foot drops known as jumps. After crossing a broad bench, they reached a second rim and found evidence of blasting used to widen a narrow shelf traversing the lower band of cliffs. They continued to descend, and once on the canyon bottom turned down the graveled wash.

When they reached the San Juan, wild horses splashed into the river and followed a submerged sandbar until out of sight. Cliffs on the far side

prevented a crossing here, so Dan climbed a terrace and found a trail running parallel to the river. Marked by cairns, it looked promising and might
lead to the ford he sought. By now it was too late to return to the rim, so
the trappers settled in for the night, with Wise cooking what he called a
"Navajo supper." He simply boiled chunks of meat in an old can until nearly
done and then poured in bacon grease to top it off. Soon the air temperature dropped, and lacking bedrolls the two trappers crowded under the
blankets next to Dan. They spent a cold night, and all three were huddled
by the fire before dawn.

After packing up his outfit, Dan shook hands with the old trapper and
thanked him for having come along. "A five mile walk," the explorer wrote,
"for one troubled with rheumatism as he is, is no joke—and down that trail
it's torture—especially when you have to think about going back up again."[1]
Wise had told him, "I wouldn't travel with no man as long as I have with you,
and then not see him across the river. I hate to see you go, anyway." Dan
and Bud Vinger took the river trail downstream and found what appeared
to be a way across. They were unaware the actual crossing was still a mile
or more downriver, above the mouth of Castle Creek.

Dan grew apprehensive as he studied the water, trying to pick out the
best route. "I don't mind telling you," he wrote, "that damn' river had me
scared. It's so full of sand and dirt that you can't see the bottom of a spoon
when you dip up a spoonful of it. It looks oily—it looks treacherous, and it
doesn't have the reputation it has for nothing. It sure looked wicked this
morning."[2] The San Juan was notoriously unpredictable. It might cease to
flow, as it had during a drought the year before, or suddenly grow into a
churning slurry so thick with silt it was more solid than liquid. Geologist
R. C. Pierce once witnessed the San Juan in flood and noted it "ran with a
smooth, oily movement and presented the peculiar appearance of a stream
of molten red metal."[3] What Dan faced was a shallow river riddled with hidden pockets of quicksand, especially dangerous for horses weakened by
long weeks of travel.

The only way to keep his animals from getting mired in the quicksand
was to avoid bad sections and keep them moving. Quicksand forms when
water percolates through sand, reducing the friction between grains. Getting stuck is not particularly dangerous for humans, since it's rare to sink
above the waist, but it can be unnerving because those who struggle will

sink deeper. And the first impulse is to struggle, which causes the sands to compact even tighter around the feet. When trapped, a person can break the suction by slowly leaning forward and getting as horizontal as possible, an acutely counterintuitive move. A horse faces a greater risk, especially when loaded down. Generally, it won't sink much deeper than the level of its belly, but it will struggle until exhausted and may not be able to hold its head above water. If the horse doesn't drown, hypothermia eventually sets in.

The young explorer rode cautiously into the shallows, leading the pack-horse at a steady pace. The bottom held for more than thirty yards until the horse Dan was riding hit a soft pocket and hesitated. Recognizing the danger, he instantly got Buck moving again, but the trailing horse stepped into the now loosened sand and sank into the quagmire above her haunches. As they lost momentum, Buck also began to sink, and Dan urged him forward while shouting at Queen. She balked, not knowing what to do, as Buck floundered, rolling over on his side. Dan jumped clear before getting caught under the horse and landed in the quicksand himself. "I was too scared to think," he wrote. "I know I could feel the suction of the quicksand—that's all."[4] To escape he splashed to shore in a frantic effort to reach solid ground.

As he caught his breath, Dan watched the packhorse sink deeper. He had to do something fast, so he decided to take his chances and waded back. First, he cut the lash rope holding the pack. Pulling off the bedroll, he stood on it to reach the rest of the gear, tossing everything in the river. He then yanked on the hackamore but was unable to get Queen to budge. Turning to Buck, he shouted and tugged on the reins with all his strength until they broke loose in his hands. Nothing was working, as both horses remained trapped and the river was inching higher. Quicksand sucked at Dan's feet, forcing him to keep moving to avoid sinking. Transferring the hackamore to Buck, he again pulled hard, desperate to free him, and whacked the horse with a piece of lash rope to keep him from giving up. "He would plunge and then fall back again—each time, however, he got out a little. At last he gave a great heave and stood on his feet; I led him ashore and believe me he didn't hesitate this time."

The young trapper, who had been watching from the bank, took off his pants and waded out to lend a hand. The two of them began by straightening Queen's forelegs. Then while Dan pulled, Vinger lifted her haunches. Each time the horse tried to rise up, she would fall back and roll on her side. Dan kept her head above water, and they tried again. "She struggled and plunged and finally stood up," Dan wrote. "I was the happiest man in the world when I led her ashore. I never want to come that close to losing those horses again. It was pure luck that we got them out at all....If they'd settled just a little faster, or if we'd been just a little slower—the San Juan would have had two more carcasses to pave its bed."

He had failed to cross the river. Alone in camp that evening, he worked on his journal as the realities of exploration took hold. "Adventure," he wrote. "As always, unexpected and unwanted."

The ascent to the rim took two days, and Queen slipped and fell back three times, nearly going over the edge. Dan was forced to unload the pack-horse and carry all of the gear up the final hundred yards. Back at the rim camp he found the trappers stretching skins and preparing to set out a trapline. Dan decided to rest his horses a few days before backtracking to Comb Wash and crossing the river at the Mexican Hat bridge. Those few days would stretch into weeks due to the weather and the old longing to explore.

In early February, Vinger rode up Castle Creek to a cowboy camp they had spotted while crossing the Clay Hills. Dan took off on foot in the opposite direction, finding a way into the canyon formed by lower Castle Creek. Reaching the San Juan, he located the elusive crossing a short distance upstream, but realized his chance to ford the river had slipped away. His horses were too weak for another attempt, knowing a second encounter with quicksand would finish them. He pushed hard and made it back to camp after dark, exhausted. To his surprise, Vinger returned loaded with cans of molasses and syrup, a supply of sugar and coffee, two pounds of salt, and fifty pounds of flour. He had raided a food cache belonging to the cattle outfit run by Harve Williams, a tough man to cross. Breaking into a cache was accepted in dire circumstances. A hungry traveler could take enough food to survive a few days, but it was considered bad form to clean out a store of food others might be depending on. No matter. Vinger had acquired the habit of ignoring both law and custom if they conflicted with his own needs. "Hope those cowpunchers don't kick," Dan wrote.[5]

A freezing night faded into a morning breaking sharply cold. A mix of snow and rain fell throughout the day, giving Dan a reason to stay in camp doing nothing. His shoes had worn out, and his horses were having trouble regaining their strength. And something else was working on him.

After having woven himself into the landscape so tightly, the explorer was reluctant to let it go. He had left the outer world behind to enter an elemental land and had grown accustomed to the long reaches of distance and the nearness of the past. The longer he stayed away, the easier it was to forget what had been left behind. Having gone so deeply into a wilderness of stone and sand, he kept finding reasons not to go back.

As his desire to explore revived, Dan saddled his packhorse and rode up Castle Wash, intending to follow the Hole-in-the-Rock trail. Vinger had found where it left the bed and thought it might lead to the elusive lakes. Climbing the bank, Dan caught his first view of the snow-covered Kaiparowits Plateau, which he called Wild Horse Mesa after the name used by Zane Grey. Soon the trail disappeared in a dune field, forcing him to pick his own way forward. After the original Hole-in-the-Rockers abandoned the route, the desert had closed in behind them, leaving few traces to follow. He continued riding until he came to a canyon cutting deeply through the underlying rock in winding twists five hundred feet deep. It was Moqui Canyon, a name unknown to him, and he descended a long falling dune to the bottom. With his needs having been reduced to such basics as water and firewood, he took delight in the flowing springs and thickets of Gambel oak he found. For the next two days he explored the prehistoric cliff houses and granaries tucked away in the cliff faces. While Dan was unaware that archaeologists had already scouted the canyon, he still found it thick with ancient sites appearing to be untouched.

He exited Moqui by climbing the sand dune he had used to enter it. Following his own trail back, he was caught by a dust storm while crossing the dune field. Tired and hungry, his horse faltered. She would balk whenever he tried to ride and drag if he tried to lead her. "I shouted myself hoarse at her," he said, "used up all of my pet cuss words, and got so mad I got blue in the face."[6] And then remorse set in for having lost his temper. Overtaken by dark, Dan finally hobbled her and continued to camp on foot.

Next day he retrieved the horse and stayed in camp all day. As snow fell, Dan and the two trappers discussed their options and decided to renew their efforts to find the lakes. For the next six days they would wander about, disoriented, as they picked up a fragment of one trail or another, only to soon lose it in the sand and bald rock. Dan walked to spare his horses. "We didn't know where in the hell we were," he wrote, "or where we'd been or where we were going."[7] Coming upon parts of an "old Mormon cross-Utah wagon," he noticed it had been built with wooden pegs rather than nails. The three of them were unable to find any sign of the lost lake, but eventually reached an overlook of the Colorado River. Dan pieced together a way down on foot without knowing he had reached Halls Crossing, used briefly by Mormon pioneers and then abandoned.

"This is old desperado country," Wise told him sitting by the campfire. "How it would look to some stranger happening along, to see us camped in the rocks, each with a six-shooter, a couple of rifles lying around, beards on our faces, and our horses hidden away in the rocks. We'd make pretty looking outlaws, all right."[8] Old Bob was having some fun with Dan, knowing he was unaware both trappers were on the run from the law.

Returning to Castle Creek, they were back on familiar ground and made camp for several days at a spring west of Clay Hills Pass. Dan spent the time exploring Ancestral Puebloan ruins and found initials and old dates carved in the mud plaster on a wall of Castle House. He added his own name and having lost count of the days scratched in the wrong date. His hold of time had again slipped, as the days became a circular progression. One day he climbed to the Clay Hills Divide with Wise. As they looked to the east, the trapper told Dan he planned to head home to Bluff before the cowboys discovered how much food they had taken. His real reason, Dan thought, was to resupply his stash of coffee and tobacco and to see his Navajo girlfriend. "That sets kind of hard on the old boy," Dan noted.[9]

The three of them descended Clay Hills Pass in late February and fought a dust storm before making camp at the foot of the Red House Cliffs. A snowstorm kept them pinned down the next day, giving them time to consider taking an alternative trail through Johns Canyon. Since the half foot of snow would make route finding difficult, they decided to stay on the known course. If they had chosen Johns, they might have witnessed a shoot-out several days later between a former sheriff and a Texas killer hiding from the law.

High winds on the trailing edge of the storm hit the next day, followed by bitter cold weather. At night they were forced to build fires to warm the ground where they planned to sleep. Even taking these precautions, Dan spent a cold night wrapped in blankets wet from snowmelt. As they crossed Cedar Mesa the following day, they lost the trail and then lost it again when they climbed out of Grand Gulch. "While we were hunting it," Dan said, "someone went through with a horse and a mule. If we had been on the trail, we might have bummed a smoke."[10] A second traveler had ridden through recently with four animals, but they never caught up with either one. They pushed on to Comb Wash, and Dan's packhorse gave out while descending. He was forced to leave Queen tied to a tree along the trail. The three men reached the line shack they had stayed in before heading west of Clay Hills.

Below the Comb

He lay in the dark interior of the cabin on the east side of Cedar Mesa, unable to sleep. Dan sat up and began dressing. His beard had grown long during his three-month journey, his hair left uncut, his face weathered. Moving quietly to the door, he was careful not to step on the blanket-covered forms of his companions on the floor. He went out before dawn and breathed in the sharp air of late winter. He stood for a solemn moment under a night sky beginning to thin. Countless grains of starlight were fading in the east where the scarp of Comb Ridge lifted the skyline high above the valley floor, stretching southward until it dissolved in the distance.

March 1, 1935

On this morning, Dan's horses were unfit to travel, his shoes unfit to wear, and his remaining food barely fit to eat. Despite the difficulties, he had no plans to end his expedition. He stood outside the line shack, thinking about the horse he had left a mile back on the trail. If there was any chance to save her, he had to try. During months of severe hardship, Dan had grown close to his horses. They had covered endless miles of broken country together, crossed a wild and icy river, fought through belly-deep snowdrifts and dust storms, descended sheer cliffs on threads of trail. The horses had depended on his judgment and care, while he had depended on their strength and companionship. Before first light Dan began hiking back up Cedar Mesa.

When he had gained some elevation, the lunar crescent surfaced above the crest of Comb Ridge, throwing enough light to soften the darkness. The trail was rocky, angling up the shoulder of the mesa close to the prominent knob of sandstone he called Pictograph Rock. It didn't take long to find the packhorse lying next to the tree where he had left her. Dan set to work, tugging and pushing, trying to get Queen on her feet. He whispered encouragement, shouted and pleaded with her, desperate to save his horse. At one point the mare almost regained her feet, but she fell back again. He built a fire and boiled some coffee, unsure what to do next.

As Dan started back to the cabin, light struck over the ridge and caught him on the open slickrock. The sunrise brought with it a great clearing, sweeping away the darkness and turning the edge of the cold. Gray tones gave way to the solid colors of day as the shadows added depth to the broad valley where dry channels braided down the open bed. The trappers were up and about when Dan got back, and Vinger agreed to give him a hand with Queen. The two of them climbed the trail to the dying horse and used every trick they knew to save her. They almost managed to get her back on her feet, but after an exhausting effort she gave up. Not knowing what was wrong, they were unable to do more and turned back to camp. The men were resigned to let events play out. As they were coming off the slickrock, Vinger saw a stranger ahead, always a concern to a fugitive. He pointed toward camp and asked, "Who's that?"[1]

Dan was able to make out a horseman, and as they got closer he realized the rider was an Indian woman. After closing the distance, the trapper shook hands with the Paiute, while in broken English she delivered the first news of the outside world they had heard in weeks. "The Pahute kept saying something about the sheriff," Dan wrote. Later, when Vinger was out of earshot, the old trapper explained the situation. "Bob told me that Bill was 'on the dodge,'" he continued. Although they had traveled together for weeks, Vinger was still calling himself Bill Jones. "It seems that some one was selling whiskey to the Utes—who got fighting drunk—and killed a couple of them. Bill got pinched for it and broke out of the best jail in Utah, and has been on the dodge ever since.... They call him the 'San Juan Dillinger.' He's supposed to be the bad man around here."

A month earlier, when the three of them had camped in Comb Wash, a rancher had recognized Vinger and notified the sheriff. A posse had come looking for the outlaw, and he feared they would be back again. After hearing the woman's report, the two trappers quickly packed up, intending to ride to the trading post at Bluff for more supplies. Dan would stay in camp and take care of the horses until they returned in four or five days. Before nightfall, he carried a bucket of water up to Queen and piled hay nearby. It was all he could do, and it was not enough. By morning the mare was dead. "I may have killed her," he wrote, "but if I did, it was through ignorance— not because I wouldn't have done anything I could for her."[2]

His family had grown increasingly worried as the weeks passed without any word from Dan. When he was long overdue, his father began sending letters and telegrams to anyone who might have information on his whereabouts. He feared for his son. A search party had begun retracing his route on horseback, following a trail grown cold, and an air search was about to get off the ground. Front-page stories were running in the Utah newspapers, and editors around the country had picked up on the search. Readers anxiously followed each development, concerned about the fate of the young man from the American Museum of Natural History who had gone missing. Cut off from the outer world, Dan had no way of knowing his disappearance had become national news.

TRACKINGS

Two cowboys descended the Horsethief Trail to the Green River on February 24, nearly three months after Dan Thrapp had passed that way. They led a string of spare horses and were packing food for ten days. The searchers moved steadily and picked up the young explorer's known trail along the river. "That took us," one of the cowboys later reported, "pretty well out of country most frequented by human beings."[1]

LATE WINTER 1935

Ten days earlier Frank Thrapp had contacted T. S. Brown, the chief of police in Green River, Utah, requesting help in locating his missing son. Dan's last letter home had been mailed from town in late November, and the family had grown increasingly concerned when the weeks rolled by without word from him. Being a father himself, Brown readily agreed to investigate the disappearance, telling Frank he would do everything possible to find his son. The lawman contacted Art Murry, the rancher who had sold Dan his horses. Murry reported, wrongly it turned out, that Dan had left his ranch carrying food for only three weeks. "Murry tried to talk the boy out of it," Brown informed the father, "but as you say the boy had a mind of his own."[2]

To mount a search, the police chief needed men who could handle themselves in the backcountry and follow a cold trail across bare rock if necessary. So he sent word to Leland Tidwell and Paul Herron, who had spent their lives in the saddle and knew the surrounding canyons as well as anyone. Realizing the young explorer might be dead, the lawman instructed them on how to take care of the body, if it came to that. Photograph the remains, he said, and gather all belongings before rolling the body in a tarp and packing it back to Green River. As they sorted their gear, the cowboys faced a difficult task. A newspaper reporter said those with knowledge of the rough nature of the terrain had given the search party only "one chance in a thousand" of finding him.[3]

The police chief kept Frank updated on developments while trying to allay his fears. "Mr. Tidwell thinks the boy alive," T. S. Brown wrote, "either lost or shelved, sayes man can live long time, there being deer and other game in that country, water in what they call wells in the rocks and river."[4] Two days after the searchers departed, Brown wrote again, still trying to strike a reassuring note. "Don't have any fear of foul play. Any one living in or going through that country will always help one in any way possible. Your boy being a rounder will be a great help to him, and gives great hopes of his safety.... A few years ago an old man was comeing through this same country, broke leg, splinted it up, shot pack mule, lived on mule meat, come out in spring OK."[5]

The search party rode onto the White Rim above the confluence of the Green and Colorado, following whatever traces still remained of Dan's trail. His newly shod horses had left sharp hoof prints, but storms and passing cattle had obscured the old tracks, adding to the difficulty of tracing him across bedrock. For several days the cowboys checked a succession of points, riding out and back, along the path taken by the explorer hunting a way to the river. They kept piecing together his route and eventually found where Dan had left the rim. The horsemen stayed on his trail down Lathrop Canyon to the Colorado. On that day an Associated Press story was reporting, "Fear Felt Daniel Thrapp May Have Drowned on Crossing River."[6]

Cut off from the outside world, the searchers reached a different conclusion. They found evidence of Dan having built a raft and followed his example. The dangerous crossing took these veteran horsemen a day and a half to complete, and once on the far side they found enough evidence to convince them Dan had made it safely across. After pushing on for another twenty miles beyond the Colorado, they were forced to turn back, having run low on supplies. "It was a disagreeable trip," Tidwell said, "due to rain and snow storms and cold winds."[7]

Frank Thrapp knew it would be many days before receiving any word from the search party. Meanwhile, he sent letters and telegrams to those who might be able to help. He learned Dan had told friends in Wyoming of his plans to undertake a solo pack trip, but little else. "I and my husband have never known such a fine boy," wrote Mrs. Milo Howe.[8] Dan had shared meals with them and occasionally spent evenings and Sundays at their ranch. "We like him so well as he is so manly and polite, not at all like other boys his age.... He got to be like one of the family."

The postmaster in Winslow, Arizona, where Dan planned to end his expedition, promised to wire if he showed up. "The boy picked a tough country and a bad season of the year to do his wandering," wrote A. R. Kleindienst, "but I would not become unduly alarmed. Ruffians would not bother him unless he has a large sum of money with him. It is quite possible that he ran into some bad weather and has put up with a rancher at some isolated point awaiting for the weather to clear."[9]

With newspapers covering the ongoing search efforts, the story of the missing scientist captivated readers across the country. And in a matter of days the national publicity had generated new leads. Rancher J. T. Pehrson informed authorities in Green River that Dan had turned up at his place two miles south of Monticello on January 4, offering to work if the rancher fed his horses. "He said he had plenty of food," Pehrson told a reporter, "but I had a 15-pound slab of cured bacon to spare, and told him to slip it in his pack. He said he was going to the other side of the Elk Mountains. That was all, and he just drove his two horses onward and never appeared for a moment to be worried by his ability to conquer the barriers of the country."[10]

Word of his appearance at the ranch brought some relief to the family, since it meant Dan had succeeded in crossing the treacherous waters of the Colorado River. And they now knew he had gone somewhere beyond Elk Ridge on the south side of the Abajo Mountains.

Unconfirmed reports of another search party surfaced briefly. A reporter claimed a tracking party of "keen-eyed Indians" was en route to southern Utah from Arizona.[11] The chances of finding the young man, the article stated, were slim. "But it is hoped that their heritage from their forefathers, who alone knew the secrets of the mysterious Dark canyon that was the young man's goal, will enable them to find his trail." No update followed. And then a government survey party returned from the field with word of having encountered the missing scientist.

The surveyors had been working near Hite Crossing on the Colorado River, downstream from Dark Canyon, when they met "a tall, rangy lad" who appeared to know how to handle himself.[12] John Trasker, the "wilderness-wise" guide for the surveyors, inspected the traveler's outfit and warned him about his lack of sufficient provisions. But he did have a seventy-five-foot rope for lowering himself into Indian cliff dwellings. Having already crossed the river at Hite with his horses, Trasker said, the young man must have drowned while attempting a second crossing to reach Dark Canyon. The leader of the party, Harry Ott, pushed the speculation even further. "When Thrapp drove his horses into the stream," he said, "and followed them at an unproved and unmarked ford, he was probably snatched up by the current, carried beyond his marked landing place, dashed against the rocks and boulders and drowned." The only trace of him that might turn up would be the rope he was carrying. "It probably will be found coiled snake-like by the water around some rock," Ott added. "That will be about all to mark where Thrapp died."

This encounter had happened sometime between November 28 and December 2 of the previous year, so the young man could not have been Dan Thrapp, as they claimed. During that period he was just beginning his journey and still on the Green River, far to the north. Trasker planned to return to the Colorado where he last saw the young man and search the banks by boat for any sign of him. The identity of the lone traveler remains unknown.

When news of Dan Thrapp's disappearance reached the American Museum of Natural History, Barnum Brown was concerned but not alarmed. "No one is better able to take care of himself in the wilds," said the curator, "than young Thrapp."[13] In his correspondence with Dr. Brown, Frank Thrapp admitted he had only a rough idea of his son's plans. He had kept his father in the dark, concerned he might launch a search prematurely if he thought Dan was dangerously overdue. "I am sure Dan did not lose his bearings," Frank wrote. "I am inclined to think he either fell or rocks fell on him. He was injured in some way and unable to reach his horses and by that means make his way back to civilization. He may have been drowned in the river. He surely would have communicated with me had it been otherwise."[14]

The curator responded with assurances that the museum was doing everything possible in the search for his son. "We all extend to you our sympathy in this great anxiety," Brown wrote, "but personally I feel quite sure that Dan will turn up safe and sound. He was not a boy to take chances and was quite capable of taking care of himself under almost any circumstances."[15] The paleontologist knew the Four Corners country and believed his assistant was investigating the ancient Pueblo ruins on his own. And based on his years of conducting expeditions in remote corners of the world, he ended with a perceptive comment. "It is so easy for a person to completely forget the outside world when carrying on an exploration." In a matter of days, Dan would begin to remember.

Museum officials thought an aerial search might be the only way to find the young explorer, if he was still alive. But they were confused about Dan's route, believing he had planned to start his trip in Arizona and head north. When the president of the museum attempted to enlist United Airlines in the search effort, it turned down his request. To divert a plane from its flight path two hundred miles north was impractical, and without knowing Dan's route the effort would be futile. A few days later the *Deseret News* contacted the museum with an offer to undertake the air search itself.

A graduate student at the University of Utah had offered to fly his own plane and take a reporter with him. Mahlon Kemmerer, an excellent pilot and son of a mining magnate, had been captain of the polo team at Princeton. Flying was his passion, and even a forced landing a few months earlier, when he walked away from a burning plane, had not lessened his enthusiasm. The museum agreed to join forces with the newspaper and recommended starting the search at the junction of the Green and Colorado. With time running out, they wanted it to begin immediately.

MARCH 1, 1935

Kemmerer and staff reporter Alfred Reck left Salt Lake City that evening, carrying messages and emergency rations to drop if they spotted Dan's camp. After crossing the Wasatch Range the pilot landed the Waco biplane in Price, Utah, and at daybreak they continued the flight. Their destination was the San Juan River, but snow squalls forced the pilot to divert to Moab, where he had to leave the plane. "An airplane roared above the yawning jaws of black-walled canyons in the Badland country of southern Utah today," a news account began, "carrying two men on an errand of mercy."[16] The searchers proceeded south by car, passing through the towns of Monticello and Blanding before arriving in Bluff.

After questioning some of the locals without success, the searchers stopped at the trading post. Inside the store they learned a trapper by the name of Bob Wise had come in the day before to buy supplies for a young

Journey's end. Dan Thrapp stands outside the town of Bluff on his return to civilization. With search parties hunting for him, the young explorer decided to end his expedition after three months. Courtesy of the Haley Memorial Library and History Center.

explorer. His name was Dan Thrapp. The reporter immediately sent word to Wise at his place on the outskirts of town, but the trapper was reluctant to cooperate at first. With an outstanding warrant for his arrest, he felt uneasy about meeting a stranger. Finally, he agreed to talk and nervously entered the trading post, not knowing what to expect. In an article for the *Deseret News*, the reporter described his conversation with the old trapper.

"Yes, I've been with a young fellow named Thrapp for about a month," Wise replied to inquiries. "He's kinda run out of grub and I came in to see if I couldn't russel some for him. Oh, he's all right, outside of one horse is dead and the other one in poor condition and he aint got no shoes and mighty little grub. I don't think he'll starve yet for awhile."

"Do you know exactly where he is?" Wise was asked.

"Shore," the aged trapper replied.

"Can you get to him?" he was asked.

"Reckon I can but my horses is tuckered out."[17]

The reporter arranged for fresh mounts, and Bob Wise promised to bring Dan back the next day before dark. The trapper rode west out of town toward Comb Wash, leading a string of spare horses. He kept riding and to meet his deadline rode through a night further darkened by rain and snow. After pushing up the creek bed for twelve miles, he stopped to build a fire and wait for daybreak. At nine in the morning he reached the line shack and told Dan that a rescue expedition had arrived in Bluff. They had a plane out looking for him, the trapper said, and everyone thought he was dead. The news took Dan by surprise, since he had never considered himself really lost.

An hour later the two of them started back. The explorer had borrowed a pair of overshoes to replace his dilapidated shoes. Moving fast, they covered twenty-two miles in five hours with Dan choosing to walk. The recent storm had brought floodwaters churning down the last wash before Bluff, so Dan mounted up and rode horseback for the final leg. At sundown on March 4 the missing scientist splashed across Cottonwood Creek, emerging from a wilderness some thought had swallowed him forever. "What's the matter?" he asked at the trading post. "Why were they worrying about me? I told them I would be gone a month, and it's only three months now."[18]

Al Reck sat down with the explorer and found he had to twist the story out of him. Dan had an aversion to talking about himself and a tendency to downplay his adventures, qualities he had admired in the old cowpunchers he worked with in New Mexico. So it took careful questioning to draw out his account of the expedition. Finally, Reck had enough material to call it in to the newspaper. "Thrapp closed his three months adventure," he wrote, "an adventure that caused the nation to worry and wonder as to his fate."[19] And then the reporter convinced him to return to Salt Lake City.

The writer, the pilot, and the once-missing scientist drove back to Monticello in a car borrowed from district attorney (DA) Don Adams. And that evening Dan learned about a shoot-out a few days before in Johns Canyon, not far from where he had camped. He wrote in his journal about "Two-Gun Jimmy" Palmer and described how he had ambushed and killed an old cattleman and a young cowboy. Palmer was now on the run, Dan added, and last seen in Arizona. The DA was attempting to involve federal agents in the case, since the fugitive had crossed the state line in a stolen automobile. "The old story about water holes," Dan summed up the incident, "the cattlemen there first and the sheepherder with squatter's rights."[20] Intrigued by the case, he would continue to follow developments over the next couple of months.

Back in civilization at last, the explorer stretched out on his first bed since November. And couldn't sleep. Despite having covered long miles on foot earlier in the day, he lay awake in a bed he found too soft. He eventually dozed off at five in the morning, only to wake two hours later in the middle of a snowstorm. As the weather eased, the three of them drove on to the Moab airstrip. Kemmerer warmed up the biplane, and the others loaded their gear before taking seats in the four-passenger cabin. They lifted off and climbed to an altitude of eleven thousand feet to clear the mountains. For Dan, conditioned to the ambling pace of his horses, it turned into a thrilling ride. "We crossed the Wasatch Plateau," he noted, "where the air was so rough it made each of my whiskers uncurl and stand straight out."[21]

The pilot landed in Salt Lake City on Tuesday morning after a two-hour flight. Al Reck refused to let Dan shave or cut his hair until photographs were taken, but he was allowed to clean up. He told the reporter he felt like old Bob Wise, who accidentally washed his hands while cleaning a pot. "Gosh," Wise said, "that little washing my hands got made them feel so good,

I think I'll wash my face."[22] The three of them posed in front of the plane with the pilot in his flight suit on one side and the reporter, nattily dressed in a three-piece suit, on the other. Dan stood in the middle, looking like he would rather be somewhere else. He wore his mud boots on loan from Bob Wise, the red sweater, and the cowboy hat he had picked up in Wyoming while digging dinosaur bones. And then they rushed off to the newspaper.

Taking seats in the editorial office, they began writing their accounts of the search and the events leading to it. A deadline was pressing, so Dan ended up dictating his story to a reporter. When they finished in midafternoon he took off to find a barber, but was hustled away for a radio interview before the job was finished. Upon returning to the barbershop, he saw the latest edition of the newspaper with the banner headline "Thrapp Brought to S.L., Missing Scientist Relates Hardships in Wilderness." On the front page was his story, already in print, and it contained an interesting omission. Dan described his adventures with Bob Wise but never mentioned his other traveling companion, Bud Vinger. He was covering for the outlaw who was still on the run.

After so many weeks of solitary travel, Dan found himself caught up in the frenzied pace of the city. Other reporters called to interview him, visitors stopped by the apartment where he was staying, and he was finally able to place a call home to his parents, who had already been notified that he was safe and happy to be back in civilization. At midnight Dan went to a nightclub with Kemmerer, feeling out of place in his red sweater and borrowed boots. Before turning in at two thirty, he wrote, "Today has certainly been one of the busiest—and most complete—days of my life."[23] Dan remained in Salt Lake, waiting to get paid for his article and enjoying the nightlife in a borrowed suit.

On March 7 the Monticello newspaper ran a story titled "Scientist Is Found, Artist Lost in S.E. Utah." It paired the search for Dan Thrapp with Everett Ruess, and that evening Dan mentioned him in his journal for the first time. A search party had been looking for traces of the missing artist at the same time searchers had been attempting to find Dan on the other side of the Colorado. At one point the pilot and the reporter thought they might be able to help. "Al and Mahlon are talking of leaving tomorrow noon," Dan noted, "to hunt for two lost would-be rescuers of an artist, Ruess, who is lost somewhere near the Escalante River, Wild Horse Mesa, or Hole-in-the-Rock."[24] The missing searchers turned up, and the air search never got off the ground.

In another entry Dan updated the Johns Canyon shoot-out. "They're going to try Palmer on a killing he's supposed to have pulled off near Sulphur Springs, Texas—where he was captured."[25] And one evening at the University Club, Dan was having dinner with Kemmerer and Al Reck when they ran into the district attorney handling the Palmer case. Don Adams had driven up from Monticello to file extradition papers against the murderer. Adams told them he was planning to travel to Texas with the sheriff to question the prisoner, and Kemmerer offered to fly them. The DA later called to cancel the flight since the sheriff, he said, was afraid of flying.

Next day an editor at the *Deseret News* asked Dan to write a feature story on the prehistoric Pueblo occupation of the Four Corners region. His three-month exploration of cliff dwellings was considered enough expertise to handle the assignment. And soon a check for two hundred dollars arrived in payment for the article he had written on the day he arrived. It was the first time he had been paid for writing, but it would not be the last. "Sure felt like a million with that dough in my pocket," Dan wrote, "more than I've ever had at one time before."[26]

His departure from Salt Lake lacked the thrills of his airborne arrival. On March 13 he caught a slow bus east, visiting family in Illinois and Tennessee before continuing on to New York City. Upon arrival he checked into a hotel and had his shoes shined and his suit pressed, wanting to make a good impression on his return to the American Museum of Natural History. While his disappearance had caused the institution some expense and a great deal of concern, he was ready to resume his duties. Entering the paleontology lab, he found one of the Wyoming crew, R. T. Bird, sitting in his old seat and pecking away at a fossil, doing the work he had once done. Then he knocked on the door of his boss, Barnum Brown, who broke the news. "Brown said there was no money," Dan wrote, "so I didn't have any job. He had assured me several times out west that I would have a job no matter how much time I took on my trip—within reason, of course. He wasn't even decent enough to write me out there and tell me."[27] Dan had lost a job but not his determination. Before stepping out of the museum and back onto the streets, he made up his mind to become a journalist.

In the wake of his son's safe return, Frank Thrapp settled accounts with the cowboys who had conducted the ground search and expressed his deep appreciation to T. S. Brown for his help. The lawman refused any compensation, telling Frank it was the first letter of appreciation he had ever received. "Dan would have made his way back alone," the father wrote, "but as it was he suffered great hardships of which he spoke only little.... Few men would have survived, except possibly men inured to such a life for years." And then he added, "Dan will tell you nothing of the hardships, you must read between the lines."[28]

Those lines stand alone. Dan Thrapp had undertaken an epic journey across the canyons of Utah in winter. He had floundered through deep snows, survived a turbulent river crossing, and struggled to extricate his horses from quicksand. He had discovered unknown rock art and the ruins of ancient cliff houses and had traveled with outlaws in a West not fully tamed. He had spent days trying to figure out ways through the maze of barrier cliffs and box canyons, and on more than one occasion had found himself lost, disoriented, or turned around. And all of this unfolded in what he saw as the last true wilderness in America.

PART 2

THE WOODCUTTER'S DAUGHTER

Lucy Garrett

THE ROADSIDE

Darkness settled over a roadside camp where Lucy Garrett sat by a fire burning low. The woodcutter's daughter had been camped among the post oak thickets and rolling farmlands for two months, helping her father haul firewood into town. Ten years before, she had lost her mother and being alone at the time was taken in by distant relatives. Her daddy had come for her after he finished serving time behind bars for stealing horses. Now a pretty thirteen-year-old, Lucy was happy just to be with him, to have a family of her own no matter what the circumstances. The tang of fresh-cut oak hung in the air as the woods closed in dark around her. On this soft April evening in Choctaw County, Oklahoma, all was right with the world.

APRIL 1934

With the country caught in a deep depression, it wasn't so unusual to find someone camped alongside a road. The killing droughts and economic collapse had uprooted a half-million farmers from their land and left 22 percent of the American workforce unemployed. People took any job they could find after millions of acres of farmland had disappeared, stripped by the winds and gullied by runoff. Swinging an ax for a dollar a day was hard work, but when women were chopping cotton for fifty cents a day, it could be worse. The Garretts lived simply, focusing on the basics of food, water, and shelter. And while they had little, sometimes that's enough.

That evening the cockfights were in full swing. Dozens of cars were parked by a barn on the outskirts of nearby Hugo, a railroad town located nine miles north of the state line. Many of the men who came for the fights had driven up from North Texas, taking the farm roads from places like Blossom and Ben Franklin, hitting the highway at Paris, and crossing into Oklahoma over the Red River. Despite being illegal in Texas, cockfighting remained so popular that the state newspapers continued to post the Oklahoma results for their readers.

The men had come to fight their roosters and bet on the outcomes, they had come for the banter and the chicken talk, to catch up on the news and use the occasion to buy a little moonshine whiskey on the side. Spectators filled the barn in a jostle of body heat and sweat, many still dressed in their Sunday best as they crowded onto the rough board bleachers. The gamblers were shouting out wagers or holding up combinations of fingers to see if anyone wanted to take the odds offered. Along the back wall the crated roosters joined the din with their full-throated crowing. Behind the seating, one of the cockfighters prepared for the next set by tying steel gaffs snugly to the natural spurs of his rooster. Curved like the tine of a pitchfork, the inch-and-a-half spikes were designed to be lethal. And being a blood sport, some argued, a quicker kill was more humane.

Inside the cockpit, a fight to the finish was under way. Voices from the crowd yelled advice as fighting roosters sparred with each other. As tail feathers arched up and hackles fanned out, both birds attacked, leaping upward with their yellow feet extended and the steel gaffs flashing ice-pick sharp. The roosters met in midair, but neither found an opening. Landing, they circled with heads low, each tracking the movements of the other. Then everything blurred in a rush and jab and dodge. The birds leaped upward again, wings chopping furiously, and dropped to the floor in a tussle. A rooster had hooked a spur in the other's back and struggled to dislodge it.

Handle! the referee shouted, and a pitter worked the gaff free, careful not to worsen the injury. The other handler, James Clinton Palmer, rested his bird and watched as blood bubbled from the beak of the wounded chicken on the far side of the pit. The fight was likely over, but even a dying rooster remained a threat. The call came for another pitting, and again they set the roosters on the fighting line, but the wounded bird floundered on its side, unable to stand. It was in its death throes, and the referee declared Palmer's rooster the winner. When the fight was over, inmate number 39467 stepped out into the mild evening air. The thirty-seven-year-old cockfighter had been released from the federal penitentiary at Leavenworth only a few months before. And more than two years behind bars had not changed his predatory nature.

Late on Monday afternoon, Lucy was taking in the wash, and Dillard was stacking cordwood. The girl with jet-black hair removed a shirt from the clothesline and began folding it when she heard the high pitch of a car running down Gay Road. She looked up as a Model T Ford came to an abrupt stop in front of their camp. Her suspicion of strangers was ingrained, and not recognizing the vehicle or the driver put her on guard.

The girl watched a man step out and strike up a conversation with her father, introducing himself as Clint Palmer. Standing five foot six, the cockfighter was only a few inches taller than Lucy. He had a friendly, disarming way about him and went on about the weather and the difficulties of making a living chopping firewood. The woodcutter waited, knowing the stranger would eventually get around to what he wanted. Lucy came over to listen as Palmer finally reached the business at hand. The stranger wanted them to take care of his rooster. "He told us," Lucy later said, "that he had fought this rooster and wanted him to rest up before he fought him again. We told him that we did not have any chickens and did not want to fool with the rooster."[1]

Palmer pressed his case with a proposition for the woodcutter and his daughter. If they agreed to follow him to Texas and keep his roosters in fighting trim, Dillard stood to make one dollar a day, with a lot less effort than his firewood business required. Palmer told them about his house in Peerless, Texas, a crossroads town that had taken its name from a brand of potato. If they came to work for him, they could live in a real house instead of remaining camped out in the woods. Dillard turned him down, but the cockfighter continued his pitch. For the next hour he hung around, trying to win their confidence and sell them on the advantages of moving to Texas. The stranger finally drove off in the Model T, leaving Lucy with a sense of uneasiness.

Clint Palmer had traveled widely in the Southwest, driving the hardtop highways and dirt tracks to match his fighting roosters. He had been drifting since he was sixteen years old, whenever he wasn't sitting in jail, where he had spent a good part of his life. Starting in 1915, he had been arrested in several western states on charges ranging from rape and larceny to passing bogus checks. Violence permeated his world, and while he was in Leavenworth his brother, Hardie Palmer, was gunned down in a field west of Hugo. Serving as a special agent, he was shot in the back by a Kansas City gangster while attempting to arrest a federal fugitive. Clint worked the other side of the law and for the past two years had been incarcerated for violations of the White-Slave Traffic Act. Also known as the Mann Act, it was intended to ban the interstate transport of females for prostitution, debauchery, or other immoral purposes. But with those purposes left vague, it often ended up being a tool used to prosecute men for having sex with underage women.

Heavy rains moved in that night and continued the next day, when the cockfighter again showed up at the camp. Palmer picked up where he had left off, trying to convince Dillard he was missing a chance to give Lucy a better life. He wanted them to see the farmhouse firsthand before deciding. Since he didn't expect them to take his word for it, he offered to take Lucy to see the place and report back. The girl had no desire to go with a stranger on what would be a 130-mile road trip. Palmer assured the woodcutter it would take only a day, and he promised to get her home by sundown. Besides, he said, another young woman needed a ride back to Texas and would be going with them. Tired of arguing, Dillard gave his consent.

Next day the young girl climbed in the Model T with Palmer, and they drove into Hugo, a brick-built town bustling with activity. He stopped at a store, telling Lucy he was supposed to meet the other young woman here. Returning without her a few minutes later, he claimed she had already left with someone else. So the two of them headed south on Highway 271 across farmlands and through stands of post oak and red oak and a half-dozen different kinds of oak. When they crossed the bridge, the Red River was running two-thirds of the way up its bank because of the rains. Ferries had stopped operating downstream due to the high flows, and one of the bridges had washed out in the storm. Still, the highway patrol was watching all of the crossings, on the lookout for Bonnie Parker and Clyde Barrow. They were on the run after a string of shootings and robberies, and reports had placed them in the area. After driving through the streets of Paris, Clint and Lucy followed a combination of muddy roads to reach the farming community of Peerless, a place the old-timers still called Fairyland.

It was late afternoon when Clint showed her the three-room farmhouse, which turned out to be a dilapidated board-and-batten field house. The foundation posts had settled at a tilt, and she had to use a makeshift step to reach the porch. He led her inside without mentioning it was where his mother had lived before leaving his father for good. Lucy wasn't impressed with its run-down appearance, and they soon finished the inspection. By the time they stopped at a neighbor's for supper, it was getting dark and too late to return to Oklahoma. So the two of them spent that night with a neighboring family.

Back at the woodlot, Dillard Garrett was growing desperate. The day had ended, and long after dark his daughter still hadn't returned. At every sound of an approaching car, he checked the road, hoping it was them and imagining the worst when it wasn't. He was worried and angry, angry at Palmer for breaking his word and angry at himself for letting his daughter drive away with a stranger. Unable to stand the agony of waiting any longer, he set off for town, walking with a limp. Years before, a glancing blow of the ax had cut into the bone of his foot and crippled him. The woodcutter reached the sheriff's office at midnight and reported his daughter missing.

Deputy L. C. Cross, better known as Red Cross, was on duty that night. "Dillard Garrett," he said, "at the time he came to my office, was very mad and tears were in his eyes."[2] Dillard told him how Palmer had taken his daughter to Texas with a promise to return that day and then asked the deputy to call his counterpart in Sulphur Springs. He complied with the request, and the Texas deputy agreed to investigate. The lawman drove to Peerless and pounded on the door to wake up Clint's father, H. P. Palmer. The fifty-nine-year-old Texan told the officer his son was not there and thought he might have returned to Hugo. When Red Cross received the report, he tried to reassure Lucy's father, without much success. Fearing for his daughter, Dillard returned to camp, unable to do anything more.

Next morning Palmer left to take care of some business, and the girl stayed with the neighbors. Returning later than planned, he claimed car trouble had delayed him. The two of them finally headed north and about three in the afternoon pulled up to the Garrett camp on Gay Road. Dillard wasn't there, so Palmer tried to talk her into coming with him to his place on Roebuck Lake, a few miles away. Not trusting him, the girl insisted on waiting for her father. When Dillard returned, all his worry and fear boiled up in anger. "At first he was terrible mad at Clint Palmer," she said, "but when I told him that we had car trouble he got alright."[3]

The Texas excursion had given Palmer a chance to learn more about Lucy, knowledge he could use to exploit her innocence and vulnerability. In the past, a series of mistakes had ended in his arrest, so this time he planned his actions methodically, taking it step by step. Except for her father, Clint now knew young Lucy was alone in the world with no one to protect her. And if he could get them to leave Oklahoma, nobody was going to miss the Garretts in the stream of migrant families heading west. But first he had to take care of the problem caused by Dillard contacting the sheriff. Palmer convinced the woodcutter to accompany him to see the officer, where he explained how a misunderstanding had led to an overreaction by the concerned father. He joked with me about it, said Red Cross, and said there was nothing to it. The deputy accepted Palmer's explanation and let the matter drop when Dillard agreed not to press charges. The cockfighter returned to his camp on the shores of Roebuck Lake, quiet and serene, a place where he could sit in the evenings and plot a murder.

Clint Palmer not only had led a life of crime, but was also criminally insane. After frequent psychotic episodes in prison, he had been transferred to the mental ward, where he spent the last six months of his term. The psychiatrist diagnosed his condition as "psychosis, with mental deficiency, periods of excitement."[4] It was so severe that the warden had a prison guard escort him back home upon his release. The two of them took the train to Cooper, Texas, where the guard turned him over to the county sheriff and passed on a message from the warden. It warned the sheriff of Palmer's mental condition and the possibility he might need to be institutionalized. But his mother had agreed to give him a home, so Clint was released into her care. Somehow he was considered too much of a threat to circulate among the other inmates, but not too dangerous to be released into an unsuspecting population. He soon left his mother's home and returned to cockfighting, working the Texas-Oklahoma borderlands.

Lucy was helping her father haul a load of firewood into Hugo when Palmer coasted up next to their wagon. He offered to buy the wood himself if it didn't sell, as long as it was delivered to his camp. In town the hours passed with no one buying, so at the end of the day the Garretts left for Roebuck Lake. Clint was waiting for them at Kilgore's clubhouse, where he took his meals, and handed the woodcutter $1.25 for the load. The chance to earn $1 a day caring for roosters was sounding more attractive to Dillard, so it didn't take much to convince him to pack up. The next day the Garretts moved their camp to the lake and went to work for Palmer, taking care of his roosters. The cockfighter knew it was only a matter of time before he would convince them to move to Texas.

ACROSS THE RED RIVER

A couple of weeks later, Dillard gave in to Palmer and agreed to relocate to Peerless. Once again, father and daughter packed up their belongings in what had become a familiar routine of their nomadic life. While they were loading the Model T, Lucy spotted H. P. Palmer driving up in a Buick. A butcher by trade, he had traveled to Hugo for the chicken fights, and his son had asked for help in moving the Garretts to Texas. Lucy was unaware Clint had told him they would be staying in Peerless for only a night or two before heading west. She was expecting to settle into the old farmhouse and make it their home.

H. P. filled his Buick with tools, kitchen gear, and bedding, while Clint packed as much as he could in his vehicle. The two cars turned onto the highway leading south to Texas and soon crossed the dark waters of the river, tinged red by the runoff. They passed Powderly and then Paris, driving across farmland cut from what had once been open prairie mixed with woodlands. They passed Stillhouse Road and a shoaly branch of the Sulphur River, where the road tunneled through the dense tree cover of the bottomlands. At Birthright they turned west.

It was evening when the cars reached Peerless, with its cotton gin, general stores, and a scatter of homes and farmhouses. Clint stopped to borrow the keys from the owner of the house. Always working an angle, he told B. C. Steen they wanted to check it out for a couple of days before renting it. He had no intention of paying him anything. They drove a mile west of town to what the girl thought would be her new home and unloaded.

Lucy spent the next day unpacking and cleaning, while the men drove over to see Clint's father, who was supposed to instruct the woodcutter on how to take care of the roosters. Instead, they spent the day riding around with the elder Palmer, collecting a debt and seeing various people on business. What that was, Lucy never knew. The girl had supper ready when H. P. dropped them off at dusk. The three of them sat on the porch afterward and talked until nine. "Well," Clint told Dillard, "if we are going over to the old man's house we had better be going."[1]

They were up to something, possibly bootlegging, but kept the girl out of it. Afraid to be left alone, she didn't want them to go. Dillard said they'd be back soon and locked his daughter in the house from the outside to reassure her. It was the last time Lucy saw him alive.

After they left, she sensed something was wrong and searched the house for Clint's pistol, normally kept in a dresser drawer. Unable to find it, her sense of dread grew. Lucy hadn't been told what they were planning; she only knew something wasn't right. The girl was left alone in an empty house with only her fears for company, and sometime that evening Clint murdered Dillard Garrett.

It must have happened so unexpectedly that the woodcutter had no chance to defend himself. He took a deep wound to his chin with an ax swung with enough force to knock him down. Standing above the wounded man, Palmer chopped again and then again with tremendous force, severing the head from the body in a psychotic rage. He loaded the woodcutter's body in his car and drove a mile out of town to an isolated section of a neighbor's farm. Carrying the dead weight of a body was difficult, especially across uneven ground at night, so he may have had help. At one point he had to cross a fence to reach a steep-sided ravine. Palmer dragged the body to the bottom and burned the clothing in an attempt to hide the victim's identity. Next he maneuvered the corpse into a pocket of the undercut bank, and finished by covering it with dirt and concealing the site with brush.

MAY 1, 1934

It was still dark the next morning when the woodcutter's daughter fixed breakfast for three, expecting the men to return any moment. She waited by herself until daylight, when she heard someone unlock the door. Clint entered alone. He told her Dillard was waiting at his dad's house, and after eating they drove over to find him. Clint immediately called H. P. outside before Lucy had a chance to say hello. For most of the morning, father

Alive and well. Lucy Garrett, shown a few years after her kidnapping, was known for her love of animals. Courtesy of Linda Sconce.

and son sat on the frame of an old car and plotted, while Lucy waited. Her father was nowhere to be seen. When Clint disappeared inside the house, H. P. walked over to the car and asked Lucy, "Do you know you are going to see your father?"[2]

"No," she answered.

"I thought I had better tell you," he said. "You might run by him." The old man was covering for his son.

Clint returned and pretended to reveal a secret. Dillard had stolen a car and wanted them to meet him in Durango, Colorado. But don't worry, he told Lucy; her father had asked him to take care of her. Clint claimed to have a ranch where they were going and assured the girl everything would turn out fine. He warned her not to speak to anyone because her daddy was on the run from the law, and if she said the wrong thing, he might get caught. The killer didn't hesitate to use the girl's love for her father as leverage, knowing Lucy would be afraid to turn to the police if she believed they were after him. Instead of viewing the authorities as protectors, she now saw them as a threat.

During their long talk, H. P. had agreed to loan the Buick to his son. So the father rode with them a quarter of a mile down the road to point out the idiosyncrasies of the car. As soon as he stepped out, they drove off. Pulled by the gravity of longing and dread, the young girl was heading west into a faraway country, unaware she was traveling with the man who had just murdered her father.

ON THE RUN

Each hour of driving took them farther west and farther away from any home Lucy had ever known. Farms gave way to ranches as the ground cover steadily thinned and the horizons spread far and wide. Clint stayed clear of the cities and bypassed the center of each town they encountered, in case the authorities had been alerted. When Lucy became suspicious, he told her only that the law was after him. She had no idea how far they traveled or where he was taking her. They drove until well after dark, when Clint found a rooming house and stopped for the night. He would get a couple of rooms, he told her, and be right back.

Lucy waited until he returned with the key and followed him inside. Entering the room, she realized he had rented only one. He tried to explain that he didn't have enough money for two, but she didn't believe him. Angry at being misled, she refused to share the room. "I told him," Lucy later said, "that I did not want to stay with him, and that I would not sleep with him. He said that I would have to, and he locked the door and would not let me out."[1] Lucy stood still as he took a seat on the bed, trying to persuade her to cooperate. Finally losing patience, Clint stood up. "He stripped his clothes off right before me," she said, "and went to bed."

When the girl refused to get undressed, Clint pulled her onto the bed and trapped her in his arms. The young girl struggled, resisting his attempts to rape her, but he simply overpowered her. "I fought him and tried to keep him away, but I could not." Afterward, she remained defiant. "He tried to sleep with his arm around me," she added, "but I would not let him."

The next morning they continued on their westward line of travel. For miles the highway shot straight across the brushlands, appearing to stretch

110

into the distance as long and thin as a telephone wire. They drove through the West Texas town of Matador and climbed an escarpment onto the Llano Escatado, an elevated plain pressed under the weight of an immense sky. It anchored the southern end of the high plains, and in the parched spring of 1934 the sun hammered down and the wind swept across it unbroken for hundreds of miles. They passed the towns of Earth, Muleshoe, and Lariat before crossing the state line into New Mexico. The two of them reached Clovis, the scene of a crime that had put Clint behind bars.

Four years earlier, he had taken his wife and her fourteen-year-old friend on a road trip. Clint had persuaded the girl to come along under the pretense of going to see her sister in Oklahoma. Instead of heading north, he turned west and drove the underage girl across the state line to Clovis, where he raped her. His wife tried to prevent him from attacking the girl, but he threatened to kill both of them. He stayed on the run for a year before being apprehended. At his trial in Santa Fe, he entered a plea of guilty and was given a three-year prison sentence at Leavenworth. The prosecuting attorney considered James Clinton Palmer such a menace to society that he recommended the prisoner serve his full term. In stating his reasons, the prosecutor described another crime committed by him. "This defendant," he wrote, "is a notorius character. Married—separated but not divorced—in 1928 transported a 16 year old girl from Allison, Colo., to Rosa, N.M. raped her and threatened to kill her with a knife if she resisted him."[2] Lucy knew none of this.

With Clint Palmer, the natural order of things had upended. Lies came to him more naturally than the truth, and he habitually chose to do wrong. He would later put the blame for his crimes on the horrors he experienced in the trenches of World War I. But he had been in trouble with the law long before he saw any action, if in fact he ever did. His military records have not survived, and his word cannot be trusted. What drove him to act mattered little to Lucy, who was caught in a world of raw consequences removed from any consideration of root causes. The girl had been wrenched from her familiar surroundings and taken into a strange and distant country by a man who could turn lethal in an instant.

Under a sky hazy with dust, the two of them worked their way westward beyond Clovis to the Rio Grande, avoiding the city of Albuquerque. Clint was probing for the blind spots between jurisdictions in case a warrant for his arrest had been issued. That evening the two of them stayed with a Hispanic family, likely in the town of Belen, where Clint had a friend. They played cards into the night, and when the game ended they left the room to sleep by themselves. Again he raped her. "He hurt me terrible," she said. "He did not even propose to marry me or anything, but that we do just as he liked. The next morning we got up and traveled on west. We traveled every day, and at night we would stay at some Mexican house or a sheep camp."[3] The kidnapper knew those living on the margins of society would be less likely to contact the authorities.

At Los Lunas they picked up Route 66, the main artery for those fleeing the Dust Bowl. In a few days a massive dust storm would sweep the Great Plains behind them, filling the sky and hiding the sun. Eyewitnesses told how the land itself boiled up in an opaque mass, growing so dark a hand held in front of the face could not be seen. The ground lost its solidity as sand shifted underfoot and the air became too thick to breathe. He kept driving.

Once away from the river valley, they entered the high desert, as Clint continued to put distance between himself and North Texas. The land now had a different cut to it, more angular, with rock surfacing in bare outcrops. And somewhere between Laguna Pueblo and Enchanted Mesa, the quality of light takes on the luminosity found in old paintings, where layer upon layer of translucent colors create a deep radiance. In springtime west of the Rio Grande, the air itself becomes charged with light.

For miles the highway passed along the foot of Mount Taylor and over the black and broken bed of a lava flow. It soon crossed the Continental Divide and began to parallel a line of redrock cliffs, a sign they had reached the Colorado Plateau. The region took its name from the great arterial river named by the Spanish for its reddish waters. Sudden storms often hit the upcountry, triggering a rush of floodwaters churning through the canyons and tinting the river flash-flood red, *colorado*.

The fugitive threaded through the outskirts of Gallup and then north across the Navajo Indian reservation. As the highway gained elevation, temperatures cooled, and ahead stood a dark spire, Gothic in profile, rising fifteen hundred feet above the plain. Ship Rock is the remnant of an ancient volcanic throat with black dikes radiating out from the base. It stands as a landmark of the Four Corners country, where New Mexico, Arizona, Utah, and Colorado meet at a single point—making it convenient for someone dodging the law to slip from one jurisdiction to another. Palmer continued to drive and every night forced himself on the girl he had kidnapped in a brutal repetition of the nights before.

Clint and Lucy crossed the bridge over the San Juan River and followed it to Farmington. They passed the ruins of ancient stone pueblos along the Animas River, known to the early Spanish as the River of Lost Souls, and continued into Colorado. For Lucy, the longing grew as she anticipated being reunited with her father. She missed him terribly. The killer and the girl reached the mining town of Durango, where Clint suggested they split up to look for him. Going their separate ways, they searched the town.

"I wanted to find my daddy," Lucy said, expressing in a few words the ache she felt.[4] But the girl was unable to find any trace of him, and her hopes were fading when Clint returned with a message. Her father had left word, Clint said, that he would have a letter waiting for her at Bayfield, a ranching community twenty miles to the east.

Next day they skirted the foot of the San Juan Mountains, a dramatic range of sawtooth peaks forming the edge of the Rockies. With the highest summits still holding snow, the road rolled and curved along the lower slopes, forested with tall ponderosa pine. At Bayfield, Clint stopped at the post office while she waited in the car. He soon came back and handed her a letter from her father with a Durango postmark to give it an air of authenticity. The girl ripped it open and began reading. The news was devastating. She learned her father had beaten them to the rendezvous point and was now on his way back east to Missouri. "He said in the letter," the girl recalled, "that Clinton would take care of me and for me to stay with him and that he would see me about Christmas or the first of the year. This is the last time I ever heard of my Dad."[5] She was so desperate for any word from him, she let herself believe he had written it. And she wanted to believe he was still alive. Carried far from any home she had ever known, Lucy only wanted to find her daddy.

A convicted forger, Clint had written the letter and mailed it during the stop in Durango. He figured she would continue to cooperate as long as he gave her a thread of hope. She tore up the letter, as he ordered, not wanting to leave any evidence implicating her father. "He told me to never mention my daddy, for on account of his stealing a Buick car that the law was after him, and that he did not want me to mention him at all to anyone."[6] Kept isolated, she rarely spoke to strangers from then on and began turning inward, the only refuge left.

The two of them reversed course and drove west into Utah. A road map from 1934 shows an enormous blank spot in the southeastern corner of the state, a region taking its character from the three rivers sunk deep below the surface. It was a land rough cut into canyons, splitting into branches again and again as they clawed back into the flanks of mesas and mountains. Shaped by water, it was also a place where water was conspicuously absent, a region of high deserts and arid expanses. Most explorers had given it a wide berth. With the barrier cliffs too rugged, too dry, with few trails and empty of roads, both Spanish and early American parties were forced to detour hundreds of miles to avoid them.

Lucy and her kidnapper now headed toward the edge of the map and the last of the outpost towns. The woodcutter's daughter had come more than a thousand miles from Texas, and no one back home knew her whereabouts or the fate of her father. Both had disappeared. With her ties to the outer world severed and nowhere else to turn, the girl was totally dependent on a man she despised. And she had no way of knowing her ordeal was only beginning.

[FIELDNOTES]

A Gun within Reach

Crossing West Texas on Highway 82, I was on my way to find where Lucy Garrett's story began. I needed to drive the back roads, to talk with those connected to the events of 1934. The highway ran under a sky stretched tight, where desert scrub eased into brushlands and oil pumps gave way to a crop of wind turbines spinning away like kinetic lawn ornaments. I passed signs to towns with names like Spur, Guthrie, and Idalou. Looneyville lay somewhere off to the north, and a Miss Lulu Road ran south.

A local radio station was airing a story on tornado hunters as I passed a rest stop with a built-in tornado shelter. And at lunchtime I pulled into a mesquite-smoked barbecue shack a long way from anywhere. Despite the remoteness, local ranchers and roughnecks filled the bench seats inside, and a handmade sign advertised "Beer—A Vacation in a Can." One of the customers asked the woman behind the counter how she got the name, Allie. "Tornado Alley," she told him. "My daddy named me for Tornado Alley." I was soon back on the road.

The high plains ended abruptly, dropping away into the land of the armadillo. The plated carcass of one lay belly-up on the side of the road, and a mile beyond lay another, and then another. By the time I reached Wichita Falls, the biomass had expanded, the horizons had pulled in, and the sky had turned hazy with moisture rising from thick rivers and wet farmlands. This was red-dirt country, and red water filled each cattle tank. The week before, twenty inches of rain had fallen, and now after a run of three sunny days the weatherman was calling it "severe clear."

Somewhere in North Texas I left the prairie behind, as thick woodlands dominated the landscape. Stands of post pine, willow, and pecan rose from the deep leaf duff, and where the fields opened wide, vultures hung overhead in a holding pattern, waiting to catch the scent of carrion. After passing Joe Bob's Gas Station, I found the turn to Peerless and stopped at a country store. Members of a congregation from the church next door were gathered on the porch, taking a break from the service. A young father sat on the steps with his son and politely asked what I was doing there. When I told him about the murder I was investigating from 1934, he traded me another killing. "I heard one guy shot another in back of the head," he said, speaking with a rolling, edge-of-the-prairie cadence. "That happened over by Birthright."[1] And driving away I found myself wondering about murder by Birthright.

Next morning I stood in the town square of Sulphur Springs, next to an imposing courthouse, appearing more castle than court of law. Inside, the sheriff had once displayed the unidentified bones of Dillard Garrett, Lucy's father, hoping someone might recognize them. I walked over to the local genealogy society, where a couple of elderly ladies sat before stacks of old documents, tracing root and branch of their family trees. Soon Judge Ronny Glossup arrived to have his picture taken by the newspaper for a story on books being donated by the court. Afterward we had a chance to talk, and I learned he had grown up hearing the story of Clint Palmer, the man who kidnapped Lucy Garrett. As he talked, prisoners in striped pants filed in with boxes of donated books. "The people of Peerless, Texas," he said, "when I lived there in the '70s, were very backwoods. They were very, very private people. You didn't go ask about anybody." And the judge added, "A lot of people from Peerless fought roosters in Hugo. That was a big thing. I never went up to the cockfights. It was considered sort of low-life."[2]

When I asked him about the manhunt for Palmer, he described in detail the pursuit and capture of the fugitive. It had taken place on back roads the judge knew well, and he took my notebook and sketched a map to get me oriented. Some of the roads were now under lake waters. He also described an article on the Garrett killing in a detective magazine, one I hadn't seen. So he called his secretary to let her know where to reach him, and we headed out of town in his pickup. During the drive I asked about his past, and he mentioned having dairy farmed for many years. And in an offhand manner he recalled his recon missions in Vietnam and a fifty-mile run he had once taken through Palo Duro Canyon.

Inside his home he checked a huge pot of catfish seasoning for tonight's fish fry, then washed his hands with a lump of stainless steel. "Best thing in the world for taking away the smell," he said. Judge Glossup led me into his office, filled with a collection of Resistol hats and a saddle mounted on a stand. "I used to do a little cowboying," he said, as I studied the hats on the wall. Going through the files, he found an obituary on Palmer, describing how he became a rodeo star in prison. The judge made a copy of the magazine article, and as we returned to town he told me about two murderers currently on death row who were distantly related to Palmer. Whether murder by birthright or simply a family tradition, I suppose in the end it did not matter much to the victims.

The following day I crossed the Red River into Oklahoma, where dew covered the grass and a sign pointed to Frogville. A tribal casino reminded me it was Choctaw country, and an old-timer in suspenders and a cowboy hat rode horseback down the median strip on some mission known only to himself. I followed the highway to Hugo.

A town cemetery reflects the character of a place, and here the rodeo and circus traditions have left their mark. Traveling circuses make Hugo their winter home, and it has become the final resting place for ringmasters and acrobats, chimp handlers and clowns. A headstone was carved in the shape of a big top, and another showed an elephant trainer standing on the head of a recumbent pachyderm. And nearby lay the grave of rodeo champion Freckles Brown, with a footstone commemorating one of the greatest moments in rodeo history. It depicted a cowboy hanging onto a bucking bull while holding his right fist high above his head. Underneath it read, "Freckles Rides Tornado," and a tornado it was.

In 1967 the oldest active cowboy on the circuit climbed into chute number 2 at the National Finals Rodeo. Freckles Brown, who would soon turn forty-seven years old, was still competing in a young man's sport. The former world bull-riding champion was going against cowboys with an average age of nineteen. Brown had drawn Tornado, awarded the title of "meanest bull alive" four times at the national finals. No one had ever managed to stay on for the required eight seconds, and the best bull riders in North America had tried and failed 220 times. Few of those present in the arena that December evening thought Brown had a chance of winning, and many worried about him coming out of the encounter alive. Over the years he had smashed, cracked, and splintered dozens of bones, including a broken neck that should have ended his career.

The arena went silent as he eased himself onto the bull's back. A crowd of nine thousand fans leaned forward in their seats or stood to watch. Brown tugged on the rope to secure his grip, and the hide of the bull tightened in anticipation. Suddenly, the gate swung open, and the bull exploded out of the chute, pitching forward when it landed and kicking up its hind legs. Then Tornado began to twist. Four times it whipped around, tucked into a tight spin. Brown stayed with him, drawing on his years of experience. His only chance was to outthink the bull, to anticipate its moves before it made them. The seconds stretched out, and the cheers began to build as the crowd realized he might pull it off. Brown hung on as the roar grew so deafening he never heard the eight-second whistle. Only when the clowns were rushing toward him did he realize it was over.

Jumping off the bull, he hit the ground running and made it to the fence as the crowd went wild. "I stood out there in the middle of the arena with my hat off for the longest time," Brown recalled. "But the applause didn't die down. It just kept going and going. And it wasn't just the fans. Even the rodeo cowboys were clapping and yelling. I finally walked off, but it didn't let up any."[3] He was coaxed back into the arena, and the crowd whooped and hollered louder than before, cheering for the cowboy who had ridden the unrideable bull.

Toughness and tenacity were qualities also found in a young girl from this corner of Oklahoma. West of town, I pulled up to the house of Clyde and Linda Sconce where horse pastures spread out under a severe-clear sky. I was here to learn about Lucy Garrett, Clyde's mother, and soon realized I was stirring up memories the family had kept private. Wearing a snap-button shirt and Justin boots, he took a seat and explained how they had talked with other relatives, who agreed it was best to get the story out in the open. His mother's aunt and uncle had known about her ordeal, but Lucy kept it secret from the rest of the family. "She didn't talk about this," Linda said. "You have to understand that."[4]

"I knew nothing about it," Clyde added. "I was a little ol' kid, and I asked her one time, 'What happened to Grandpa? She kind of set there for a little bit and said, 'A man shot him through a window.'"

Over the years a few hints surfaced, and Clyde decided to find out what had happened. He was sitting with his mother on the back porch of a farmhouse when he asked about it. "She wouldn't answer nothing," he said. So he told her he had read something about it. "She looked at me and said, 'Palmer kidnapped me and raped me.' That's all she'd ever say."

And Linda added, "It's something that was never talked about." Lucy's uncle had kept a scrapbook of newspaper clippings about the incident, which eventually came into their possession. "That was the first time we knew much about it," Linda said. "The whole family kept it quiet. None of them said a word about it."

Linda, in her role as family historian, brought out binders filled with articles, court records, and even a comic-book version of the dark events of 1934. She opened a photo album, giving us a way to ease into the story. The album contained a photo of a young man in a beat-up wide-brim, and Linda thought it was Lucy's father, Dillard Garrett. "He was the world to her," Clyde said.

And Linda added, "She thought the sun rose and set in her dad. She thought so much of her dad, there was no way she would do anything to jeopardize him." Linda then showed me a black-and-white snapshot of Lucy herself, taken when she was about twenty-one years old. It shows a pretty woman petting a dog next to an old Bonnie and Clyde–style Ford, and her warm smile came as a surprise. The young woman in the photo projected an unexpected vitality. She had survived a year packed with violence and tragedy, but I saw no trace of what she had suffered.

Lucy loved animals, I was told, and as an example Clyde related the time his parents were skidding logs near Antlers, Oklahoma. "They were living in a tent," he said. "A storm come in, and she insisted on bringing the horse inside the tent so it could have shelter." And she had a sense of adventure. "We'd follow more fire trucks than you'd ever believe," said Linda, "just to see what's burning. And she liked to play pranks." When a relative from Oklahoma came to see them in Texas, Lucy served a goose egg for breakfast. She told him, "You know, we always grow big chickens in Texas."

Then I asked Clyde if he remembered anything about her that might suggest the trauma she had gone through. He thought a moment and said, "She was always suspicious of people."

"And she always had a gun within reach," Linda added. "She wasn't going to let that happen again. What she went through made her a strong lady. She was a strong-willed lady, and sooner or later she always got her way." Linda paused a moment and added, "She wasn't afraid of anything." Unless it was the threat of violence.

"One night," Clyde said, "we were sitting around the dining room table talking, and something was said about somebody breaking in. And I made the statement, 'It wouldn't bother me at all. I'd blow somebody's damn head off like that.' And she went all to pieces, raised hell with me. 'No you won't!' she said."

Driving south out of town, I turned down Gay Road, where Palmer first met young Lucy. The place was now rolling farmland, threaded with creeks and ponds set near the houses. Clover ran down to the pavement, and junipers grew along the fence lines. I passed the Sweethill Cemetery and a weathered roadhouse called Frankie's. In 1934, deep in the Great Depression, Lucy was camped with her daddy at his woodlot next to the road. The day Clint Palmer stopped to talk was the day her world began to unravel.

EMPTY QUARTER

Lucy and her kidnapper next surfaced in Monticello, riding into town on horseback. Palmer had taken her to the southeast corner of Utah, one of the least inhabited regions of the country, where a handful of graded roads connected a few trading posts with outlying settlements. Tough and stoic, the Mormons who settled these communities did not inquire too closely into the private affairs of others. And that suited the fugitive.

After crossing into Utah, he began passing Lucy off as his wife. "She's older than she looks," he said, introducing her as Johnnie Ray to everyone they met.[1] Palmer never mentioned he was still married to another woman, long estranged, who was raising his child. He began using his first name, and the locals came to know the couple as Jimmy and Johnnie Ray. The Texan had spent years on the run, leaving behind a string of broken laws and ruined lives. The girl despised him, even suspecting he had murdered her father. But Lucy desperately needed to believe Dillard was alive and thought Palmer was her best chance of seeing him again.

SUMMER 1934

A few days later, the two of them gravitated south to Blanding, where an older couple invited them to camp in their back lot until they were rested. William and Mary Jane Oliver were known to take in destitute strangers and to feed the local Ute Indians when times were difficult. Mary Jane felt sympathy for the hard-pressed travelers, especially Lucy. She later remembered her as "such a frail, little frightened girl that I felt sorry for her. She never said much, but I knew she was afraid of Jimmy."[2]

121

Last of the frontier lawmen. After retiring as sheriff, William Oliver turned to full-time cattle ranching, using Johns Canyon as his winter range. Courtesy of the San Juan County Historical Society.

Bill Oliver, with a gray mustache and work-thickened fingers, was a heavyset man in a lean age. "He didn't waste words or mince around about it," recalled a daughter years later. "He would tell you how he felt. What he felt, he told."[3] For many years, Oliver had hauled freight between Colorado and Utah, driving a six-horse team on round-trips lasting ten days. Motorized trucks put him out of the freighting business, so he ran for sheriff of San Juan County and served four years. His livelihood now depended solely on his cattle operation. The seventy-six-year-old stockman ran his livestock on ranges far to the west. Following the custom among Mormon ranchers, he lived in town and traveled to his cow camps whenever the work required rather than make his home on an isolated ranch. While quick to anger and just as quick to forgive, the former sheriff was not in the habit of backing down from a confrontation. "He was a man that wasn't scared of anybody," a cowboy recalled. "The devil himself wouldn't frightened him."[4]

The people of southeastern Utah who came to know Jimmy and Johnnie Ray often remarked on the differences between them. He dressed western, wearing high-top boots and a white Stetson, while she preferred a news-boy cap. With his eyes shifting constantly, Palmer had a feral quality to him, "quite edgy," said one of his gambling friends. He talked nonstop, while Lucy remained silent and had an air of sadness about her. Ray Hunt, a cowboy who later worked at Goulding's Trading Post, remembered how Palmer kept her under his control. "Palmer didn't want the girl to be left alone with anyone," Hunt said. "He always made sure that she never said anything. He must have pounded that into her over and over, 'You musn't say anything, because they still might get your father.'"[5]

While in Blanding, the Texan took advantage of another Palmer's hospitality by posing as a relative. He fed his horses, keeping them in his corral for a few nights, while they camped at his place. And during this period Clint Palmer began to steal horses. He would show up with suspicious mounts, and before anyone knew if they had been acquired illegally he traded them for other horses. After a month in town, they continued south toward the San Juan River.

Palmer had promised to take Lucy to her uncle in Kanab, Utah, but on reaching Bluff sometime in July, he told her they were unable to continue. He was broke and applied for public assistance with the local caseworker, requesting food and clothing. Eventually, Palmer and the girl settled on Lem Gaines's place, a short distance upriver from town. After a day clearing brush from the fence lines, he would often ride into Bluff, looking for a card game. He liked to sit down with the locals and play pitch, a trick-taking game involving heavy betting. "All he did there in Bluff," Lucy remembered, "was to gamble."[6]

One time an argument over cards ended badly, with Palmer storming out. He returned with a gun in his belt, only to find the other man had been taken away by friends. "I'm going to have to kill that fellow for what he said to me and how he abused me," Palmer threatened.[7] With him, violence always lay close to the surface.

During this period, Palmer traveled to Johns Canyon and recognized its natural advantages as a way station for stolen horses. He began spending time there and eventually cleared a steep trail onto Cedar Mesa for a place to hide them. The mesa top afforded decent grazing but infringed on the range belonging to the Nielson family. When his horses turned up on their land, the Texan was told to remove them. Instead of backing down, he pushed back, arguing it wasn't any more their range than it was his. "They got into a feud," DeReese Nielson later said, "and he told my uncle he was going to kill him."[8] It was a threat they took seriously. "That man was half crazy," he added, "and I think he would just as soon have shot somebody than to look them in the face."

FALL 1934

Harry Goulding ran one of the most remote trading posts in America, requiring a journey of 180 miles to reach the nearest railroad. Built on the Arizona border, it backed up against the cliffs of Rock Door Mesa and overlooked the dramatic spires of Monument Valley. "Me and another old boy," Goulding once told a reporter, "come ridin' through here with a pack outfit in 1920. And when I saw this valley I said to myself, if they's ever a chance to throw my hat on one of these rocks, I'm gonna do it."[9]

Returning to Monument Valley five years later, Goulding brought with him a wife he called Mike, having had difficulty spelling her given name, Leone. They built a trading post on a section of land leased from the state. And in the middle of the Great Depression, most of his trade with the Navajo came in the form of blankets, wool, and sheep. No one had any money, and he was unable to sell the sheep at fair prices. To the anger of the Navajo people, the federal government had begun enforcing a drastic stock-reduction program in an attempt to save the reservation from overgrazing. Tensions were running high, and Goulding was caught in the middle. The Navajo watched his sheep graze on the land returned to them, while their herds were being devastated by order of distant authorities. The government program had a profound impact on the Navajo and on some of the agency workers involved. Anthropologist Edward T. Hall, who was assigned to the sheep-reduction program as a young man, criticized the slaughter. "It haunts me now, more than a half century later," he wrote, "and it still haunts the Navajos even more profoundly."[10]

At first the trader ran his sheep on land known as the Paiute Strip, lying between the San Juan River and the Arizona border. Then the federal government transferred the strip from public domain to the Navajo tribe, threatening his business. Ordered to remove his sheep, Goulding could only trail them north onto rangelands already fully stocked. He had no other choice.

After delaying as long as possible, the trader drove two thousand head of sheep across the bridge at Mexican Hat in early January 1934. In a year of hard drought, he entered the stark beauty of a land known then as the Garden of the Gods, a garden of rock and sand.

Stockmen in the nearby towns strongly objected to his pushing onto their range. The sparse grass and undependable water barely supported their own cattle. Goulding arranged with other sheepmen to combine their herds until September, when another influx of sheep arrived from the Navajo lands, forcing him to locate a new grazing area. Goulding was cornered and growing desperate. Knowing he would face resistance from those who controlled the range, he needed a firm hand to help manage the herd. At that moment Palmer showed up, looking for work, and the trader offered him a deal. The Texan would take over the daily operation of the herd, grazing the sheep westward along the blackbrush benches toward the Goosenecks of the San Juan. This would crowd Bill Oliver at Johns Canyon, but it couldn't be helped. As partners, they would each get a cut of the wool and lambs until the Texan was able to buy out Goulding's interest. The trader would provide food and supplies until the first turnover, allowing him time to get on his feet financially.

Goulding wanted to avoid trouble with Oliver, so he instructed Palmer not to water the herd in Johns Canyon except in emergencies. He also told him to let the former sheriff decide where the sheep could graze, attempting to minimize the impact on his cattle operation. The trader was asking Palmer, known for his volatile temper, to handle sensitive negotiations as diplomatically as possible. Goulding may have counted on Palmer's knack for making friends, but his misjudging of Palmer's character would prove to be a fatal mistake. He also loaned him a pistol and a Winchester rifle to keep coyotes away from the herd.

After two months in town, Palmer took the thirteen-year-old girl deeper into the backcountry. It was September when they left Bluff and headed west, riding fifty miles on horseback. They followed a rough track threading between the twisting gorge of the San Juan River on one side and an unbroken escarpment on the other. Far across the river, the buttes of Monument Valley roughened the skyline, and when the road began hugging Cedar Mesa it cut below the sharp prow of Muley Point. Turning into a box canyon, they found themselves ringed by cliff and talus forming a wall twelve hundred feet high. Dependable water and grazing had drawn stockmen to the canyon since the 1880s, when John E. Adams gave the place his name. With only a single road entering Johns Canyon, Lucy felt trapped.

The girl knew Palmer wanted to homestead here, and they moved into an old shack barely able to keep them dry. Oil prospectors had abandoned the board-sided cabin after drilling a dry hole, and it was now being used by cattleman Bill Oliver. The old sheriff had claimed the canyon as his winter range for the past twenty years. Now Palmer began using Johns as his base of operations, and he wasn't only raising sheep. Lucy remembered seeing him put his JP brand on stolen horses, and cowboys later found several dozen head of horses he had taken. For the next four months, Palmer managed the sheep, bringing food and firewood to Goulding's Navajo herder and scouting for the best grazing areas. Lucy had her own concerns.

"I was pregnant and beginning to get big," she later recounted.[11] So a few days before Thanksgiving, Palmer allowed her to leave and stay with the Gouldings. At the trading post, she would sit by the fireplace in the living quarters on the second floor with Pueblo pots on the mantel and Navajo rugs covering the floors. Jimmie Rodgers might be playing on the hand-crank Victrola as she leafed through a Sears, Roebuck catalog, looking at the dolls with Goulding's wife. "She said one time," recounted Ray Hunt, "'I wish I had one.' Mike said, 'Well, Honey, you don't want to be looking at them. You're going to have a real one before too long.'"[12]

Lucy stayed with the Gouldings until December 11, when she was taken to Monticello to have the baby. Letting others care for her, Palmer returned to the herd. The girl stayed with a local woman, and on December 31 the very young mother gave birth to a baby boy who lived only a week. Alone among strangers, she had difficulty handling the acute loss of her child. No doctor was in attendance, and the death certificate stated the baby was never normal and died of convulsions. Rumors later circulated that Palmer had suffocated the child, but he was in Johns Canyon at the time. "Clinton Palmer was sent for when the baby died," Lucy said, "and came to the funeral."[13] Harry Goulding drove up from his trading post to handle the burial, and a week later Lucy had healed enough to travel. Palmer took her back to Johns, where trouble was building.

SKELETON MURDER CASE

Two days before Lucy Garrett gave birth in Utah, the bones of her father were discovered in a ravine outside Peerless, Texas. On a cloudy Saturday in late December, twelve-year-old Stanley Graham was playing with his friends near his family's farm. As he crossed a fence on his way home, the boy stepped on what he thought was a rock. Looking down, he saw a human skull on the edge of a cut bank and ran to tell his father. Rube Graham immediately drove to Sulphur Springs, only to find the sheriff was out of the office, investigating a case of cattle rustling. He turned the skull over to the deputy.

From the skull's condition, the lawman estimated it had been exposed to the elements for at least six months. The two of them returned to the scene, where more human remains and a bed of charcoal were dug out of the side of a ravine. The deputy retrieved parts of the skeleton, hair, and burned clothing, which he placed in a basket and turned over to the sheriff. It was obvious someone had hidden the body and burned the clothing to prevent identification of the remains.

"A man," said Sheriff W. C. Reneau, "does not burn his own clothes and then decapitate and bury himself."[1] He knew he had a murder case on his hands and opened an investigation. The local farmers had not noticed any suspicious activity in the preceding months, and his check of the missing-person reports led nowhere. The bones were put on display in the courthouse, where they stirred up interest in the case but did not result in an identification of the victim. The sheriff, unable to tell if the bones were male or female, had little to go on. And with the mystery intact, the newspapers began calling it the "Skeleton Murder Case."

Sheriff Reneau decided to enlist the aid of William W. Looney, a professor at the Baylor University College of Medicine with the reputation of being an expert anatomist. Taking the basket of bones, he drove to Dallas, where Dr. Looney inspected them. He not only was able to tell the gender but also provided the approximate height, build, and age of the victim. And to the sheriff's surprise, the professor was able to describe how the man had died. Clean cuts to the head and neck indicated the bones were green at the time of death. If dry, they would have shattered. And since it took considerable force to make the wounds, they could not have been self-inflicted. With suicide ruled out, murder was the most logical explanation.

The sheriff now had a description of the victim and returned to question the residents of Peerless. After conducting interviews through the month of January, he finally got a break in the case. A tip came in about a woodcutter from Oklahoma last seen in Peerless with his daughter the previous spring. Reneau learned his name was Dillard Garrett, and his physical description matched the skeleton. The father and daughter had spent two days at a house on the outskirts of town, a place loaned to James Clinton Palmer. Finally, the sheriff had a suspect.

Reneau tracked down Clinton's father, H. C. Palmer, who had not seen him since April. At the time, he claimed, Clint was taking Lucy Garrett to meet her father in Hugo. The sheriff made several trips to Oklahoma, working with the Choctaw County sheriff, only to reach an impasse. Reneau had better luck when a check of Palmer's background uncovered an extensive criminal record. He quickly broadcast descriptions of the suspect and the girl, while dispatching Deputy Jeff Branom to New Mexico, hoping to pick up the fugitive's trail. Meanwhile, he tracked down Dillard's brother and asked him to come to his office in Sulphur Springs. The sheriff pulled out the basket, and Mack Garrett studied the bones. Based on a deformed finger and an old wound to the foot, he was able to identify the remains of his brother. Dillard Garrett had been murdered, and the man who had killed him had disappeared with his daughter.

THE SHOOT-OUT

The girl in a newsboy cap rode horseback next to the sheep wagon as it lurched and joggled along the rough track. Trailing far behind the herd, Palmer drove the wagon with his saddle horse tied to the back. Where the road swung north into Johns Canyon, the two of them passed beneath a promontory of red sandstone piercing a sky so blue, a deeper shade would turn it to night. Boulders had tumbled from the rim long ago and lost momentum on a bench between the mesa cliffs and river gorge. The sun was now high up, and she scanned the road ahead, expecting trouble.

WINTER 1935

Earlier, in the middle of January, Palmer had brought Lucy back from Monticello to the confines of Johns Canyon. Upon arrival he caught the Navajo herder letting the sheep wander unattended. The Texan, looking for a pretext to fire him, ordered the Indian to cut his own sheep from the herd and leave. Knowing Harry Goulding would soon hire another man, Lucy asked for the job. The trader agreed to the arrangement, and a few days later Palmer directed her to water the sheep in Johns Canyon. They had continued to do this about once a week whenever Bill Oliver and his son were not around.

Goulding left the trading post in early February to resupply Palmer and the girl. He tracked them to Johns, where the Texan had taken the sheep without his knowledge. To avoid trouble, the trader told Palmer to remove them as soon as possible and to inform Oliver it had been the fault of the Navajo herder, who had let the herd drift onto his range. Goulding stressed the need for Palmer to work with the rancher on where to graze the sheep to lessen the impact on his cattle.

Having to draw his living from the land, Bill Oliver had been pressed hard by the years of Dust Bowl conditions. "We had quite a large herd," he wrote in his diary, "and as the drought came, feed and water became scarce."[1] The arrival of the sheepmen only compounded his problems. "We had a permit and had run our cattle in John's Canyon for many years. As cattle will not graze or drink where sheep have been, our feed and water became a real problem. This naturally created friction between us." To avoid trouble, he had informed the authorities he was willing to abide by any decisions they made regarding the fair distribution of the grazing lands. But when he learned of sheep being moved onto his winter range, Oliver knew he had to act to protect his interests.

His wife asked him not to return to Johns Canyon, afraid events would turn violent. When he insisted, she begged him not to take his gun. He believed he had to stand firm or risk losing everything. So he enlisted the aid of his grandson Norris Shumway, a good-natured twenty-four-year-old who could help with the cattle and do the driving. Oliver was comfortable on a horse or handling a freight wagon, but had not mastered the automobile well enough to take it on rough roads. He loaded his camp outfit in the Model A Ford, packing extra oil for a leak in the main bearing, and tucked his rifle out of sight. With his grandson at the wheel, they drove south out of town and met Joe Weston along the road to Bluff. The range inspector later said, "They were bound for the north breaks of the San Juan River to drive sheep from the range which they claimed."[2]

Conflict between sheepherders and cowboys had continued in southeastern Utah after it subsided elsewhere in the West. Before becoming a federal prosecutor, Knox Patterson had successfully argued the case of cattlemen charged with the murder of two Basque sheepherders. And in another he had defended ranchers charged with conspiring to control the public range by slaughtering horses belonging to sheepmen. "It is hard," he said, "to pin anything on anyone in warfare like that." And he added, "When a sheepman meets a cattleman, trouble begins."[3]

Reaching Johns Canyon, the cattleman encountered Palmer, and an argument took place. Oliver ordered him not to water the herd on his range, but the Texan insisted the sheep had to drink and drove them to the springs anyway. After watering, they were herded back to open range, beyond the canyon. Bill Oliver and his grandson set up their camp at the Seeps, a few miles back on the Johns Canyon road. Palmer and the girl camped a half mile away from them on a point above the San Juan River. A confrontation was building, and the next day Palmer ordered her to let the herd of thirsty sheep loose, knowing they would head straight for water. It was a Thursday, the end of February.

Bill Oliver ended his diary with a last entry. "I asked Goulding to remove his sheep from my grazing land," the cattleman noted, "but he refused. I went to the authorities in Monticello and asked them to order that the sheep be removed from our range. Things did not look good. Goulding had hired some sheepherders who I did not trust, so I began carrying a gun again."[4]

As they headed up the Johns Canyon road, Lucy spotted sheep moving toward her. They were funneling through the rocks and spreading across the benchlands in a hunt for every nibble of grass. Someone must have turned them back from the spring, and the girl searched the road ahead, where she spotted a horseman driving the herd. The wagon came to a stop, and she watched Palmer climb down. Wearing a sweat-stained Stetson and carrying a .32 revolver at his side, he stood, waiting for Oliver to close the distance.

"What do you mean, old man, driving my sheep away?" Palmer asked as the former sheriff reined in his horse next to him. "Don't you want to get along?"[5]

"No, you son-of-a-bitch," Oliver responded, "I don't want to get along with you!"[6]

Lucy watched as the horseman accused Palmer of packing a gun to scare him into abandoning the range. Refusing to be intimidated, Oliver said the only way he would leave was if they carried him out. She remained on horseback as the Texan returned to the wagon and took a seat, appearing to have backed down. She saw Oliver ride up and stand in his stirrups, staring at Palmer without a word being spoken. Getting no reaction, he turned back to the sheep, intending to finish driving them away from his water.

She waited as Palmer eased himself down and walked to the back of the wagon. He slowly untied his horse and mounted. Riding up to Oliver, he drew his pistol and without hesitation started shooting. The horses jumped as gunfire ripped apart the silence. With hooves churning the ground, both riders fought to control their mounts. The first shot had passed through

Oliver's right hand and lodged in his stomach. Blood flowed bright red from a mangled finger as the cowpuncher struggled to work the rifle with his wounded hand, managing to get two shots off.

The girl sat gripping the reins, a witness to the terrifying scene playing out a few feet away. With the horses rearing and dust kicking up, the shots were flying wild, despite the point-blank range. The Texan emptied his pistol, while Oliver managed to stay on his horse. So Palmer pulled a rifle out of the saddle scabbard and fired. The bullet tore through the sheriff's right arm, ripping tissue and breaking bone as it passed through his body and exited his chest, leaving a gaping three-inch hole. "I saw this," Lucy said in disbelief, "and saw the old man fall off the horse."[7]

The sound of the last shot died away as Palmer dismounted and tied the fallen man's own lariat around his neck. The sheriff was still alive. "I saw him put a rope to the old man and drag him off," she said. "He dragged him down the road."[8] Lucy was stunned. A deep silence settled over the scene as the girl turned her horse and left to round up the sheep.

March 1, 1935

He awoke in the dark, remembering yesterday's events and remembering what he had left unfinished. He got up and struck a match to light the woodstove, the flare filling all but the darkest corners of the cabin. Before flickering out, it disclosed the form of a girl curled asleep in a crumple of bedding on the floor. The fire caught, and the Texan stepped outside before dawn.

An older moon, worn to a thin edge, rode the night sky in Utah's empty quarter. It was late winter in the high desert. During the dark hours, heavier air had slipped off the mesa top and settled into Johns Canyon, carrying the cold with it. Palmer crossed the yard to the horse he had kept close for an early start. Working mechanically, he placed a Navajo blanket on its back, heaved a saddle on top, and tightened the cinch. He retraced his steps inside and stoked the fire as young Lucy let go of sleep.

Finding the girl awake, Clint told her his plans. He would go back and burn the body of the sheriff. But first he had to find the man's grandson Norris Shumway, known to them as "Jake." The young cowboy was camped at the Seeps, six miles back on the road to town, waiting for his grandfather to return. "Clinton told me," Lucy said, "that he was going over to the

Oliver camp to see Jake Shumway and see if he missed the old man and if he suspicioned that he had killed Bill Oliver."⁹ And she added, "If Shumway didn't talk just right that he would kill him."¹⁰

Leaving the girl behind, he mounted the big bay and turned through the gate. A pistol was strapped to his waist and a .401 Winchester rifle tucked in the scabbard. He knew what waited ahead and what he had to do. Palmer rode across the shelfrock above a pool of dark water, passing a string of cottonwoods bristling stiff and leafless. As he descended into the wash, the clomp of hooves on bare rock was amplified by the stillness. He crossed a thread of creek and rode on. Cliffs massed darkly to his left, and on the right a lower tier dropped into the void of Johns Canyon. Riding the horse of the man he had killed, he was on his way to murder again.

The wagon track threaded between the angled talus and the cliff edge, turning rocky where the road crimped at the head of a ravine. This was where the Texan had pushed the body of the old sheriff over the edge. A grainy light had spread above the eastern rim, pulling shapes out of the flat expanse without revealing any sign of the dead man. He rode on, no sound but the steady creak of saddle leather. The horseman entered a boulderfield, passing the scene of the shoot-out. He crossed the trampled ground and continued through benchlands studded with blackbrush and a few tufts of bunchgrass. The road turned east and followed below an escarpment running for miles along the flank of Cedar Mesa. On his right the ground sheared away on the edge of an inner gorge where the San Juan flowed unseen.

Suddenly, the sun breached the rim ahead in a flood of light, and the rock flared red. Less than two miles away the curve of cliffs formed an amphitheater, and several hundred head of cattle ranged nearby. That was where Norris Shumway had his camp. The old sheriff and his grandson had set their bedrolls under a block of sandstone, mottled with patches of brown and red as if the rock had begun to rust. Deeply undercut, it gave enough protection from the elements for a cook fire and a small sleeping area. A line of smoke rose from the boulders, and a Model A Ford was parked nearby. Palmer rode steadily on, alert in case the cowboy had heard yesterday's shooting. He could be hiding anywhere in the mass of rocks above, sighting down the barrel of a gun.

Nothing moved but the steady gait of the horse, the sound muted by the sand. The Texan warily approached from the blind side of the camp,

The last camp. William Oliver and his grandson Norris Shumway made camp at the Seeps, where the young cowboy carved his initials and the date. The following day he was murdered next to this rock. Courtesy of Scott Thybony.

screened by rock and tree. As he drew close, Norris stepped into the sunlight and stopped, surprised to see the Texan on his grandfather's horse. Before he could react, Palmer raised the pistol. Norris lunged toward the gunman, instinctively lifting his right hand to shield his face. A single shot rang out, tearing through his wrist. The bullet creased his face and lodged in the right shoulder, knocking him back. Dazed, the cowpuncher kept on his feet.

Palmer jumped off the horse and grabbed an ax leaning against the woodpile. He swung the ax in an accelerating arc, crushing Norris's skull with the first blow and knocking him to the ground. The killer lifted it high overhead and brought it down again and again in a feral rage. He dropped the ax only when the head was all but severed. Quickly grabbing the cowboy's hat, he caught the blood gushing from the neck. As it drained, he thought through his next moves.

Once the flow eased to a stop, Palmer began to methodically cover up the murder scene. He set the hat aside, rolled the dead man onto a piece of canvas, the head dangling by a single strand, and dragged him to the Ford coupe. With his slight build, Palmer struggled to maneuver the dead weight of a 195-pound body into the trunk. He then unsaddled the horse, swung the saddle on top of the body, and found a place in the car to wedge the hat. Blood had stained the ashy soil sloping down from the fire pit, so to hide the evidence he built a fire over it using the stacked wood. Next to him was an inscription cut into the ledge rock at the mouth of the shelter reading, "NS FEB 28 1935." Without knowing it, Norris had carved his own headstone the day before.

Palmer brushed out all traces of the encounter as he worked back to the car. Climbing behind the wheel, he drove several hundred yards to the road. In case a passing cowboy or trapper had heard the shot, he needed to find somewhere to hide the body. He searched the terrain while steering the car along the bouldery roadbed. It threaded between the rising cliffs and countersunk gorge, leaving only enough room in places for a single car to pass. Here the San Juan had carved through the core of the land in great serpentine loops twenty-two hundred feet below the mesa. Crossing a landscape of rock and red sand, the road snaked about in bends, matching those of the river.

The killer reached the last ravine before the straightaway leading to the Mexican Hat road. He parked the car where the open view ahead gave him some assurance of not being surprised. Unloading the mangled body from the back, he dragged it behind a slab of sandstone and rolled it off the cliff. The body hung up on a shelf ten feet below instead of falling out of sight. Studying the curve of the road, Palmer felt confident no one driving by would spot it, so he walked backward to the Ford, brushing away his tracks. He turned the car around and began the ten-mile drive back to the cabin.

On the way he stopped to search the site of the previous day's gunfight and found the dead man's rifle, a Savage High-Power .22, capable of bringing down a deer. It was only a matter of time before the law would be after him, and he might need another weapon. The unfiltered sun had angled overhead, while a scrim of clouds lined the horizon to the west, prefiguring a change of weather. As Palmer drove up to the cabin, sunlight glinted from the pools of springwater and tangled in the branches of the cottonwoods. He worked fast to load the two-door car with saddles, chaps, and all the camp gear he could pack in. He stashed the rifles behind the seat and looked for Lucy, anxious to leave.

Hundreds of sheep had drifted up the flanks of the canyon where she sat horseback, watching the herd. She had seen the Model A drive up and now heard him shout, telling her to come down and get ready. The girl rode to the cabin and unsaddled her horse, graining it before attending to her own needs. As Palmer finished packing, she questioned him about the bloody Stetson. Palmer admitted killing and throwing the body over a cliff. Taking the hat inside, he soaked it with gasoline and burned it in the stove. He ordered her to get in the car.

The two of them drove away from the cabin, fleeing down the only road out of the canyon. Having spent most of his life either in prison or on the run, Palmer was back on familiar ground. With a posse bound to follow, the predator had once again become the prey. Soon a rear tire blew out on the overloaded Ford, forcing him to inch along on the wheel rim. They rounded the Gothic spire of Muley Point and continued along the bench. As he drove, Palmer tried to justify his killing the young cowboy, telling her Norris had taken cover in the rocks and was shooting at him.

The road passed close to a stand-alone boulder where ancient symbols had been stone-chiseled into the desert varnish, exposing the underlying red. Carved pronghorn tracks crossed a rock face, and on the adjacent side two human figures, solidly pecked, carried a third person between them.

The middle figure was only outlined in dots, giving the impression of a body lacking substance, of someone either dead or dying. And below the human forms a rattlesnake approached, suggesting the old story of danger and death.

The killer reached the spot where he had dumped the young cowboy's body and continued driving beyond the last headland, not far from a series of entrenched meanders called the Goosenecks. Pulling off the road on high ground, he had a wide-angle view ahead, stretching from the Valley of the Gods south to where Monument Valley broke the skyline with sharp-cut monoliths. From this perch he'd be able to see the dust of any approaching car.

Lucy was now on the run, an unwilling fugitive in an alien land a long way from anyplace she might have called home. She had witnessed the chaos of dust flying and horses rearing, the rapid shots echoing off the canyon walls, and the bleeding rancher stretched out on the ground. The incident had been a throwback to an older West, a time of high noons and range wars when force went unchecked. Now the two of them waited for dark while clouds thickened to the west and shadows stretched long and blue. At this hour everything stirred but the land itself. Waves of light began washing across the scene, and between each pulse the canyon grew steadily darker. With night almost upon them, the sun wedged through the western clouds to suddenly illuminate the rim below. A last band of light capped the cliff for an instant and then vanished.

HAUNTED CANYON

Before dawn I crossed the Divide on Highway 89 and began a long descent toward a dry river and the desert beyond. The road kept disappearing behind me as quickly as it emerged from the darkness ahead until suddenly the sun broke the horizon. A couple of hours later I passed El Capitan on the threshold of Monument Valley and continued north beyond the San Juan River. Where a road branched toward Johns Canyon, I turned onto it.

Straight ahead stood the lithic mass of Cedar Mesa fronted by a thousand-foot cliff half-buried under rubbled stone. At the foot of the scarp I drove along a bench chopped by tributary canyons running down to the river. My plan was to spend a couple of days covering the ground where the violent events of 1935 took place. Sunlight glanced off the rock surfaces, heating the air, while the shadows remained cold. It was the end of February, the time of year when the shoot-out occurred. Before long I spotted a cowpuncher working his cattle and stopped to talk. He told me the Ute Indians never entered Johns Canyon on account of the ghosts. "They think it's haunted," he said.[1]

And it's not only the Ute. After the shoot-out Ray Hunt and two hired hands arrived to round up Goulding's sheep, spending the night in the old cabin. "After the sun went down," he recalled, "they just froze. They could imagine spooks and spirits and everything else walking around down there. We were all so spooked that we were scared to go down and get a bucket of water."[2] Thirst finally overcame fear, so he grabbed the bucket and stepped outside. That night I camped near the Seeps, where Norris Shumway had

Johns Canyon cabin, 1935. When out on the range, William Oliver used this abandoned cabin for his cattle operation. Lucy Garrett and her kidnapper stayed here at
the time of the shoot-out. Courtesy of Northern Arizona University, Cline Library,
Phillip Johnston Collection.

been murdered, but the only nocturnal forms moving about turned out to
be a straggle of cows.

After making coffee next morning, I drove to Shootout Point. The road
curved into the upper canyon where the bench narrowed between cliff
and gorge to form a bottleneck. It was here Lucy Garrett sat on her horse
watching the gunfight. Neither the sheepherder nor the cowboy could have
avoided the other without one of them backing off, and neither was of a
disposition to do so. Two hundred yards farther the road looped around
the head of a ravine, and I pulled off at the spot where the killer had rolled
his victim over the edge. After climbing twenty feet down the first drop, I
descended twice that height at the next cliff to where the body had come
to rest. Directly below it an eighty-foot drop ended in a slope of red ledges
and stepped cliffs, pitching sharply downward for hundreds of feet.

Back on the road I crossed the creek and left the truck at a grove of cottonwoods, the limbs reaching out gray and barren this time of year. The
cabin site lay nearby, and a stub of drill casing marked a failed attempt to
tap an oil pocket in the early 1900s. I walked through what little remained

of the place—a scatter of boards, a root cellar, an outhouse placed in the shade of the only juniper left standing. A fence line ran nearby, stretching across the canyon, and on the other side of it Clint Palmer had built a dugout within sight of the cabin. He had simply cut into a sand terrace and roofed the trench with ax-cut cottonwood beams. Being about ten feet wide and sixteen long, the accommodations would have been cramped at best. The only sign of comfort was a fireplace, laid with quarried stone and set against the back wall. He claimed to have filed on a section of land in Johns Canyon, and local tradition identifies this rough shelter as his attempt to make the required improvements. The dugout resembled a bunker more than a home.

After retracing the Johns Canyon road to the highway, I turned east toward Bluff. Screened by old cottonwoods, the San Juan River runs on one side of town and a crest of cliffs on the other. About 250 members of the Hole-in-the-Rock Expedition settled here in 1880, and while the population hasn't grown much since then, the mix of residents has changed. River guides and artists, field scientists and various urban transplants and drop-outs now outnumber the Mormons by a wide margin. Bluff has the reputation of being one of the most remote towns in a remote region. It lies more than 140 miles from the nearest interstate highway and went without electricity or paved roads until 1957, a time when some Ute Indians were still living in tepees. Nearly a half century later, it does fine without a stoplight, bank, or a grocery store. And for me the sense of isolation depends on where I've been. If I've just spent days in the backcountry or long hours rattling down dirt roads, Bluff turns into a metropolis.

I pulled up to a house across from the Navajo Twins, a pair of standing rocks named for Monster Slayer and Born for Water. Melvin Gaines was in his yard inspecting a collection of old tractors and heavy machinery when I arrived. The core of his home, beneath the siding and additions, dated back to the 1890s. As we shook hands I noticed he was wearing a pair of intricately patched pants, displaying a lifelong habit of thrift. My original conversation with him in Mexican Hat had led to my interest in Lucy Garrett, and I wanted to talk with him about the time the girl and her kidnapper had lived with his family. Gaines invited me in and introduced me to his wife, Betty. As we sat down he started talking about the summer of 1934, mentioning how he knew the fugitive as Jimmy and the girl as Johnnie Ray.

"He took that girl," Gaines said, "and came straight down the river to Bluff. They had saddle horses and a couple of horses they packed all their stuff on. They came down here to Bluff and scouted around, wanting a job. They was hungry, didn't have nothing to eat."[3] His father gave Palmer a job building fence, and the pair ended up staying through the summer. He told me his dad, Lem Gaines, was "an ornery old bastard" who had been run out of Mexico by Pancho Villa. His family had two hogans, earth-covered shelters traditionally used by the Navajo, and they cleared out one so Palmer and the girl could spread their bedrolls on the floor. "I remember Johnnie Ray," he said, "who was just a kid, but I thought she was an adult. Us little-bitty kids, she used to set out there and play with me, bug the heck out of me."

Betty cuts in. "You probably bugged the heck out of her."

"They would eat at our table every night," Gaines continued. "One night, which is really fresh in my mind, Johnnie Ray was sick, sitting at the table. Jimmy Palmer reached down and got his pistol, said, 'If you don't eat, I'm goin' to shoot ya!' My dad grabbed him, threw him down, and took his damn pistol away from him and said, 'You don't pull a gun at my table. When you settle down, I'll give you your damn pistol back.' My dad kept his pistol and stuck it in his pocket. Palmer was always after my dad to give him back the pistol. He said, 'Well, if you don't have sense enough to handle a pistol, you don't need it.' He said, 'When you leave, I'll give you back your pistol.'

"I remember the day they got on their horses. Palmer had done all the work he could do, and nobody else had any jobs or nothing. He's always telling Johnnie Ray, 'We're going to meet your dad at such-and-such-a-place.' That's how he bribed her along. He was gonna meet her in New Mexico, and now he was gonna meet her in Bluff and all that kinda story. Anyway, I remember the day they left. My dad had a little Bull Durham sack and put all Palmer's bullets in the Bull Durham sack. He handed him his pistol, handed him his bullets, and said, 'Now you can go. There's your gun; there's your bullets.' So they rode off."

Jimmy and Johnnie Ray headed across the San Juan River and entered Monument Valley a step ahead of the law. "I remember," Gaines continued, "when this detective came up to our hogan. She was a redheaded woman, driving a Model A, and she was armed to the hilt—two guns on her. She was a detective or law officer of some kind and had a badge. Anyway, she come alookin' for Jimmy Palmer. She got out, talked to my folks about this wild cowboy that had this young girl.

"They told her, 'Why hell, he left weeks or months ago.'

"'Do you know where he went?'

"'No, we don't know where he went.'"

The detective suspected Palmer of having murdered a sheepherder near Fruitland, New Mexico. "If she had found him, I'm sure she would've took him back, or she would've shot him—one way or the other. My dad said she looked like a mean one, something he didn't want to tangle with."

Gaines, a Korean War veteran, has spent most of his life in southern Utah, so I asked him about the men who had traveled with explorer Dan Thrapp in the winter of 1935. "Bud Vinger," Gaines said, chuckling as he pronounced the name as "vinegar." "He was kinda an ornery damn guy. He used to beat the hell out of some of them people up at Dove Creek, I remember that." Gaines paused a moment. "Ol' Bob Wise, he was quite a character. He never had any serious charges against him, outside of getting drunk and raising hell. He had a farm here, up the river a ways, a pretty nice damn layout. He trapped all during the winter. He was a trapper, and he'd come in with furs, coyote furs—the damn horse stacked plum to the gills—all on spreaders. Made a lot of extra money that ways, and then he'd farm all summer."

According to Gaines, no one in town knew much about his past. "We figured that wasn't his name," he said. "We never did know his name. We think he came out of the Texas area. He talked to some of the old-timers one time when he was drunk. It seemed as though he got in trouble in Texas, and he escaped the law. So he just called himself 'Bob Wise'—wise enough to get away from them. We know damn well he was an old outlaw, but his past never did foller him up."

"He'd ride down from the farm with an old dog, named Mike. Damn dog, he'd jump the fence and beat the hell out of our dog every time. My mother, Beuna, kept on to him about beating the hell out of our dog. He got pissed off one day and opened the gate and come on in, and my mother knocked the living hell out of that old man and throwed him over the goddamn gate. He got up from there just madder than hell. He got back on his horse and made off. He told my dad, 'I don't know how you put up with that woman. She's the meanest woman I've ever seen.'"

Beuna could hold her own. "My mother," he said, "was mean and stout, stout as a bull. When I was just a little boy, these women all worked out in the fields. My mother, I seen her get out in the fields all day long, following a turning plow. She would plow the ground and harrow it, getting it ready to plant. And I'll tell you something, you don't just walk up and decide you're going to whip a woman like that. A female, when they get mad, if they're strong like that, you can get the damnedest beating from one of them that you ever got in your life. They don't know when to quit."

Realizing it was time for me to quit, I said good-bye and took the road north to Monticello, where I met Rigby Wright at his home. During his career in law enforcement, he had chased prison escapees, raided meth labs, aggressively pursued pothunters, and hunted for missing persons. During one search he was stranded without a bedroll and forced to spend the night in a cadaver bag. Without the cadaver. "I'm still haunted by some of the bodies I've handled," he said. "I wake up in the night, you know. Some of them really bother me."[4]

Earlier a friend had called, telling me I needed to meet Rigby Wright, a former sheriff of San Juan County.

"Rigby is the kind of guy," said Chuck LaRue, "who knows where all the bodies are buried. He knows about the shoot-out in Johns and where the sheriff's body was hidden. If we can meet him at Mexican Hat in two days, he'll show us."[5]

That gave me only a day to get up there and back, since I had to be in town at the end of the week. It meant leaving in the dark and returning in the dark and in between a madcap trip covering hundreds of miles and some rough roads. But it might be my only chance. "Tell Rigby we'll meet him."

At Mexican Hat, the retired sheriff climbed into my truck with a friend of his, and soon the four of us were rattling down the Johns Canyon road. It skirted the foot of Cedar Mesa, rising like an island from a sea of rock and sand. Wearing a camouflage ball cap and work boots, Rigby settled in next to me, perfectly at ease on these back roads. He had read the case file on the 1935 shoot-out and knew the region well, having spent twenty years chasing lawbreakers across it, often at night. "There's a hell of a lot of this country I haven't seen," he said, "except in the cone of the headlights."[6]

As I drove, Rigby let the landscape jog his memory. He had investigated murders and chased pothunters here, searched for those who had disappeared, rescued the injured, and retrieved the bodies. He talked about the prehistoric sites he'd explored and the mummies recovered from looters. And then he mentioned events during the Posey War in 1923, known to some historians as the last engagement of the Indian wars. "They call it the last Indian uprising," Rigby said. "Bullshit. That's Bluff, Utah, any Saturday night." The Ute call it the last white-man uprising.

Eventually, the talk got around to Lucy Garrett. I recognized similarities between her ordeal and the 2002 kidnapping of Elizabeth Smart outside Salt Lake City. In both cases the girls had passed up chances to escape, which I found curious. For Rigby, it was only natural. "She wasn't in control," the sheriff told me, remembering victims he had interviewed over the years. "She was being used. What do you do when you're thirteen years old? No kid will testify against their parents for abuse—hell, that's their security blanket. That's all they got, and they don't want to lose that."

The road curved into the canyon, and the bench narrowed. "Along in here might be where they found him," Rigby said. "Stop here." We got out and walked to the edge of a cliff, falling in two jumps to the canyon bottom. "I don't think there'd be any reason to go down there," he said in case I thought otherwise. I stood with Rigby as he pointed out where the old sheriff's body had been hidden by James Clinton Palmer long ago. "This is where he throwed him over," Rigby said. "He just throwed him over—and he's gone."

I looked across the canyon at a line of red cliffs and then down at the gorge below. My eye traced the path a body would take as it rebounded down the slope. After the shoot-out, Rigby told me, Jimmy Palmer proceeded to hunt down the sheriff's grandson and brutally murder him. His recounting of these events raised a number of questions. What had happened here in the winter of 1935 to trigger such a violent confrontation? And how had the girl survived a year on the run with a man who might kill her at any moment?

When I asked about the Johns Canyon troubles, he called it a range war. The grazing was so limited in the canyon that Rigby figured it could sustain only several dozen head of cattle or a few hundred sheep. "They'd be hard-pressed. I could see them fighting over it immediately." And such a dependable source of water, surrounded by desert, would make it especially desirable. "That's the story of the West. More people have been killed over water than women."

Before I left, he mentioned a pair of incidents so strange that the mood stayed with me long afterward. They happened sometime in the years before World War II. A cowpuncher, Rigby said, often rode to the mouth of Red Canyon on the Colorado River. One day as he sat horseback, a pack string of three horses drifted by, having drowned somewhere upriver. And later he noticed something that caught him completely off guard. Floating past him was the body of a blonde woman. The Colorado moved strong and fast, making it impossible for him to try retrieving her, so he never learned what happened. Perhaps she died attempting to ford the river, or a flash flood may have swept her away. He couldn't say. It was as if the cowboy had found a few pages torn from a book without knowing the beginning or end. All he was left with was the haunting memory of a body floating past.

THE MANHUNT

The Model A Ford slipped past Mexican Hat late at night. Overloaded with saddles and bedrolls, it could have been a family of Dust Bowl refugees instead of a murderer on the run. The girl rode next to her kidnapper in silence, afraid of him and afraid of those in pursuit. Turning onto the one-lane bridge over the San Juan River, he steered the stolen car up the rough shelfrock beyond. The road they followed skirted sand-filled hollows as it headed toward a horizon of standing rock, silhouetted against the dark sky. He inched the Ford along the rocky stretches, running on two flat tires, and reached Monument Valley. Turning onto a spur, he drove past Goulding's Trading Post to a hidden pocket in the cliffs. It was past midnight, and no lights had come on.

EARLY MARCH 1935

At daybreak the rock monuments stood massive and sharp cut against the sky with the red desert spreading below. Clint Palmer scanned the expanse, making sure no one had followed them. By late morning on Saturday, March 2, heavy storm clouds had pushed in from the west, and he walked a quarter mile to the stone-built trading post. The fugitive banged on the door. The Gouldings were still in their living quarters above the store. Mike stepped onto the balcony and asked in Navajo who it was, "Ha'át'íishą́'?"[1]

Palmer called up, saying he was in trouble and needed to speak to Harry. He climbed the ladder to the upper story and waited until Goulding finished shaving. As the two of them descended to the store, the trader noticed the manager of his sheep operation had a gun strapped to his side. Goulding asked what had happened, and Palmer told him straight out, "I have killed two of those sons-of-bitches." As Palmer spoke, the trader noticed "a gruesome, cold-blood expression came over his face."

"My God," he asked, "what did you have to kill anybody for?"

Working himself into a furor, the Texan claimed Oliver had hit his wife with a twist of his lariat, and the next day Norris had attacked her. The old sheriff then took a shot at him, and being unarmed he got his gun and killed both men. The bodies, he told Goulding, had been hidden so well no one would ever find them. Palmer lied without hesitation to his friend, the man who had given him work and buried his child. And he kept lying. "They thought they could get away with anything," he said.

The news sickened Goulding, leaving him stunned. "I thought perhaps he might kill me," he recalled, "if I did not cultivate his confidence and do as he said." The trader advised Palmer to turn himself into the authorities since it was a case of self-defense. "The only way I will even go to Monticello," Palmer said, "is with my legs stiff from my toes up, because if they don't get me for this they will get me for something else."

The two of them returned to the hideout, where the heavily loaded Model A had been driven up the wash as far as it could go. Lucy Garrett was lying on bedding below an overhanging cliff. "Show him where those sons-of-bitches hit you," Palmer told the girl, but she refused to play along. Any marks she might have would have been ones he had given her. Throughout her ordeal, Lucy had been repulsed by her kidnapper, but fearing for her life she had kept her feelings buried. He now taunted her by asking, "Do you like this better than killing Mormons?"

If it were true Oliver had mistreated the girl, Goulding said, they should give themselves up. The comment set Palmer off again, and he began a tirade about the way Goulding had been treated by those across the river. Growing furious, he told the trader he would not let them get away with it.

Goulding responded, "I am not trying to give you orders about what to do, but you ought to think this over good." Palmer ignored his advice and demanded to be driven to the railroad at Flagstaff, 175 miles to the south, under the pretext of having to pick up supplies for the store. As he talked he kept his hand on the grip of the revolver. Goulding felt he had no choice but to comply and walked back to the trading post to make arrangements.

"Get me those low cuts of yours and a small hat," the killer said. "I have to get out of this cowboy rig."

Palmer switched the battery from Goulding's car to the truck, and the trader went inside to tell Mike about the killings. When she heard Harry was planning to drive them to the railroad, she recognized the danger. "Give him anything," she said. "Do not leave here."

Back outside, Goulding said he couldn't leave his wife alone. So Palmer ordered the trader to gas up the car and give him all the money he had. When the vehicle was ready, he handed over forty dollars. Driving back to the box canyon, Palmer told Lucy to get in. The sheriff was already on his trail, he said, and they had to leave in a hurry. Palmer loaded a bundle tied in a blanket and the guns, leaving everything else in the stolen car.

By early afternoon the girl and her kidnapper were on the run again, heading south into Arizona. They were driving Goulding's 1931 Chevrolet, equipped with wide doughnut tires for the sand. The rains had begun to fall, so they pushed on fast before the roads became impassable. At Kayenta they turned west toward Marsh Pass, a notorious stretch of road in wet weather. Palmer threaded between Black Mesa and the red cliffs of Skeleton Mesa, speeding through the gap before it became saturated. Once beyond the pass, the two of them continued to the Red Lake Trading Post, and outside of Tuba City they turned south across the Painted Desert toward the cloud-hidden San Francisco Peaks. Below the mountains ran Route 66, the highway John Steinbeck came to call "the road of flight."[2]

That evening Sheriff Lawrence Palmer was staying at the home of his parents in Blanding. Unrelated to the murderer, the young lawman shared only a last name with him and had held office only since January. "I was 25-years old," he remembered years later, "and the kid sheriff of San Juan County."[3] That summer he had been fired as a ranch manager when he ran off to get married and then was elected sheriff on a seventeen-vote margin. The job paid a slim nine hundred dollars a year, but it was the middle of the Depression, and he needed work. Breaking the stereotype of a tough western lawman, he is shown in a newspaper photograph dressed in a fedora, bow tie, and glasses with round black rims. Now after only two months on the job, the soft-spoken sheriff had his hands full.

Reports were coming in about attempts to raise the dead at the Home of Truth, north of Monticello, and he had been notified of a young scientist,

Dan Thrapp, who had gone missing in his county while searching for Indian ruins. Another young man, Everett Ruess, may have crossed the Colorado River into his jurisdiction before disappearing. And then there was Bud Vinger. After his jailbreak, someone had spotted the outlaw in Comb Wash, and Lawrence Palmer had searched the area without success. The kid sheriff was in over his head, he admitted, and events would soon test him beyond his abilities.

It was after midnight when voices below his window woke him. Harry Goulding and two other men were calling for the sheriff. He let them in, and the trader reported that Clint Palmer admitted having killed two cattlemen in Johns Canyon and hidden their bodies. Whether another lie or a confession, he also claimed to have killed a deputy sheriff sometime before going to work for the trader. Goulding stalled for as long as possible, he said, before turning over his car and all the cash on hand. Palmer had then taken the girl and left for parts unknown. The trader went on to explain how a government agent had arrived at the post around two in the afternoon, soon after the killer had left. They drove to Kayenta, hoping to alert the authorities, but the phone was down. So he borrowed the government pickup and reversed course back to Utah.

A steady rain had set in and soon turned to snow. With road conditions treacherous, his progress slowed, and he didn't reach Blanding until after midnight in the middle of a blizzard. Goulding went straight to the home of Paul Black, a county commissioner he knew, and woke him up. After they alerted the sheriff, word of the killings spread quickly. The sheriff wired lawmen throughout the Four Corners country, warning them to be on the lookout for Clint Palmer, who was wanted for murder. He next gathered a posse to search Johns Canyon for the bodies. Neighbors and relatives of the victims were shocked by the deaths of two good men. "Oliver himself," said the sheriff, "while an old Indian fighter, was quiet and peaceful if left alone, Shumway just a bashful kid."[4]

As the manhunt got under way, Lawrence Palmer had one last duty. At three o'clock on Sunday morning, he went to Bill Oliver's home and broke the terrible news to Mary Jane. Both her grandson and husband were dead, he told her, and their bodies still missing. She had feared a confrontation with the sheepman would lead to this. "I thought," she said, "I would go wild with grief."[5]

At dawn the young sheriff took off in pursuit, hoping to overtake the fugitive, despite knowing Palmer had a twenty-four-hour head start. The car Palmer had commandeered lacked chains, so he might be stuck somewhere ahead. Riding with the sheriff was his deputy, A. E. Shumway, the uncle of Norris, and Barton Lyman. They were followed by the search party and Goulding, who was returning to Monument Valley. As details of the incident emerged, anger at Goulding had grown. Many of those in the posse believed he had purposely delayed reporting the incident to give Palmer a head start. "I was afraid," said Paul Black, "someone was going to kill Goulding before I could get him back down the road and home."[6]

Reaching Goulding's Trading Post, seventy-three miles from Blanding, the sheriff learned from an Arizona deputy that Palmer and the girl had been able to clear Marsh Pass during the early stages of the storm. The fugitive had also stopped at a string of trading posts in Arizona, asking directions to Flagstaff. So the sheriff pushed on to Kayenta and notified radio stations in Salt Lake City and Phoenix, asking them to broadcast descriptions of Palmer and the car he was driving. Then he picked up the trail and reached Marsh Pass, where conditions had deteriorated. The road had turned into gumbo, and even with chains the mud stuck to the tires in such thick layers that the car lost traction. It bogged down repeatedly, and for three miles the passengers had to get out and push. When that wasn't enough, the kid sheriff joined them, steering with one arm and pushing with the other.

Covered in mud, they reached Tuba City at ten that night and learned Palmer had passed through six hours before the sheriff first heard of the shoot-out. They had little chance of catching him now, but if he went deeper into Arizona, the sheriff thought, the authorities would arrest him. Exhausted and uncertain of the route taken by the fugitive, the posse stopped for the night.

Newspapers around the country began to cover the breaking story on Monday, allowing readers to follow the events in southern Utah as they unfolded. As new details of the crime came in, one story buried another. Follow-up articles framed the conflict as an anachronism, closer to a Bret Harte tale than a contemporary murder case. Some editors considered it a throwback to the frontier days of a half century earlier, when bloody feuds had erupted between cattlemen and sheepherders. One headline read like a line from a western page-turner, "Six-Guns Blaze by Wild West Waterholes as Range Wars Flare."[7] By the 1930s that sort of thing was supposed to happen only in movie theaters.

A reporter described Bill Oliver as being famous for his leadership as sheriff in the last battle between the Indians and white settlers of San Juan County. News accounts referred to the killer as an outlaw, a desperado, and as "Two-Gun Jimmy."[8] But the girl remained a mystery. At first Johnnie Ray was identified as the fugitive's wife, and only days later did details of her kidnapping emerge and her real name surface. Eventually, readers learned she was Lucile Garrett, the daughter of a woodcutter murdered by Palmer. And those who knew him believed her life was in danger.

Next morning the sheriff decided to follow a tip that Palmer might have turned north into the remote country beyond the Colorado. So the posse renewed the chase and crossed the river at Marble Canyon. They picked up what was thought to be the fugitive's trail at the House Rock Trading Post. An attendant reported a car matching the wanted vehicle had stopped late Saturday night. The driver appeared nervous, and a woman was sleeping in the back. After paying for the gas, he took off at a high speed. Crossing back into Utah, the posse lost the trail in Kanab and decided to pursue another possibility. The sheriff knew the girl had an uncle in Las Vegas, and Palmer had mentioned his plan to leave her in a safe place as soon as possible. So they pushed on into Nevada, reaching Las Vegas at noon on Tuesday. From the local sheriff they learned the uncle had moved, and no one had seen Lucy or the killer. "We checked the gambling joints, Palmer being a natural gambler," the sheriff said, "and checked the used car lots for any trace of the car."[9] Nothing. It was now obvious they had been following a false lead.

Turning back, Sheriff Palmer reached St. George at two in the morning, where he received a telegram informing him of Palmer's arrest in Texas. Later that morning he briefed a federal agent who had been brought into the case under laws passed the previous year to hunt down the notorious gangster John Dillinger. They granted agents at the national level new powers to carry guns and make arrests in certain crimes, including crossing state lines to avoid prosecution. But with Clint Palmer now in custody, the local authorities would handle the case. That day the front page of the *Deseret News* announced in a banner headline, "UTAH SLAYER IS CAPTURED."[10]

At the start of the manhunt, the second posse had left to search for the victims. A handful of men followed the sheriff in two cars and stopped in Bluff to pick up John Oliver, the brother of the dead rancher. They had been close, and he had been up all night unable to eat or sleep after hearing the news of his brother's death. And believing the trader had instigated the confrontation, the seventy-five-year-old farmer wanted vengeance. "He was crazy mad at Harry Goulding," Black recalled.[11]

The searchers took the fork leading to Johns Canyon and proceeded slowly on what was little more than a wagon track. Checking the camp at the Seeps, they found Oliver's horse grazing nearby and the inscription Norris Shumway had cut into the rock, but no sign of the victims. They continued to the cabin at the springs and again found nothing. But the presence of an angry John Oliver, armed with a Colt .45, was impeding the search efforts. They were afraid he might shoot somebody, so Paul Black agreed to take him home and recruit more men to help. As they reached the main road, John forced the commissioner to stop the car. He insisted on being driven to Goulding's, but Black refused to comply. It took him twenty minutes to defuse the situation and convince the brother to go home.

On Monday, March 4, nearly twenty reinforcements arrived with supplies to last until the remains were recovered. They drove the Johns Canyon road again, inspecting every spot a body might be hidden. Without finding any trace of the victims, they turned back to the cabin, and while rounding a tight bend one of the searchers saw something below a tier of cliffs. They stopped the truck, and men climbed down to where the remains of Bill Oliver had snagged on brush. If the body had rolled any farther, it would have disappeared over the edge of a sheer drop. Retrieving it was a gruesome task due to the state of decomposition, the bullet-torn flesh, and his bruised and lacerated face. Several men struggled to lift the body up the ledges.

Back on top, Paul Black noticed drips of oil on the road and remembered that Bill Oliver's car had a leak in the main bearing. He realized it might be a way to find Norris's body and told the other searchers to keep their eyes open for oil spots. On their way out, they found more drips at the last bend and stopped. The body of young Norris had been dragged behind a boulder next to the road and rolled onto a ledge below. Their grim mission now complete, the posse transported the remains back to Blanding.

Not a single doctor practiced in the southeastern corner of Utah, so one had to be summoned from Moab to hold an inquest. That evening at the home of Addie Black, a daughter of Bill Oliver, the bodies were laid out on the kitchen table, grandfather next to grandson. The doctor performed an autopsy and confirmed both men had been murdered. When he was finished, preparations for burial began immediately, since the bodies could not be embalmed. Lacking an undertaker, volunteers cleaned the remains and sewed the wounds as best they could, using crude stitching to reattach young Norris's head. A carpenter began work on a simple pine coffin, having one of his children hold a coal-oil lantern as he sawed the boards. Water was put on to boil, which he used to curve the boards before nailing, and the local women sewed the burial clothes. Because spring flowers had not yet appeared in the high country, the women worked late into the night making artificial flowers. When all was ready, the bodies were placed in the coffins and packed with snow. To further prevent decomposition, the windows were left open to the icy gusts, turning the room into a makeshift cold storage.

Winds swept across the mesa while volunteers dug the graves, shoveling away the deep snow and chopping through the frozen ground. On Thursday friends and relatives filed past the open coffins, banked by hundreds of paper flowers. Among them were local Indians who came to pay tribute to a man who had earned their respect, despite having once fought against them. As the deceased lay in state, a memorial service was held in the afternoon at the Latter-day Saints church. Nearly a thousand mourners packed the hall and listened to the choir open with "Though Deepening Trials," followed by eulogies for the dead.[12] The speakers reminded those in attendance of what they had lost. They noted the upstanding character of the deceased and mentioned that Bill Oliver had left behind seven children, sixty-three grandchildren, and fifty-three great-grandchildren. Sheriff Palmer had driven all night from St. George to attend, and district attorney Fred W. Keller arrived after having interviewed Harry Goulding. He cleared the trader of any responsibility for the killings, a judgment not shared by many of those in attendance. Next morning, more than a week after the shoot-out at Johns Canyon, the two men were buried.

TO THE SULPHUR RIVER

The murderer had made his initial escape and was speeding east on Route 66, detouring around the center of each town they passed to avoid being spotted. Clint Palmer was now an old hand at evading the authorities. Beyond Gallup he followed the route he had taken after previous crimes, entering Texas by way of Clovis. As they fled farther east, Lucy kept alive a flicker of hope, believing she might still be reunited with her father. The two of them sped across the high plains through country lightly inhabited and seldom patrolled.

On Monday afternoon Palmer stopped outside Wichita Falls to pick up three girls standing by the road with their thumbs out. He introduced Lucy as his daughter and soon dropped two of the hitchhikers off at their homes in Bowie. Helen Smith, a girl about Lucy's age, accepted Palmer's invitation to go with them to the Fort Worth Stock Show, an annual extravaganza combining an auction, fair, and rodeo. But Palmer turned east before reaching the city, telling the red-haired girl he had changed his plans and needed to see his father. He continued to avoid towns while making his way back to Peerless.

The fugitive parked Goulding's Chevy in the yard of his father's home at two on Tuesday morning. He had covered more than twelve hundred miles since fleeing the scene of the Utah shootings, and it had been nearly a year since H. P. Palmer had seen his son. During his absence Clint had become the prime suspect in the death of Lucy's father, and murder charges had been filed against him the month before.

"What are you doing here?" his father asked, surprised to see him.[1]

"I'm hot in Utah," he answered.

"Well, you are just as hot here as you are in Utah."

Father and son stepped outside for a private conversation, and on his return Clint sat down at the table for a quick meal. As he ate, Clint kept his pistol next to him, covered with a napkin. When he was finished, the three of them disappeared again into the early-morning darkness of North Texas.

They headed to a crossing of the Sulphur River at Deep Well. If they could get to the other side, a choice of roads fanned out in several directions, making pursuit difficult. The ford was easily passable during dry seasons, but the same storm that allowed Palmer to escape his pursuers in Arizona now turned against him. The river flowed high and strong due to the rains, but he took a chance and eased into the current. When the water reached the bottom of the doors, the engine stalled, and he was unable to restart it. Stranded in midriver, Palmer told the girls to strip off their clothes and push. Their efforts succeeded in moving the car back to shallow water, where he decided to wait until daylight before finding help.

Next morning the girls waded the river and found a farmer willing to pull them to higher ground with his mule. Starting back the way they came, Palmer met a pair of hunters and asked about an alternate route. They directed him to a track climbing the hillside to Tater Dickson's place, near Posey, and Palmer took it. Having recognized him as a wanted man, they drove almost to Sulphur Springs before finding a phone to call the local sheriff. Palmer and the girls headed east, searching for another crossing, and while driving full throttle on the rain-slick road he missed a curve. The car veered across a yard and ran over a mattress set out to air. He next took a chance by stopping at a farmhouse, where Mrs. O. P. Nations fixed breakfast for them. While eating he identified himself as a detective working on the Skeleton Murder Case and wanted to know what she had heard. "The only reason why I hate to trace this Clint Palmer," he told her, "is on account of his poor old daddy. I don't think his daddy had anything to do with his murder. He might have helped put him in the cave and put the brush over him. That's all."[2]

A posse of eight officers quickly assembled in Sulphur Springs, armed for a fight. They left in two police cars and reached Deep Well Crossing in the early afternoon. The fugitive had fled, so the lawmen followed the main road on a ridge between two branches of the river and continued past Birthright and Sulphur Bluff. Catching sight of the fugitive's vehicle, they gave chase. Palmer was desperate and took a back road east of Needmore. He knew his chance of escaping was slim, so he provided the girls with a cover story in case they were caught. He told them to pose as sisters from Bowie, Texas. "I was supposed to go under the name Lorena Smith," Lucy said. "He told me to be sure and deny that I had ever known him, to never admit seeing him before he had picked me up. And we girls were to get hacksaw blades and give them to him as soon as they turned us loose."[3]

The road looped down to the Sulphur River bottom, but it soon became impassable. Palmer backed off and got stuck in the mud as he turned around. With rifles bristling from the windows, the posse closed in. The lawmen jumped out and surrounded the Chevy, ready to open fire. The sheriff ordered Palmer to surrender, and he stepped from the car with his arms raised, giving up without resistance. A search of the vehicle turned up stolen plates and the weapons used in the Utah murders. The twenty-eight-mile chase had come to an end, and Sheriff Clint Reneau cuffed the wanted man at 2:40 in the afternoon.

Word of the capture spread, and by the time the posse got back to Sulphur Springs a large crowd had gathered at the county jail next to the courthouse. The curious lined the walkway to get a look at Palmer and the two girls, who were dressed colorfully, while he wore a checked shirt and cowboy hat. All three were placed behind bars until the sheriff could sort out the degrees of involvement. When Sheriff Reneau had Palmer brought into his office for questioning, he remained silent. "I kept hammering away at him," the sheriff said. "In another hour he cracked but not dangerously."[4] He admitted killing the Utah cowboys as an act of self-defense, but refused to confess to the murder of Lucy's father. He told the sheriff they were fools to believe they could pin a murder on him with only a pile of unidentified bones as evidence. He was taken back to his cell and Lucy escorted in.

At first she refused to cooperate with the sheriff. For a year Palmer had instilled in her a fear of the police. If she spoke to them, he told her, her father would end up in prison. "I tried fatherly admonition," Reneau said, "frankness, friendliness, pity, and stern rebuke on her. None of it worked."[5] Getting nowhere, he decided to confront her with the news of her father's death. Lucy refused to believe the sheriff. Having convinced herself he might still be alive, she was unable to face the truth. So he went to the storeroom and returned with the remains of Dillard Garrett. "I hated to put this child through the ordeal," he said, "but there was no other way."

Placing the bones on his desk, Reneau pointed out a deformity in a finger and identifying marks from an old injury to his right foot. The blood drained from her face as the realization sunk in, and a moment later her shock turned to anger. "If my daddy's been killed," she said, "then it was Clint Palmer who killed him. I know it!"[6] And Lucy Garrett now wanted revenge for his murder, for the kidnapping, for a year of living in terror. "She told me the whole pathetic story of her life," Reneau said. And as she opened up to the sheriff, the evidence against Palmer became overwhelming.

After Reneau completed interrogating the prisoners, reporters crowded into the jailhouse, shouting questions at Clint Palmer, who was back behind bars. He denied having killed Lucy's father, but readily admitted the Utah slayings, claiming self-defense. "I killed Oliver and Shumway," he said, "trying to protect my wife and my land. I am ready and want to go back to Utah and have the real story of the entire shooting told. In fact, I am eager to go."[7] A cell mate interrupted, saying he had the hot seat coming. "I haven't got any hot seat coming," Palmer said, "but if I have let 'em pour it on me."[8]

When the newspapermen questioned Lucy in her cell, a different story emerged. She denied being married to Palmer and told them her life with him after her father disappeared had been terrible. Oliver, she added, was perfectly right in keeping their sheep out of Johns Canyon, and he had never harmed her. The girl had witnessed his death and told how Palmer had killed Shumway the next day. And having identified the bones of her father, she was now certain her kidnapper had killed him. "I am going to kill Palmer," she said, "just like he killed my daddy. I am not through with him."[9]

Knowing the importance of her testimony, the authorities held Lucy Garrett in jail as a material witness. They also faced the difficulty of seating an impartial jury, since the bones of Dillard Garrett had been on display in the Sulphur Springs courthouse for weeks. Thousands of citizens had seen them and formed opinions on the Skeleton Murder Case. So they moved the trial to Greenville, in the adjacent county, and set a court date for the following month.

Sheriff Lawrence Palmer and county attorney Donald T. Adams arrived by bus from Utah on Thursday, March 14. They presented extradition papers, signed by Governor Henry H. Blood, to the Texas authorities. But the Texans were already moving ahead with their plans to put Clint Palmer on trial and turned down the request. They placed a hold on the prisoner to prevent him from being released before Utah authorities could take custody. Sheriff Palmer and the county attorney were permitted to question the prisoner and found he was now being held in Greenville. "There was fear of mob violence," said the Utah sheriff, "by the people of Sulphur Springs where Palmer had killed Dillard Garrett before fleeing to Utah."[10]

As the prisoner sat in his cell, he gave a self-serving account of events leading to the shoot-out with Bill Oliver and the killing of Norris Shumway. "It was the most brutal murder I had ever heard of," Sheriff Palmer recalled, "and the people of San Juan County were determined that Palmer be brought back and tried and given the death sentence."[11] When he was finished with Palmer, the sheriff interviewed Lucy Garrett. She recalled that she was a victim of Palmer's deception and how he had forced her to live with him as his common-law wife, holding her as a virtual captive for a year. At the end of the week, the sheriff and county attorney started on their return trip to Utah, driving Goulding's stolen car, and arrived in Monticello four days later.

APRIL 1935

Jury selection began on Tuesday, April 9, and the trial of James Clinton Palmer opened the next day. Spectators and reporters crowded into the courtroom, where the defendant sat with his mother on one side and his sister on the other. His court-appointed lawyer had him dress in a gray suit with his hair neatly trimmed. After Palmer entered a plea of not guilty on the charge of murdering Dillard Garrett, the prosecution began calling a string of witnesses, one after the next. By the time court was adjourned in late afternoon, twelve witnesses had testified, helping the district attorney establish the identity of the skeleton as Dillard Garrett and the nature of the wounds as being consistent with murder. He also established a relationship between Palmer and the victim, while preparing the ground for his star witness, Lucy Garrett.

On Thursday morning the fourteen-year-old girl took the witness stand. As the crowd continued to push into an already packed courtroom, the doors were locked. Lucy testified for most of the day, beginning her story in Hugo, Oklahoma, and ending with the capture of the defendant near the Sulphur River, nearly a year later. She detailed how he had tricked her into going west with him, how he had forged a letter from her father, and how she had given birth to a premature baby who died a week later. She told of fleeing back to Texas and testified she was able to recognize the bones of her father. During cross-examination, the defense attorney tried to shake her identification of the skeleton, but she was certain the remains were those of her father.

The trial resumed on Friday, with the prosecution calling a few follow-up witnesses before resting its case. To the surprise of many, the defense decided not to put any witnesses on the stand, claiming the state had failed to positively identify the skeleton and tie Palmer to the alleged murder. Each side was given two hours for closing arguments, and Palmer interrupted when the judge reminded the prosecutor his time was about up. "Give him all the time he wants, Judge. Before God, my conscience is clear."[12] After demanding the death penalty, the state rested its case.

The jury began deliberations at ten Friday evening and retired an hour later. At eight the next morning, the ten farmers, a plumber, and a traveling salesman returned with a verdict of guilty. They recommended Palmer serve ninety-nine years in prison instead of being executed. As the deputies led the prisoner away, he shouted, "An innocent man gets 99 years in the penitentiary. And they know as well as I do that I'm not guilty!"[13]

Sheriff Reneau telephoned Lawrence Palmer in Blanding with the news that Lucy Garrett's testimony had put Clint Palmer behind bars for life. Justice had moved swiftly.

PART 3

THE SOLITARY ARTIST

Everett Ruess

TRACKS BLOWN OVER

He was awake before dawn under a red moon descending. Everett Ruess got up and stoked the fire and watched the world slowly emerge from the darkness, the sky separating from earth along a broken horizon of buttes and rock spires. Dust suspended in the air obscured thousand-foot monuments, the rock formations that gave the valley its name and mark the heart of the Four Corners country. Everett saddled one burro, pulling tight the cinch, then packed the other burro and threw a double-diamond hitch to secure the load. Breaking camp below the H. T. Goulding Trading Post, he set out on foot under a yellow sky with his burros trailing behind.

The twenty-year-old from Los Angeles rounded a mesa and took the desert track toward Kayenta, a day's travel to the south. Set against such a vast expanse, the young artist and his burros appeared to be barely moving, three figures lost in the great scale of things.

MAY 1, 1934

Highway maps called the way through Monument Valley a road. And when it wasn't washed out, covered by drift sand, or lost in a confusion of possible routes, it served as one. After a few miles of walking, the young artist mounted Leopard, and Cockleburrs followed under a mound of gear. They passed a hump of bald sandstone known as Promise Rock, where Navajo customers were always promising the local bootlegger to pay him later. Mystery Valley, with its hidden ruins and blind canyons, opened to the east, but he stayed on course, needing to cover ground. Everett and his companions entered a broad flat, purple with locoweed, stretching to the distant cliffs of Skeleton Mesa. Shaking in the wind, the plants struggled to stay rooted in the drift of red sands as the air thickened with dust and the light diffused in a dead haze. Behind the rider, blowing sand covered the tracks as quickly as they were made, leaving no trace of his passing.

The miles turned into hours as the distance shifted into pure duration. He stopped for lunch only when he found enough grass for his burros. While they grazed, he huddled behind a swell of brush-anchored sand and pulled out *Death Comes for the Archbishop*. He ate his jerky and for a moment let himself get drawn into Willa Cather's story of the old Southwest. Returning to the road, he faced a full blow, which would make it more difficult to reach camp by dark. Storm clouds were approaching from the west, darkening the sky, as he urged his burros on. That was when he began to sing. He rode with his shirttails flapping, singing full throated into the wind. In the past he had sung from loneliness or grief, as if the pain within could express itself only through the human voice. Now he sang from the pure exhilaration of being young and on the loose, far away from home and the life he had known.

The way ahead led toward the red flank of Tyende Mesa, and soon the top of Agathla Peak poked above an intervening ridge to the southeast. Passing below it late in the day, Everett faced a solitary pinnacle rising skyward more than twelve hundred feet. The prominent landmark, better known to travelers as El Capitan, was a volcanic neck, its dark and ragged facets contrasting with the purple shadings of soft mudstone next to the road. Everett, always the romantic, saw a castle in its form, and if so, the walls had tumbled into ruins long before. The late light angled through a split in the clouds, painting the gray face of El Cap with a wash of red. The artist stopped, unwilling to pass up the chance to paint it, and pulled out his sketch pad and palette. This was the way he saw himself, the artist-adventurer surrounded by the beauty of a storm-swept landscape. He worked fast, knowing camp was still five miles down the road, but the light soon failed.

Rolling up the sketch, Everett tucked it inside a tube and rode until the slow pace forced him to dismount. He drove his burros into a lope, shouting to get them moving as they crossed an elevated valley toward the dark ridgeline ahead. It was the tail end of Comb Ridge, a great flex in the earth's surface exposed and weathered into a sharp flange of cliffs curving north into Utah for 120 miles. The road threaded through a pass toward Laguna Creek and the outpost of Kayenta beyond. He paused where the trail to a hogan branched off at a pile of stones. Night had overtaken him, and camp was close. Then without warning the burros bolted, and whether spooked by something real or imagined the result was the same.

"They were off like a shot," Everett wrote, and he was right behind them, listening to the pack thumping in the distance.[1] They carried all of his food, water, and bedding. So the artist, who had earned only an average mark in his high school phys-ed class, chased after them like a track star. He ran until his lungs were burning, and only when he lost sight of them did he admit they had made their escape. Following at a walk, he retrieved the Navajo saddle blankets that had slipped off and continued down to the creek. No sign of the fugitive burros turned up. "The desert," he wrote, "might have swallowed them up; they might be anywhere."

He headed for the trading post to get help, fearing the worst. While he had chased strays before, this time was more serious. He imagined finding all of his equipment scattered and broken in the morning, his camera crushed and his paintings lying in the rain. But a mile from Kayenta he stopped to reconsider. He knew the incident would become the talk of the small community and the source of a few jokes at his expense. He could handle that, but what caused him to hesitate was the need to prove to himself he could manage whatever problems came along. On earlier trips, he usually had someone around to get him out of a tight bind. So he turned back and circled through the rocks, unable to find any trace of the escapees. Everett felt his way through the darkness and finally reached the hogan.

Beginning with his first trip to the Navajo country three years before, Everett made himself at home whenever he found an empty hogan. The traditional earth-covered dwelling, oriented to the rising sun, was designed to replicate the natural world. The floor represented the earth, with the main posts supporting the roof the way the four sacred mountains held up the sky. Every structural detail corresponded to an aspect of the Navajo cosmos. Family life revolved around the central fire, like stars circling the North Star. The smoke hole was left uncovered, letting rain from the male sky reach the female earth below to ensure the continuation of life. Some of the hogans Everett stayed in may have been used seasonally by families moving between summer and winter camps, but others stood empty for a reason he may not have known. When someone died inside a hogan, the custom was to abandon it or burn it to the ground. The Navajo believed life left the body with the last breath at the moment of death. What remained behind was a menacing force, the *chindi*, capable of bringing bad luck, sickness, or death to those who came in contact with it. Prudent Navajos stayed clear of a *chindi* hogan to avoid trouble.

Inside the dwelling, Everett built a fire and stretched out on the sand floor with a saddle blanket for a pillow. He smoked a cigarette to take his mind off his hunger and watched the clouds scud across the night sky, framed by the smoke hole. He fell asleep, and when the fire burned low the cold woke him. Building it up, he dozed off again, spending a restless night trying to stay warm. And at dawn the rain began.

He set out to find his burros and a mile or so away crossed their tracks. Following them, he soon came face-to-face with Cockleburrs standing perfectly still, pretending to be invisible. To Everett's surprise, the hitch had held the pack securely in place. Not far away he found Leopard, with the saddle hanging under his belly. Both burros looked tired and subdued after their night on the loose. Everett combed the area until he turned up his missing camera and canteen. Straightening the saddle, he gave the girth a good yank and mounted. Herding the other burro, he rode past layers of Jurassic sandstone tilted at such a sharp angle that they resembled the bristling scales of a horny toad. Before long the hogan came into view with a curl of smoke rising above.

All was well. He hobbled the animals and fed them extra oats. Then he attended to his own needs, cooking not only breakfast but also the supper he had missed. His adventure on the road to Kayenta gave him enough confidence to travel beyond the safety net of trading posts, Navajo camps, and ranger stations. He detailed his adventure in a letter to Emily Ormond, a friend from California. "Though not all of my days are as wild as this," he wrote her, "each one holds its surprises, and I have seen almost more beauty than I can bear. Many times in the search for water holes and cliff dwellings, I trusted my life to crumbling sandstone and angles little short of the perpendicular, startling myself when I came out whole and on top."[2] The young artist had acquired a taste for the aesthetics of danger. For him, the pursuit of beauty meant a willingness to risk everything.

His passion for art had not happened by accident. Everett's mother recognized his talent at an early age and shaped his formative years to draw it out. Stella Ruess believed art was essential for a meaningful life and constantly encouraged him to express himself in painting and poetry. He read the best literature and listened to the finest music. Born in Oakland, California, Everett lived in a succession of homes as his father, a graduate of the Harvard Divinity School, switched jobs. Christopher Ruess worked as a probation officer and sales manager, with a brief stint as minister before returning to probation work in Los Angeles when the Depression took hold. Everett attended Hollywood High School and soon after graduating in January 1931 made his first solo journey to the Four Corners country. Now on his third exploration, Everett planned to visit many of the same places he had seen on his first trip, wanting to recapture the magic of the original encounter. When his brother dropped him off in Kayenta on April 14, it was the last time any of his family would see Everett again.

After reuniting with his runaway burros, the artist reached the outpost of Kayenta. A pair of trading posts anchored the nascent community, which included a tuberculosis clinic and a school run by the Indian Service. It had become a staging area for trips to Monument Valley and Rainbow Bridge, both on the Arizona-Utah border. From it Everett continued south to the even more isolated trading post of Chilchinbito. There, at the foot of Black Mesa, his thoughts turned to a friend he had left behind in San Francisco. From his surviving letters it's difficult to know the exact nature of the relationship, but Everett must have fallen in love, or something close to it.

He sent a letter to a young woman named Frances containing an undercurrent of longing and regret. "I was sorry, though," he wrote, "that our intimacy, like many things that are and will be, had to die with a dying fall. I do not greatly mind endings, for my life is made up of them, but sometimes they come too soon or too late, and sometimes they leave a feeling of regret as of an old mistake or an indirect futility.... But much as I love people, the most important thing to me is still the nearly unbearable beauty of what I see."[3]

Again he wrote Frances upon returning from the Lukachukai Mountains, responding to a letter in which she had mentioned his greed for life. Having it put so bluntly came as a shock, but he admitted it was true. "I am not willing to take anything but the most from life," he wrote, and went on to describe the intense beauty of a night ride into the mountains.[4] "We traveled in an ominous, murky calm, occasionally slashed with lightning.... By moonlight we climbed to the rim of the mountain and looked over vast silent stretches of desert. Miles away was the dim hulk of Shiprock—a ghostly galleon in a sea of sand." He reminded her of the moments of beauty they had together and why he often acted so unrestrained. It was, he told her, because "always I sense the brink of things." For Everett, there was no turning back.

About this time he came upon a Navajo healing ceremony deep in one of the canyons. These multiday undertakings bring together the wider community in an effort to effect a cure by restoring beauty and harmony. Everett likely entered the ceremonial hogan uninvited, as was his habit, when sand paintings were being made. At this stage of the sing only the chanter and his apprentices are allowed to attend the patient, along with the family. Everything would have stopped at the appearance of an unexpected stranger. The disruption of a ceremony can have serious consequences if not handled properly. Everett mentioned spending three days at the sing in what was ultimately an unsuccessful attempt to cure the patient, a young Navajo girl.

JUNE 1934

In mid-June the Californian returned to his base of operations in Kayenta, having covered more than four hundred miles in less than two months. His love of humanity had a way of expanding the farther away from people he got and constricting whenever he found himself back at an outpost of civilization. His stopover in Kayenta put him in a surly mood, which found expression in a letter to Bill Jacobs. Everett began by criticizing his friend, who craved material security, and for his fear of death. Apparently, Jacobs was writing short stories and attempting to publish them in magazines.

"Your stories," Everett lectured him, "if polished and published, would serve to divert various morons and business people. They would help them to occupy a few hours of their lives in reading about the imagined activities of fictitious characters. Then, more thoroughly satisfied with their own more peaceful or otherwise superior lives, they would use the magazine to start a fire or sell it to the junkman."[5] Everett went on to castigate the Anglos he had met in the Navajo country and their fixation on money. "And when they have it, they seem to be comfortable enough in their stupid way, but they do not live." In contrast, Everett had grown closer to the Indians on his travels, overcoming his earlier dislike for them. He had begun wearing a fine Navajo bracelet with turquoise stones set in cast silver. It had cost all his money and forced him to scrimp for the next month. "I have often stayed with the Navajos," he wrote. "I've known the best of them, and they were fine people. I have ridden with them on their horses, eaten with them, and even taken part in their ceremonies.... Their weird, wild chanting as they ride the desert is often magnificent, with a high-pitched, penetrating quality."[6]

Everett was full of unchecked enthusiasms, and his knowledge of art and literature attracted those who shared his interests. But he demanded a lot from people, whether friends or family, and if they fell short, his criticism could be caustic. He had a habit of turning a casual invitation to visit into a prolonged, and not always welcomed, stay. And while crossing the reservation, he would barge in on a Navajo family to their surprise, showing up with a smile and making himself at home. His mannerisms often struck people as being a bit strange, due partly to his scorn for social conventions and partly because he missed the normal social cues. His mother saw his quirks as a sign of superior intelligence, and some of his friends were fond of "his little odd, peculiar ways."[7] Others were less tolerant. Everett's inclination to hang around a trading post for hours, starved for conversation, could wear thin for the trader when the young wanderer never made a purchase.

Everett now sat down with John Wetherill, the renowned trader he had met on his first southwestern trek in 1931. Wetherill had spent a lifetime exploring the Four Corners country, trading with the Navajo, and guiding various expeditions and a parade of travelers, from archaeologists to artists. He had built the Kayenta trading post in 1910, a year after leading the discovery expedition to Rainbow Bridge. Unrolling a map, he showed Everett how he could travel from Kayenta to Escalante, Utah, passing through the heart of a spectacular region with fine cliff dwellings he could paint. Wetherill went on to tell him about the Hole-in-the-Rock crossing of the Colorado River and the remote Wilson Mesa country beyond. When the two of them finished, they had roughed out the route of Everett's last journey.

While resting and resupplying in Kayenta, the artist met members of the Rainbow Bridge–Monument Valley Expedition, "likeable and intelligent young fellows," who were preparing to spend the summer conducting archaeological investigations in Tsegi Canyon.[8] He decided to visit them on his return from Navajo Mountain, a landmark lying near the geographic center of the Colorado Plateau. To reach it, Everett headed north again through the now familiar landscape of Monument Valley and into another dust storm. The heat of midday forced him to restrict his travels to dawn and the evening, often riding at night under the stars.

"Before me," he wrote, "the desert drops sheer away into a vast valley, in which strangely eroded buttes of all delicate and intense shadings of vermilion, orange, and purple, tower into a cloudless turquoise sky."[9] His route took him by Goulding's Trading Post about the time Lucy Garrett and her kidnapper were getting to know Harry Goulding and his young wife, Mike.

By June 29 Everett had reached War God Spring, two miles below the top of Navajo Mountain, called Naatsis'áán by the Navajo people. The word means "Head of Earth," and earth being female, it is regarded as the Head of Earth Woman. She stretches southward, with the red summit of Tall Mountain representing her heart and Black Mesa her torso. Medicine men visit the spring in dry years to perform rain-bringing ceremonies, but Everett saw no one while on the mountain.

"The perfection of this place is one reason why I distrust ever returning to the cities," he wrote Bill Jacobs. "The beauty of this country is becoming a part of me. I feel more detached from life and somehow gentler."[10] He was entranced by the unreal world surrounding him and had no intention of breaking the spell. Then he talked about his growing alienation and thought his incompatibility with others was due to having gone too far alone. Even his friends, he found, misunderstood his solitary travels and his determination to live so intensely. "I was never one to be content with less than the most from life."

From the summit he scanned the impenetrable slickrock expanse reaching toward the junction of the Colorado and San Juan Rivers, a lithic sea of heaving sandstone riven with deep gorges and twisting slots. In the far distance spread the Escalante country, a remote canyon-cut desert he would enter later in the fall. For Everett, the scene opening before him was more than scenery; it was a revelation. The unbounded space stirred a need in him to go farther, deeper into a landscape saturated with beauty.

INTO THE DREAM

When only sixteen years old, Everett began his first exploration of the Southwest. He hitched rides to the Navajo Indian reservation in Arizona, entering a land of sand and slickrock, of hard skies and limitless space. As he approached Kayenta, sandstone crested in waves along the east flank of Skeleton Mesa, and toward the north a scatter of rock spires floated weightless on the far horizon.

THE YEARS 1931 AND 1932

Everett outfitted himself with a six-dollar burro and all the necessary supplies, paying exorbitant prices at the trading posts, due to the high shipping costs. His plan was to support his travels by selling block prints and watercolors, but his work didn't stir much interest at this stage. He had received some prize money for an earlier effort, but mainly relied on his parents to underwrite his adventures. At first he hid what dollar bills he had in his shoes and then noticed the printing was starting to wear off. The problem soon took care of itself when he no longer had enough money to worry about.

The young artist began his walkabout by trailing north through Monument Valley to the San Juan River in search of a job on a road crew. He found work but no job. In exchange for meals, he spent a week helping a mining outfit build a road to their holdings and learning to cook for the crew. One day he forded the river at a crossing between Castle Creek and Mikes Canyon, where he spent a languid Thoreau-style afternoon transported by the beauty of his surroundings. Indian trader John Wetherill, who was working on the crew, sketched a map for Everett, showing some of the better cliff dwellings to explore. Wetherill had guided many of the early expeditions to the region and was the most knowledgeable source Everett would meet on his travels.

With map in hand, he retraced his steps to Kayenta and continued west into Tsegi Canyon, entranced by the country he was passing through. Each branch hid intriguing sites abandoned centuries ago. Betatakin and Keet Seel, immense cliff houses embedded within sweeping walls of sandstone, had been set apart as a national monument. And dozens of other cliff dwellings were scattered throughout the archaeological wilderness. At one point the Californian lost his shoes in quicksand as he worked to free his stuck burro, but the difficulties he encountered only intensified the experience, adding to his exhilaration.

On April 18 he again wrote Bill Jacobs. "These days away from the city have been the happiest of my life, I believe. It has all been a beautiful dream, sometimes tranquil, sometimes fantastic, and with enough pain and tragedy to make the delights possible by contrast. But the pain too has been unreal. The whole dream has been filled with warm and cool but perfect colors, and with aesthetic contemplation as I jogged behind my little burro. A love for everyone and everything has welled up, finding no outlet except in my art."[1] He added, "Music has been in my heart all the time, and poetry in my thoughts. Alone on the open desert, I have made up songs of wild, poignant rejoicing and transcendent melancholy. The world has seemed more beautiful to me than ever before."

Insightful moments appear in his writings, and he could lay out descriptive passages so fine they continue to strike a chord with those who know the country and stir those who don't. But they are buried among page after page of routine diary entries and often querulous letters. While admired for his commitment to art and passion for the wilderness, he had his flaws. He killed rattlesnakes for sport and collected prehistoric artifacts whenever he had the opportunity. Returning from Tsegi, Everett sent his brother several packages containing an assortment of potsherds, ancient corn, and a shell pendant picked up at Keet Seel. He also mailed a human jaw bone. The young artist was steeped in the emerging ethic of wilderness preservation, the desire to preserve the pristine natural world. But he had not transferred this concern to prehistoric remains, despite the antiquity laws. Collecting artifacts was such a common practice in those days that he felt no need to justify it to Waldo. What he felt a need to defend was his choice to leave the city for a wandering life in the wilderness.

Everett sparred with his brother in an exchange of letters on the issue of how best to live. He criticized Waldo for holding down a job and not living life to the fullest. The older brother shot back, reminding Everett of his financial dependence on the family, always a sensitive point. This put the younger brother on the defensive, and he claimed to have asked only for necessities. He went on to itemize his meager purchases, giving Waldo a full accounting, and admitted he had been unable to find paying work. Laying out his plans for the future, Everett intended to spend a year or two in the open, honing his artistic skills in preparation for a career with his own studio and places to exhibit his work. Upon returning to civilization, he planned to take full advantage of the cultural activities found there and intended to visit more distant places. And then he ended on a prophetic note. "I must pack my short life full of interesting events and creative activity.... Then, and before physical deterioration obtrudes, I shall go on some last wilderness trip, to a place I have known and loved. I shall not return."[2]

Traveling on to Canyon de Chelly National Monument, he spent nearly two weeks exploring the dramatic gorge before heading for the Hopi mesas, getting lost for a couple of days before reaching the Indian pueblos. He roamed through northern Arizona, crossing the Painted Desert and spending five weeks at the Grand Canyon. He made one excursion into Utah, to Zion National Park, before colder weather pushed him south into the cactus country of central Arizona. At the end of December, the artist returned home to Los Angeles with the knowledge that he had finally found a landscape to match his dreams.

The city didn't hold him for long. A few months later he was on his way back to the desert with Bill Jacobs and another companion. Everett began his 1932 exploration where his first one left off, in the Salt River country below the Superstition Mountains. The three young men trekked into the rugged Four Peaks region beyond Roosevelt Lake and explored the prehistoric cliff houses of Tonto National Monument. After two months, Everett had a falling-out with his friends. He considered them too soft for his style of travel and didn't think much of their having to write home for money, despite being dependent on his own parents. What they thought of Everett went unrecorded.

Traveling solo again, he headed north and spent the next couple of months branding cattle and wrangling horses on ranches south of Holbrook. The young artist became a cowboy and began to dress the part by wearing a black Stetson and a silk neckerchief of the same color. But restlessness took hold, and Everett made his way back to Canyon de Chelly in early July. A letter to his brother told of his fascination with roaming alone through the West. "I'll never stop wandering," he added. "And when the time comes to die, I'll find the wildest, loneliest, most desolate spot there is."[3]

Loneliness set in at this stage of his explorations, and he felt the need for a great love, realizing solo travel had its limitations. The solitude he had sought was losing its appeal, and a growing physical weakness was causing him concern. Whatever ailment was troubling him, his eating habits didn't help. He often fixed a rice and raisin dish called Spotted Dog, one of his favorites, and a steady diet of foods like fried peanut butter sandwiches and fried macaroni may have contributed to his troubles.

The Californian camped in a deserted hogan and read poetry out loud by flashlight, needing to hear a human voice even if it was his own. Matching his mood, he recited the works of Edgar Allan Poe and Walt Whitman's elegy for a slain president, "When Lilacs Last in the Door-yard Bloom'd." The next day he rode horseback up Canyon del Muerto, passing Mummy Cave to reach the empty hogan he had stayed in the previous year. He found a stone seat he had made still undisturbed and settled in. Dark thoughts filtered into his journal. "I think I have seen too much and known too much," he wrote, "so much that it has put me in a dream from which I cannot waken and be like other people."[4]

The following day one of his horses dropped dead so suddenly that he didn't know what caused it. Stunned, he carried the saddle up the cliffs, caching it in a hidden ruin, and that night he sang tragic songs to mourn his loss. The next morning Everett continued up Del Muerto, leaving the canyon and moving on to Lukachukai. He crossed the mountains to the town of Shiprock, homesick and suffering pain from an undiagnosed condition. He led his packhorse down the main street of town, whistling symphonies and singing at the top of his voice, not caring what others thought. By the end of the month, he had crossed into Colorado and reached Mesa Verde National Park.

Parallel canyons carved the tilted mesa into long fingers reaching toward the south, and Everett spent weeks exploring them and the ruins they contained. At the end of summer, the Californian released his horse into the wild and hitchhiked to Grand Canyon, where he grabbed a pack and headed below the rim. Doubts about his abilities as an artist continued to surface, leading him to reconsider his future.

Back home in Los Angeles, he followed a friend's suggestion and enrolled at the University of California for the fall semester. But Everett bristled at the routine and couldn't handle a style of learning so detached from the wild beauty he had known. His grades suffered, and he dropped out at the end of the semester. By June 1933 the snows had melted enough in the High Sierra for him to take a lengthy pack trip along the crest of the range, ending his journey at Yosemite. He sold his burro and rode the rails to Oakland, following the rough plan he had sketched out two years before.

For the next four months he lived the life of a struggling artist in San Francisco, visiting the galleries and art exhibits, attending symphonies, and working his way into the artistic circles of the city. Maynard Dixon, a prominent painter of the American West, gave Everett his most important lesson in painting: simplicity. Leave out all but the most essential elements. That's how the young artist wanted to paint, and that's how he chose to live. Before leaving the city, Everett got swept up in a Young Communist League demonstration that turned violent. Normally apolitical, he attended the protest with friends and found himself sympathizing with their concern for the plight of the lower classes and the stand against military spending. Five minutes after it started, a special police unit known as the Red Squad raided the demonstration, using raw force to disperse the crowd. Another reason for leaving.

After spending a month at home in Los Angeles making preparations, he headed for the Navajo country on his third and final trip to the Southwest.

Skeleton Mesa

Returning from Navajo Mountain, Everett Ruess took the trail through an upper branch of Tsegi Canyon. The young artist headed straight to the main camp of the Rainbow Bridge–Monument Valley Expedition, where his enthusiasm and ability to cook landed him a job. The tents at base camp stood among a patch of Gambel oaks in what the crew called Water Lily Canyon, a branch of the eastern arm of Tsegi. Camp Anasazee gave them access to Twin Caves Pueblo, a stone village tucked under a soaring cliff of Navajo sandstone. And it put them in position to investigate a burial site in a cave high on the rim of Skeleton Mesa. Everett would spend the next five weeks among the ruin-sheltering cliffs and wild expanses of the Tsegi country.

Summer 1934

The expedition had first fielded teams of scientists the year before in an ambitious plan to survey prehistoric ruins throughout an enormous region, south of the San Juan River between Navajo Mountain and Monument Valley. Ansel Hall, the first chief naturalist of the National Park Service, had secured private funding to launch the expedition as an educational venture aimed at producing scientific results. Driven by near-missionary zeal, Hall had a reputation for making things happen. As a ranger at Yosemite, he established the park museum and initiated experience-based educational programs. He also encouraged Ansel Adams in his photographic career by giving him what may have been his first camera. In the middle of the Depression, Hall was able to recruit college students willing to pay for the adventure of working with professional scientists in a spectacular natural setting. He posted notices on campuses, knowing the call would be hard to resist: "WANTED: 10 EXPLORERS."[1] So many students responded that he handpicked dozens of them for what ultimately became the last of the grand expeditions to explore the American Southwest.

Whereas the college students had to pay $3.50 a day plus transportation expenses, Everett signed on to work in exchange for meals. He spent the first few days helping around camp before being assigned to a crew planning to excavate Woodchuck Cave, located six hundred feet above base camp. Visible from the canyon floor, the rock shelter resembled a heavy-lidded eye, seventy feet long and sunk thirty feet into the rimrock. Some of the more daring expedition members had used their Sunday off to work out a climbing route to the cave. During the ascent, they found a string of ancient footholds, known as Moqui steps, carved into the cliff face and leading up a crack system to the top. Once inside the rock shelter, the young archaeologists discovered human bones protruding from the sand. The cave was identified as a Basketmaker II burial site, dating back to the earliest period of the Ancestral Puebloan, a prehistoric people who built the remarkable cliff dwellings scattered throughout the canyons. After a preliminary investigation, the expedition leaders decided to mount a full excavation of the site. They organized a pack string to carry the needed supplies by a long roundabout route and recruited Everett and his burros to aid the effort.

With Navajo packers to guide them, the party left base camp and threaded up the wash to the head of Dowozhibito Canyon. To reach the mesa top, they ascended the hazardous Horse Ladder Trail, built by Navajo herders who cut steps up the canyon wall and widened them with a rough cribbing of juniper limbs and rubble. Carrying only half loads, the burros had to be pushed and pulled up the cliff side. The risk they ran turned real for Everett when he noticed the carcass of a horse that had slipped and fallen off the route sometime before. In a black-and-white photograph taken at the time, he is seen climbing the precarious trail behind a reluctant burro loaded with gear. An archaeologist tugs on the lead rope from above as Everett glances back tentatively, his face appearing even younger than his twenty years. Carrying a pack, he wears a black cowboy hat, jeans, and the turquoise bracelet picked up on his travels among the Navajo. In an unguarded moment, he's another Huck Finn, lighting out for the territory.

Trail to Skeleton Mesa. Everett Ruess glances back while ascending the Horse Ladder Trail, a Navajo bracelet visible on his wrist. Another member of the Rainbow Bridge–Monument Valley Expedition, Jim Russell, coaxes a reluctant burro upward. Courtesy of Fort Lewis College, Center of Southwest Studies, Ansel Hall Photograph Collection (P 008).

Once on top the trail branched and branched again, unraveling into multiple strands. The pack string soon got lost and had to bivouac for the night. They also ran out of water, so a volunteer rode back in the dark to a spring they had passed earlier. Next day they found the right fork and traversed a long finger of the mesa. At noon they reached the cave, soaked by a cloudburst. The crew pitched a tent to store supplies on the rim above the rock shelter, where they would live and work until finishing the dig. At an elevation of seventy-two hundred feet, a few ponderosas had taken root in the slickrock, while old-growth piñons and junipers dominated the tablelands, each gnarled tree matching the branching pattern of the canyons below. The site overlooked a landscape of falling cliffs, bone white with streaks of red spilling hundreds of feet down the side of Skeleton Mesa. "We had great fun up there by ourselves," Everett wrote home, "discovering something new every day, and looking out over everything from our sheltered cave."[2] The artist found the canyon country to be more spectacular than anything he had encountered on his earlier travels in the Sierra Nevada.

Inside the overhang a scatter of sandstone spalls and rubble rested on the sand-filled floor, and seepage along the back wall supported clumps of monkeyflower, goldenrod, and penstemon. Alignments of upright slabs marked a few of the grave sites. To bring the past alive, archaeologists have always sought out the dead. From experience they know that graves contain a concentration of clues to such things as social status and belief in an afterlife, physical appearance and clothing, what people valued, and how they died. A burial is seen as a time capsule, and for an archaeologist in 1934 to express qualms about disturbing the dead was considered unprofessional. The Navajo packers would have seen it differently, knowing that contact with a corpse could bring misfortune and even death.

A half-dozen men set about excavating the site, including the head archaeologist, Lyn Hargrave. He wore a wide-brim field hat, and others were dressed in khakis or jeans with the cuffs turned up, and one worked with a pipe stuck in his mouth. When the crew began digging, Everett joined in. Using shovels and trowels, it didn't take long to expose a cluster of burial cists, and then the pace slowed. Excavating the fragile remains required painstaking work using dental picks and camel-hair brushes. And as they exposed more and more of the remains, they found something unexpected.

All of the adult bodies were headless, and many were missing the leg bones. The site appeared to have been ransacked at an unknown period, causing artifacts from different burials to get mixed together. This puzzled the diggers. If it had been looted for valuables, the grave robbers had done a hasty job and missed some impressive items. The archaeologists recovered a beautiful necklace of five hundred jet beads spaced at intervals of fifty with white shell beads, among other pieces of jewelry. They also found fragments of coiled baskets painted red, a skin bag painted blue, and another bag containing paint pigments. Remnants of a rabbit-fur robe trimmed with bird feathers turned up, along with yucca-cord sandals, gaming dice, and broken atlatls—a chaotic mix of artifacts.

During noon breaks the crew pulled out the sack lunches Everett had prepared and ate among the dead. Some of the archaeologists had moved their air mattresses and bedrolls inside the shelter rather than camp on top. "We were all thrown together on equal footing," wrote crew members Jim Russell and Russell White, "university men, Boy Scouts, and Ph.D's. We drank from the same bucket (or occasionally from the same mud hole) with

The climb to Woodchuck Cave. Expedition members Jim Russell, head archaeologist Lyn Hargrave, and crew chief Clay Lockett climb an ancient hand-and-toe route. This was the direct way to reach their excavation site from the base camp on the floor of the canyon. Courtesy of the Museum of Northern Arizona (MS-122-932), by D. F. Walkington.

the mules. One wore a tenderfoot's outfit, or nothing at all, as he chose. One could shave every morning or never; there were cases of both. One could swear or pray; again there were cases of both. The one concentrated effort was the desire for information."[3]

As the dig progressed, they recovered fifteen burials dating to AD 200, and most of the bodies were in a flexed position and wrapped or covered with rabbit-fur robes. In a letter to his family, Everett expressed his fascination with the work. "One mystery lies in the fact that all of the skeletons are headless," he wrote, "though there are some lower jaws. Evidently the graves were robbed—perhaps by the Pueblo people, but it is a difficult problem to ascertain the facts."[4] The crew members continued to speculate among themselves about the puzzling burials. Expedition director Ansel Hall told reporters he wasn't sure if the human remains represented "grave robbing for ceremonial purposes by a later people or a hitherto unknown rite of the Basketmaker tradition." They had uncovered a past without a history.

During the dig, Everett gravitated to crew chief Clay Lockett, describing him as "a grizzled young chap of twenty-eight, widely experienced and a magnificent humorist."[5] Lockett was also an artist and had brought his own watercolors. Sitting inside the cave, the two of them had long talks, studying paintings together and critiquing the finer points. "I had an excellent chance to really know Everett," Lockett wrote, "because he spent most of his time in this burial cave with me for about two weeks."[6] The young artist, he said, seemed drawn to danger. "Everett was always anxious to get into situations which provided thrills and excitement. When these situations arose he would think about them, write about them or often paint them."

In his free time, Everett joined some of the other diggers in exploring the prehistoric climbing routes in the vicinity. He talked with enthusiasm about scrambling "up almost sheer sandstone cliffs, clinging by worn footholds hundreds of years old, or on narrow crumbling ledges."[7] Below the cave, the crew had rigged a hand line on the most dangerous pitch of an aerial route leading to base camp. Downclimbing is always more risky due to the difficulty of seeing the foothold below. The climber descends, blindly feeling for the weathered indentation with a foot, easing weight onto it, and then groping with the other foot for the next step. To mail his letters, Everett had to descend by "a very precarious way down the face of the cliff with footholds in the stone hundreds of years old."[8]

By the summer of 1934, he had gained confidence in his ability to handle himself. He was now on his third solo journey through northern Arizona and parts of Utah. "I have seen more wild country than on any previous trip," he wrote his brother, Waldo.[9] "I almost lost one burro in the quicksands—he was up to his neck—and the other fell over backward in trying to climb a cliff. I myself had endless difficult climbs and descents—like one time when three of us came down a cliff by moonlight, using old worn-out hand holds." He found himself taking greater risks than he had on any of his earlier travels. And his response to a dramatic summer storm showed his willingness to push the limits.

Thunder rolled through the canyon below Skeleton Mesa as the sky split open in a violent rain, pounding the slickrock benches. Every crease in the bare sandstone channeled the runoff toward a single nick point on the rim. Within moments a flash flood leaped out into empty space, plunging into an immense amphitheater of overhanging cliffs. In one sheer drop the stream fell more than four hundred feet before hitting the canyon floor. Everett had to move fast, knowing the storm would end as suddenly as it began. He grabbed his sketchbook and hurried across the wet slickrock along the edge of the precipice. As the rain eased somewhat, the artist found a vantage point on the very brink of the canyon. He worked fast, hunched over his watercolor sketch to give it some protection, trying to capture the wild dynamics of the storm. By now other members of the excavation crew had left the shelter of the cave to watch the event unfold. Clay Lockett was among them, and Everett surprised him by taking such a chance. As crew chief, he was responsible for the safety of his team, and he found the artist's risk taking unnerving. "I personally was scared to death," the archaeologist wrote, "just watching him perched on the edge of the cliff."[10]

If any single incident can throw light on what was driving Everett, it was the rainstorm on Skeleton Mesa. It shows not only an element of recklessness, but something more fundamental as well. No artist would head into a storm and expect to return with a fine watercolor. Everett took his art seriously and knew he would end up with a rain-smeared sketch at best. That didn't matter. For him, the act of creating was more important than the final result. By risking everything for a painting, he was living up to the image he had created of himself, the artist-adventurer swept up in the great forces of nature. He was on a journey of self-discovery, throwing himself into experiences meant to shape his own life into a work of art, no matter what the cost. He was painting a self-portrait, and the canvas was himself.

When the excavation ended at Woodchuck Cave, the crew packed up the artifacts and human remains and backfilled holes they had dug. They returned the way they came by the difficult horse trail. The head archaeologist had instructed them to take tree-ring samples from prehistoric beams in a cliff dwelling on their way back to Camp Anasazee. During a brief stay among the ruins, Everett did more excavating and cooked for the crew of seven. "The last night's work," he wrote his brother, "was done by firelight. Huge shadows played on the orange wall of the cave, which reaches upwards into the darkness. Outside, rain hissed down, and once we heard wild geese honking as they flew south."[11] With the work now finished, it was time to continue his journey alone.

Next morning Everett snugged the cinches on his burros and said goodbye to the archaeologists. He left the expedition and resumed his solitary journey, heading up the opposite wall of the canyon by another horse-ladder trail. With Everett there was always a leaving. Each journey was a string of leavings—first his home, then a last good-bye to his brother, and finally the ephemeral friends met along the way. Each arrival meant another departure.

Topping out on a finger of Skeleton Mesa, Everett followed the Gunsight Trail down the eastern flank, going against the folded layers of rock curving upward in great tongues. He descended the mesa through a scattering of juniper, taking in the views of El Capitan, the flaring cliffs of Comb Ridge, and the dark mass of mountains on the far horizon. By now he had traveled too far into the dream to turn back.

THE CAVE

A trip to Skeleton Mesa was in the works. Nothing solid yet, but momentum was building. My curiosity about this corner of the Navajo country came from letters written by Everett Ruess during his final journey. In 1934 he spent more than a month on the edge of a cliff, helping to excavate a prehistoric burial cave. The young artist came into his own that summer, and to understand what he experienced I wanted to see it firsthand.

The remoteness of Skeleton Mesa makes it difficult to reach, so I stopped by a friend's house for suggestions on the best route to take. A field biologist with a passion for the past, Chuck LaRue knew the area well, having grown up in nearby Kayenta. Entering his house, I found it packed with skulls, journals, and rabbit sticks. On one shelf sat the cast of a saber-toothed skull, with its jaws spread wide and fangs bared. Around it lay the skulls of various carnivores and a beaver with orange teeth almost as menacing as the Ice Age predator. A bighorn skull rested in a corner next to pots bristling with wild turkey feathers, a bundle of arrows in different stages of manufacture, and a stuffed toy condor.

Chuck scooted his chair closer to the computer and brought up images of the Tsegi Canyon country. But my attention kept drifting to the archaic weapons he had made lying nearby. Arrows filled a quiver made from an agave stalk next to a bundle of fireboards and spindles. Above his desk hung a huge bison skull with stone knives dangling from one horn and a finely crafted atlatl from the other. Chuck had visited museum collections around the country to inspect the original artifacts and reproduce them as accurately as possible. His room had the feel of an eighteenth-century naturalist's study, packed with curiosities brought back from distant travels.

As the two of us discussed various approaches to the rock shelter, Chuck unrolled a map. I could try driving up Tsegi Canyon, he said, but Mr. Gray Eyes lived at the mouth and would chase me out if he caught me. And besides, the tribe had closed it to outsiders. Chuck marked two trails coming up the east side of Skeleton Mesa and considered the advantages and disadvantages of each. While we were talking, a Navajo friend of his called from Kayenta. Chester Salt's family had lived in the Tsegi region for generations, and he planned to drive up the canyon in a couple of weeks to visit the grave of his father, who had worked as a cook for the Rainbow Bridge–Monument Valley Expedition. The two of them discussed the options, including a route traversing a knife-edge ridge known to the locals as "Where You Scoot across on Your Ass." The name, unfortunately, never made it onto the maps. A few homes were near the trailhead, Chester said, so it might take some diplomacy to get permission. After listening to suggestions and studying the map, I decided to enter from the west, where I could leave my truck with a Navajo sheepherder I knew. Doing it as a two-day backpack, I would descend into upper Tsegi and reach the cave on the second day.

Next morning, an hour before I left Flagstaff, Chuck called and said he would join me, being unable to pass up a chance to revisit what he considered to be the center of his world. After picking up tribal permits in Cameron, we continued north into the Painted Desert and took the back road to Tuba City. As we crossed the one-lane bridge over Moenkopi Wash, Chuck pointed out where the deep-cut arroyo had begun to fill in. I found the dynamic nature of a landscape, the cycle of down-cutting and deposition, intriguing. Nothing remains stable for long, especially in a land of sand and sandstone. Reaching Highway 160, we skirted the flank of Black Mesa and eventually turned north on a sand road. It ended at a sheep camp with a stunning expanse of canyon spreading below. Chuck was back on home turf, excited by what lay ahead.

The two of us strapped on backpacks and descended the trail to Laguna Creek, the carver of Tsegi Canyon. Because of the dependable water and sheltering cliffs, prehistoric Pueblo Indians lived here for centuries, building spectacular cliff dwellings. Chuck wore jeans, a khaki shirt, and a pair of binoculars slung around his neck. He might get by without his pants and shirt, but being an expert birder he would be naked without the binoculars. Crossing the stream, we picked up a horse trail and looped past Kachina Mother Rock, eventually finding our way into a side canyon, where Chuck knew a hidden route up Skeleton Mesa. It followed a narrow break in the cliffs tucked into a fold of Navajo Sandstone.

We made camp at a spring, which Chuck proceeded to dig out by hand. Above us the rock walls graded from red to the color of dry sand, rising from a green thicket of oak and piñon into a sky weighted with blue. And at the head of the canyon, sheer cliffs framed a deep pocket of aspens and a scatter of Douglas fir. Navajo cowboys sometimes used the place and had rebuilt a pair of folding metal chairs, cleverly weaving the seats and backrests with bailing twine to make them more comfortable than the originals.

With a lot of ground to cover, we were on our way the next morning as soon as the darkness thinned. The route climbed steeply up loose scree and passed a cluster of petroglyphs. Near the top of the cliff, I used a set of Moqui steps to aid the climb. At a notch we found the masonry walls of a prehistoric structure overlooking our route and another coming up the other side. It appeared to be guarding the way into the canyon, but may have been simply a storehouse used by the Ancestral Pueblo who farmed the mesa top. Being familiar with the route, Chuck led the way to a ridge above Dowozhibito Canyon, an arm of Tsegi. The two of us stood and gazed across a sandstone landscape cut wide and deep. Big, dramatic country. "Ahh," he said. "This just sets you free."

We descended toward the rim, hitting it above an amphitheater of immense undercut cliffs. In canyon country the rim marks the boundary between an upper and lower world, each with its own mix of trees and its own weather. Here piñons and junipers had taken root on the cliff edge, and thickets of Gambel oak crowded the bed of the canyon below. At our feet the sandstone cliff plunged downward more than four hundred feet in a mural wall stained with long, tapering strands of desert varnish. During cloudbursts, runoff pours over the lip of Skeleton Mesa in a tremendous waterfall so ephemeral it may last only a few minutes. Hitting the floor, it runs down canyon in a surge of churning water, flowing past cliff ruins and old hogans until absorbed by the sands.

Finding a break in the rim, we scrambled down to an exposed ledge leading to Woodchuck Cave. The expedition archaeologists had taken the precaution of roughening the slickrock with picks and lining the safest path with stones. As we entered the rock shelter, I noticed the archaeo-logical site number, "NA 3112," pecked on the wall. Bits of charcoal from the original campfire still remained, mixed with sand and an old can or two. And nearby rested a branch of ax-cut firewood, the same piece I had seen in a black-and-white photograph taken during the 1934 field season. Woodchuck Cave had remained virtually unchanged since the archaeol-ogists left it seventy-five years ago. The photo shows the crew at work in the shade of the overhanging cliff. At the back of the cave, Everett Ruess is starting to dig a test pit. His foot pushes on the shoulder of a shovel, sink-ing the blade deep into the sand, and a young archaeologist stands next to him, gripping another shovel.

As the two of us discussed the excavation, Chuck mentioned that the scientists had recovered marmot jawbones from a burial but misidentified them as woodchuck. He told me the marmot does not occur in Arizona, so he thought they must have been traded into the area prehistorically. A more appropriate name for the place, he suggested, would be "Yellow-Bel-lied Marmot Cave."

Several years before the archaeologists arrived on the scene, the National Park Service put in motion plans to set aside a huge section of the Navajo country as a new national park. It would be anchored on key natural features such as Monument Valley, Rainbow Bridge, and Canyon de Chelly. About the time Everett joined the crew, the *New York Times* ran a story on how the expedition was producing the detailed maps needed to mark the park boundaries. Under the leadership of Ansel Hall, the Rain-bow Bridge–Monument Valley Expedition was drawing national attention to America's empty quarter, a wilderness region with high national park potential. But the Navajo leaders in Window Rock had their own ideas. That summer tribal representatives expressed opposition to the plan, and their objections would eventually force the Park Service to shift the boundaries outside the reservation. And as opposition grew in Arizona and Utah, the idea of a major national park in the region was shelved.

In 1934 Everett was in his element as the field season peaked. He found himself in a wildness of stone, digging into the past with other young men who shared his passion for pushing the edge. Together they took risks they might not have taken alone, climbing the cliffs using weathered foothold routes and sometimes going at night. For Everett, the adventure was a means

The dig. A crew of archaeologists spent weeks excavating a Basketmaker site on Skeleton Mesa. Everett Ruess (*standing second on the right*) helps with the shovel work. Courtesy of the Museum of Northern Arizona (MS-122-929A), by D. F. Walkington.

to something more essential. Another artist, Eugene Delacroix, put it this way: "Without daring, without extreme daring even, there is no beauty."[1]

After investigating the rock shelter, we looped back to our camp by a different route. Not far from Woodchuck Cave, we found one of the vertical trails Everett must have explored. It followed a ledge of sandstone as it arched down the canyon wall for hundreds of feet with increasing steepness. The rock face it descended leaned outward into empty space, and along the route Ancestral Puebloan climbers had carved hundreds of hand- and footholds. They had also pecked images of bighorn sheep, water birds, and a human form with legs ending in dizzying spirals, perhaps meant to convey the sensation of downclimbing such an exposed face. The two of us inspected the improbable route before giving it a pass, suddenly remembering we had a lot of distance left to cover.

LOST MESAS,
BLUE MOUNTAINS

The artist and his burros trekked south along the valley floor until finding a steep ravine cutting back into the flank of Skeleton Mesa. Everett Ruess then picked his way upward through the broken terrain, searching for a hidden cave. In 1916 a pair of young archaeologists from Harvard, Samuel Guernsey and Alfred Kidder, excavated the rock shelter and discovered a portal into the lives of the people who inhabited the region twenty-four hundred years before. Everett, drawn by his feral curiosity, soon reached an immense cave opening sunk in shadows. The entrance arched 125 feet overhead and led into a deep chamber.

LATE SUMMER 1934

Inside the shelter early Basketmaker people had buried their dead in cists, much as they had at Woodchuck Cave. The archaeologists found that the dry sands had preserved a remarkable assemblage of artifacts, including a 240-foot rabbit net in near-perfect condition. They also uncovered the mummified remains of a dog the size of a terrier with a shaggy black-and-white coat. The light coloration of another dog no larger than a small collie gave the site its name, White Dog Cave. Everett could have passed dogs bearing a close resemblance to them herding sheep on the flats below. The archaeological report noted that a section of the vaulted ceiling had collapsed sometime after the occupation of the cave, and in a letter home Everett took it a step further by mentioning that a "sandstone block had fallen and crushed the cliff dwellers."[1] He finished exploring the site and made his way east to Kayenta.

A brief stop was all he could afford this time, as he needed to keep moving to reach the Hopi mesas in time for the Snake Dance. After loading his pack burro at the hitching rack in front of the school, he walked out of town, with his animals following loyally behind. The most direct route to the Hopi pueblos crossed Black Mesa, and he likely followed the pack trail west of Chilchinbito Trading Post, an area familiar to him from previous travels. The trail climbs onto the mesa, north of a rock formation known as Three Fingers, which he had painted before. Everett waited for the heat of the day to ease. "I rode up from the desert floor to the rim of Black Mesa by moonlight," he wrote, "camping among the pines."[2] Having ascended fifteen hundred feet in elevation, he was back in the green and solitary world of tall ponderosas.

The next day he continued down a canyon, probably the head of Din- nebito Wash, only to leave it when conditions turned rough. Under a wide sky he headed across a rolling plateau without landmarks, using the sun to guide him. He veered to the west, where a lattice of intersecting trails made navigation difficult through stands of piñon-juniper and across sage- brush flats. And without knowledge of the local terrain, finding water was problematic. Everett saw no one until late on the third day, when he began to encounter a scattering of sheep camps. Reaching Blue Canyon, he spent the night with a Navajo family among the banded cliffs and pale hoodoos before continuing his trek. At dawn on August 24, the day of the Snake Dance, he rode into the pueblo of Hotevilla, on Third Mesa.

He arrived at the climax of a nine-day religious ceremony, a solemn and deeply spiritual undertaking of the Hopi. Many of the visitors simply came for the thrill of watching painted and feathered men dancing with live rattlesnakes in their mouths. For the Hopi, it was a prayer for rain, espe- cially critical in the drought-stricken summer of 1934, and all the bless- ings associated with rain. Joined by the spirits of the dead, they danced to renew life by drawing on the primal forces underlying the surface world. And contained within the chants and prayers of the ceremony was the tale of a young man on a journey into the unknown.

The origin of the Snake Ceremony recounts the story of Tiyo, the Hopi word for "boy." He lived at Navajo Mountain in a time of drought and every day watched the Colorado River flowing by, wondering where the water went. The river ran through a deep gorge beyond reach, while the corn-fields turned to dust and the people faced famine. Every day the boy prayed, until finally the river told him, "I'll take you with me."[3]

Tiyo made a raft of cottonwood logs and began a solo journey down a wild river knotted with rapids. He floated through the great canyons, past "swirling water and a strong, whirling wind."[4] His epic journey was filled with adventure and tests of courage as he searched for the knowledge needed to end the hunger and despair of his people. When all motion stopped, he discovered he had reached the ocean and set off inland. Eventually, the young Hopi met the Snake People, who gave him the ritual songs and offerings needed to attract the rain clouds. With the beautiful daughter of the Snake chief as his wife, Tiyo returned overland to Navajo Mountain. The young Hopi introduced the Snake Dance to his people, the ceremony Everett had come to watch.

Among the spectators gathered for the event were members of the expedition Everett knew from Tsegi Canyon. He teamed up with one of them, Vernon DeMars, who liked to sketch and perform Indian dances. Vernon traded for a Hopi kilt, gourd rattle, and other paraphernalia used in the dances. The following day the two of them traveled to Second Mesa, where they were invited into a kiva at the village of Mishongnovi. They spent the night in the ceremonial chamber, watching the Hopi practice the Buffalo Dance, a social dance performed in winter, and what he called the Antelope Dance. Writing to his parents about his stay at Second Mesa, Everett mentioned participating in the dance a few days later. "My Hopi friends," he said, "painted me up and had me in their Antelope Dance. I was the only white person there."[5]

Everett had made friends among the Hopi and enjoyed their company, but his reference to the Antelope Dance is curious. Outsiders sometimes refer to the rite conducted on the day before the Snake Dance as the Antelope Dance, but it is not a separate ceremony. And while the dance begins with the Antelope people, they are soon joined by members of the Snake society. The Hopi spend weeks practicing the intricate steps and songs necessary to perform the dance, so it's unlikely Everett was included in the official ceremony. The Hopi had taken the young artist into their lives for a few days. And knowing his interest in their customs, they painted his face and bare chest and taught him the rhythmic down tread of a Pueblo dance, probably for the fun of it.

By early September Everett set off for the Grand Canyon. Whenever he had a clear trail before him this time of year, he traveled at night to avoid the heat. He left the Hopi mesas and crossed the Painted Desert to the Little Colorado River, where he ran into trouble. In a brief note to his parents, he mentioned losing a burro down the gorge of the Little Colorado. Because he was able to recover some of the pack, the burro may have become trapped in quicksand, a common hazard. Everett avoided going into details and assured his parents he had already replaced the burro with a larger one. He arrived at Desert View on the rim of Grand Canyon during the night of September 9.

In a letter to a friend, he gave a quick sketch of his travels. "In my wanderings this year I have taken more chances and had more wild adventures than ever before. And what magnificent country I have seen—wild, tremendous wasteland stretches, lost mesas, blue mountains rearing upward from the vermilion sands of the desert, canyons five feet wide at the bottom and hundreds of feet deep, cloudbursts roaring down unnamed canyons, and hundreds of houses of the cliff dwellers, abandoned a thousand years ago."[6] The year was not over, and wilder country lay ahead.

Leaving his burros with a friend at the rim, Everett made a side trip to Flagstaff to visit his crew boss from Skeleton Mesa. Clay Lockett considered him a "strange kid," but they shared many of the same interests. Everett had taken him up on his offer to stop by and then overstayed his welcome. After a week he was encouraged to pack up and do some painting in nearby Oak Creek Canyon. The first snows had fallen on the San Francisco Peaks by the time he returned to Flagstaff, and the aspen were changing. On October 1 he was back at Desert View.

The artist found himself drawn to the great gorge on each of his southwestern treks and once wrote his brother, "Nothing anywhere can rival the Grand Canyon."[7] Faced with such immensity, where space itself becomes a force, he did not attempt to write more than a few lines about his experiences. On his first journey he spent five weeks in the national park and twice crossed rim to rim with a burro and a little dog named Curly. The burro balked at crossing the bridge and had to be persuaded across with a shovel. Returning the next year, Everett slung a pack over his shoulder and headed below the rim. "I stopped several days at the Grand Canyon," he wrote a friend, "descending alone to the depths, to submerge myself in the steep silence, to be overcome by the fearful immensity, to drown everything in the deafening roar of the Colorado."[8]

Now in early October he hiked below the rim again and spent a couple of weeks exploring the inner canyon. On October 15 he ascended the Bright Angel Trail to pick up his mail and buy supplies for the next leg of his trip, returning to Indian Garden the same day. Everett now headed for the North Rim with his burros, Cockleburrs and Chocolatero, taking the Tonto Trail east along the edge of the Inner Gorge. Reaching the South Kaibab Trail, he followed it another fifteen hundred feet lower to a suspension bridge spanning the Colorado River.

Fear gripped his new burro, Chocolatero. Already spooked by having to pass through a dark tunnel on the approach to the bridge, the burro refused to cross. The dizzying motion of fast water flowing below and the narrow span were too much. When a packer arrived, Everett asked for help, and the cowboy dragged the burro across behind his mule. Those who encountered Everett often remarked on his love for his animals, but the hardships of travel forced him to do what he felt necessary to keep going. Once across the Grand Canyon, the artist continued into Utah on his way to Bryce Canyon.

Everett reached what was then a national monument on November 1, and during his two-day stay he told the owner of Ruby's Inn about a plan to spend some months with the Navajo. And he made friends with the chief ranger, who invited him to his home in the town of Tropic, below the flank of the plateau. For the next few days, he was a guest of Maurice Cope and his family of nine children, spending a pleasant interlude picking apples and attending the Friday-night dance with Gene Cope and his sister Rhea. After the dance, he met a couple of "wandering Navajos" and stayed up most of the night talking and singing with them, eating roast mutton, and drinking black coffee.[9] It was a tradition at this time of year for Indians to travel from the Navajo Mountain area and trade in the towns of southern Utah.

A friendly partnership had grown between them, and the local families gave the trading parties nuts and candy as early Christmas presents. The route followed by the Navajo and Paiute traders crossed the San Juan River, climbed over Wilson Mesa, and went down Cottonwood Canyon. They reached the Colorado River at Hole-in-the-Rock, and by early November the water levels had dropped enough to allow safer crossings. They used an old wooden boat resembling a water trough, kept hidden in the willows, and swam the horses across the fast, turbulent waters. On the west side, the spectacular trail cut by the Mormon pioneers through the upper cliffs was no longer passable by horse. Halfway to the rim notch the alternate route turned upstream toward Jackass Bench, where it ascended steps cut into the slickrock and pitches so steep the horses had to be unpacked and the loads carried up on foot. Once on top, the trail angled back across the slickrock and sand flats to intersect the Hole-in-the-Rock road.

A trading party would follow it north to the settlement of Escalante, while a couple of them might split off to hunt deer on the Fiftymile, a local name for the southern end of the Kaiparowits. In town the Navajo would trade their boldly patterned blankets for horses. "They came to town loaded with blankets," recalled Arnold Alvey, an Escalante rancher skilled in breaking horses.[10] And when those ran out, they would trade their jewelry, moccasins, and even their tack. "They'd trade everything they had for horses. They'd go out of here riding bareback with only a bridle." Before winter set in, the Navajo returned south of the rivers, driving herds of up to one hundred head of horses.

On Sunday Everett went with Cope and his family to the Mormon church. When asked what church he attended, the artist had some fun with them, saying he was "a pantheistic hedonist."[11] While staying in Tropic, he had a long conversation with the ranger on his proposed trip south of Escalante. Cope told him of the harsh conditions on top of Kaiparowits Plateau in winter, and Everett decided to keep to the lower elevations near the river to avoid the heavy snows. "He intended to visit with the navajo indians," the ranger later wrote, "after reaching the other side of the river."[12]

The artist finally left town on his way to Escalante, nearly forty miles farther east, leading his burros down the street and waving to friends he had made. "If I had stayed any longer," he wrote his older brother, "I would have fallen in love with a Mormon girl, but I think it's a good thing I didn't. I've become a little too different from most of the rest of the world. I don't think I could ever settle down. I have known too much of the deeps of life already, and I would prefer anything to an anticlimax."[13]

In 1934 the Escalante road took a wide loop to the north, so he attempted to follow a more direct trail leading over the north end of the Kaiparowits. He found himself untethered again, on his own with no responsibilities beyond himself and his animals. The great adventure he had dreamed about kept unfolding before him, and he was pulling it off. Even the villages he passed through had a sense of remoteness to them. His route of travel took him into the Blues, a stretch of barren shale eroded into badlands, where stark hillsides can appear as soft blue or somber gray depending on the light or the mood a traveler brings to them. Everett soon found himself tangled in the ravines cutting into the side of the plateau and lost the trail. When the way forward became impassable, he was forced to backtrack and lose a day. He tried another approach, crossing miles of rough terrain, bushwhacking his way through sagebrush and oak thickets. He had to drive his burros down slopes so steep they almost lost their footing, but he was able to press on.

Finally reaching the top, he found a trail and made camp on "what seems like the rim of the world."[14] He was on the divide between the Paria and Escalante Rivers, with the surface falling away on both sides of him. "Below," he wrote Waldo, "are steep cliffs where the canyon has cut its way up to the rim of the divide. Northward is the sheer face of Mt. Kaiparowitts, pale vermilion capped with white with a forested summit. West and south are desert and distant mountains.... Often as I wander," he continued, "there are dreamlike times when life seems impossibly strange and unreal. I think it is, too, only most people had so dulled their senses that they do not realize it."

His camp sat below a summit now called Canaan Peak, and from this perch he could look out upon a rockscape carved by the Escalante River, his destination. The last unknown river in the West was named by Almon Harris Thompson, the intrepid leader of a Powell Survey party in 1872. They had entered a vast blank spot on the map, and by the time they left the main topographic features had been sketched in. Thompson climbed a high point overlooking the surrounding country and viewed the incredibly rugged topography. "A large portion of this area is naked, sandstone rock," he wrote, "traversed in all directions by a perfect labyrinth of narrow gorges, sometimes seeming to cross each other, but finally uniting in a principal one, whose black line could be traced, cutting its way to the Colorado, a few miles above the mouth of the San Juan River.... No animal without wings could cross the deep gulches in the sandstone basin at our feet."[15] Everett had reached the threshold of the perfect labyrinth.

The Powell Survey relied on the skills of packers hired from the fledgling Mormon settlements in southern Utah. When these men returned home at the end of the field season, word of the new lands spread. The Escalante Valley had good grazing, water for irrigation, and a climate mild enough to grow fruit trees. With the pioneer impulse still running strong, families packed up and headed across the high plateaus to found the town of Escalante in 1875. The following year, while preparing to celebrate the Fourth of July, they discovered no one had brought along an American flag. Accustomed to improvising, they came up with a substitute. When the day arrived, they raised a Navajo blanket patterned with red, light gray, and blue stripes. And then they proceeded with their celebration.

NOVEMBER 1934

Escalante, Utah, remained in the grip of a heavy and prolonged drought, and that summer conditions had taken a biblical turn with a plague of grasshoppers. "Billions of them," recalled a town resident.[16] To combat the infestation, two riders would stretch a tarp between them and sweep the fields repeatedly, filling it with grasshoppers. Caught in the Depression, two-thirds of the residents were receiving government relief and still struggling.

Fall had taken hold, and most of the cottonwoods along the river were bare of leaves when Everett arrived. He rode into town on a burro, trailing the other behind. Being horse country, heads turned. Being desert country, the residents tolerated a wide range of eccentricity and gave it a shrug. But the boys in town found his arrival with a pair of burros to be an entertaining distraction. No one raised them locally, and some of the boys had never seen one of these long-eared novelties before. They led the wandering artist through town to a campsite across the river at the end of Center Street.

In his writing Everett expressed a longing for solitude, but as his last journey progressed he took obvious pleasure in the company of others. In Escalante he teamed up with a couple of boys to hunt arrowheads and ride horses and then took them to see the Saturday feature at the local theater. They watched *Death Takes a Holiday*, a popular movie where Death assumes a human form to experience life and find out why people fear him. The next night Everett sat around the campfire with his new friends, roasting venison on sticks and burying potatoes in the coals to bake. The stillness of open spaces amplified the sounds close to him, and he listened to the tinkling of a bell in the field as his burros cropped alfalfa. Content, he settled into the long November evening.

In the letter written to his brother on the Escalante Rim, Everett explained what kept drawing him deeper into the unknown:

> As to when I shall visit civilization, it will not be soon, I think. I have not tired of the wilderness, rather I enjoy its beauty and the vagrant life I lead, more keenly all the time. I prefer the saddle to the street car, and the star sprinkled sky to a roof, the obscure and difficult trail, leading into the unknown, to any paved highway, and the deep peace of the wild to the discontent bred by cities. Do you blame me then for staying here, where I feel that I belong and am one with the world around me? It is true that I miss intelligent companionship, but there are so few with whom I can share the things that mean much to me that I have learned to contain myself. It is enough that I am surrounded with beauty and carry it with me in things that are a constant delight, like my gorgeous Navajo saddle blankets, and the silver bracelet on my wrist, whose three turquoises gleam in the firelight.[17]

A Navajo party, camped south of town, had completed their trades and were preparing to return home. They had the horses corralled, ready to be driven back to their lands across the rivers. Everett stopped by to say hello and practice a few words of the language he was learning. One of the boys rode by after school and saw him with the Indians. Late in the day the young artist, wearing his turquoise bracelet, stood between two Navajo men with his arms around them. He sang with them in a steady, rhythmic pulse, singing for all he was worth.

Next morning he left for the Escalante Desert wearing a red shirt, sun bleached and weather worn. Arnold Alvey lived with his family on the outskirts of town where, as a six-year-old, his chore was drawing water from the well and pouring it in the trough. "I was standing out there when he came up with two burros, walking," Alvey remembered. "He was going down the desert. He had a floppy hat on and a pink shirt flapping in the wind. His shirt was as thin as smoking paper. He said he was going down in the desert to stay all winter. I knew he didn't have enough grub to do him two weeks. I thought it funny he didn't have a coat."[18] And having never seen a burro, he found them fascinating.

"Can I water my burros?" Everett asked.

"Sure, go ahead." And when he was finished, Alvey watched him fade into the distance, heading down the road to Hole-in-the-Rock.

Fall was in the air as Everett Ruess left civilization behind. Carrying his canvases and provisions for an extended trip, he set out alone into the great solitude of canyons near the confluence of the two rivers, into the big reaches of distance lying close to the human heart. The banded escarpment of the Straight Cliffs stretched unbroken to the west, while rabbitbrush and a few junipers anchored the sandy benchlands on both sides of the road. The possibilities opened wide as the young artist entered the desert, and the deeper he went the wilder it became. The long drought finally broke on November 17 when a rainstorm swept in, catching Everett on the trail.

The slow-moving system lasted several days, and he took shelter at a sheep camp near the head of Fiftymile Creek, known locally as Soda Gulch. Although no one lived permanently in the outer reaches of the Escalante Desert, a number of ranchers used it as winter range. Everett spent two nights with herders Addlin Lay and Clayton Porter, questioning them closely about the surrounding canyons and the route to Navajo Mountain. Initial reports said he stayed at their camp until November 19, which fits the time frame and weather conditions better than later accounts, which put it at November 22. Leaving early on the third day, he turned down an offer of a lamb quarter, saying he needed to travel light, having already bought thirty dollars' worth of provisions in town. That morning the sheepherders watched as the artist headed down the trail, never to be seen again.

Everett found his way into nearby Davis Gulch, so narrow that most of the canyon remained in shadow at this time of year. Yet the fall leaves of the box elder obliterated any sense of gloom with a yellow so radiant that the trees seemed to emit their own light. His last days were saturated with deep autumn colors.

UNKNOWN.
RETURN TO SENDER

Far to the west in the city of Los Angeles, a mother and father waited for their son to return. Christopher and Stella Ruess lived in a middle-class neighborhood between Santa Monica Boulevard and Melrose Avenue. They lived modestly, and by the standards of the Great Depression living modestly was doing pretty well. A letter Stella had written to her son lay on the table among other papers.

She had fixed a pair of Christmas Seals to the back of the envelope before mailing it, and each displayed a red cottage in a field of snow with the words *Season's Greetings 1934*. It was something a mother would do to brighten the holidays for a son who would not be home for Christmas. On the face of the envelope was a canceled three-cent stamp and a postmark bearing the date of December 22. It was addressed to "Mr Everett Ruess, Escalante Rim, Utah."[1]

WINTER 1935

After holding the letter for more than a month, the postmaster in Escalante crossed out the address and added the handwritten notation, "Unknown. Return to sender."[2] A message never received became a message of a different kind. Everett Ruess was missing in the distant canyons of Utah.

The twenty-year-old artist had last written his parents in November, giving them only a vague idea of where he was going on the next leg of his journey. With his two burros he was planning to head south toward the Colorado River through wild country, he wrote. He might try crossing the river at Hole-in-the-Rock, above where the San Juan joined the Colorado. Or he could end up making a long, difficult traverse to reach the bridge at Marble Canyon. On the other hand, his route might eventually loop north to Boulder, Utah, a village so isolated that the first road to it was still under construction. With so many possibilities and all of them passing through uninhabited country, he warned his parents he might not be near a post office for a couple of months.

What he wrote was an accurate sketch of the uncertainties he faced, tailored not to alarm them. But what he was telling people on the ground in Utah differed in scope from what he had outlined in the letter. The young artist mentioned to several people he met on his travels of his plan to cross the Colorado and spend some months living with the Navajo Indians. And he left the impression he might not return until July. That would keep him out for nearly six months instead of two. This idea hinged on a number of factors, including the severity of the weather and the danger of the river crossing. Having to stay flexible, he didn't want to needlessly worry his mother and father about an extended trip. He could get word to them later when he made it to trading posts in the Navajo country.

After having the first of their letters returned in early February, Everett's parents were troubled but not fearful. What they needed was more information. On February 7 they wrote postmistress Mildred Allen in Escalante, asking for help in locating their son. She had met Everett when he passed through town in the fall and alerted her husband, Jennings Allen, of his disappearance. A rancher who served as a Garfield County commissioner, he would play a key role in the initial searches.

This was only the beginning of an intense letter-writing campaign initiated when they received no word on Everett. His parents sent inquiries to every postmaster in the Southwest where their son was known to have traveled. They wrote to the sheriffs and local cattlemen, to the Indian agents and traders, to the forestry officials and conservation officers. Next they contacted the newspapers and radio stations, then combed through their son's letters and wrote every person mentioned in them. By mail and word of mouth, what the Navajo called *jiní jiní*, the news rippled out to every corner of the region.

A reporter for the *Los Angeles Evening Herald* heard the story from a forest ranger in Arizona, and the first newspaper account of the disappearance appeared on Valentine's Day, February 14, 1935. The wire services picked it up, and reports soon appeared in papers across the country. In the following weeks letters of support poured in. Those who had met Everett during his four seasons of travel were convinced he knew how to take care of himself and tried to reassure the family. While his parents had confidence in their son, they couldn't shake the fact that he was a month overdue.

Everett had often landed in trouble of one kind or another on his travels, the normal difficulties of wilderness exploration. Burros had died, food had run low, violent storms had swept in, and he had faced flash floods and quicksand. The young artist also had a knack for getting turned around. "He had been lost for days repeatedly," said his father, "and always kept his head and found his bearings in a few days."[3] Because he had survived so much, his parents had come to trust his ability to handle himself in the wilderness.

Toward the end of February, Stella received a Western Union telegram sent collect from a miner who claimed to be working in the district where Everett disappeared. Neal Johnson offered to conduct a search for her son and suggested using "Indian scouts" who knew the lay of the land. He also added a note of urgency. Her son was depending on meltwater from snows that were fast disappearing. If the search didn't start immediately, Everett would soon run out of water and die.

His warning increased their apprehension. So far, no solid clues had turned up, and no one had offered to search for Everett. Christopher responded to the miner with a thoughtful letter, trying not to discourage him while mentioning the difficulties of mounting a search. He believed his son had holed up for the winter with some hermit, maybe a sheepherder, or possibly with Indians. He advised patience. "We are worried," Christopher wrote, "but not stampeded."[4] The father then asked how much a search would cost.

MARCH 1, 1935

A week later, on March 1, Johnson turned up in Los Angeles, claiming to be in town on business. About thirty years old and clean shaven, he didn't fit the image of a wild-eyed desert prospector. His dark hair was neatly combed back, exposing a receding hairline. Christopher, who worked for the city, took him out to lunch, and they talked about the disappearance and what could be done. The father invited the Utah miner home and introduced him to his wife, who showed him Everett's watercolors and read passages from her son's diaries.

Johnson told the couple he would not accept any money for himself, but needed to cover expenses for the Navajo searchers he planned to send out. What the miner didn't bring up in their conversations was his criminal past. Convicted of forgery, Johnson had spent time in the Utah State Prison and a year after his release got into more trouble with the law. Police in Idaho arrested him for passing a bad check, and when Johnson went on a hunger strike they threw him into solitary confinement. The punishment broke him. Twice he tried killing himself by bashing his head against the cell bars. A couple of months after his release, he began working placer claims along the Colorado River, attempting to wash enough fine gold from the sands to make a living.

The only thing Johnson had to offer the Ruess family was hope. A parent losing a child suffers an incomparable loss. A life cut short overturns the natural order, throwing everything out of balance. And the disappearance of a child, the not knowing what happened, adds an agonizing layer of despair. Faced with such a terrible loss, the father and mother couldn't bear to lose hope. With his firm belief that Everett was alive, Johnson gave them what they needed, and in return they grubstaked him on the outside chance he might find their son. The miner stayed with them that evening, sleeping on the couch, and next morning left with seventy-five dollars, an amount equal to nearly half of Christopher's monthly salary. He promised to find their son.

On the day Neal Johnson was meeting with the Ruess family, a search party was gathering in the Mormon village of Escalante. Jennings Allen had stirred up the interest of the community, and a handful of men had volunteered to accompany him on a ten-day sweep. He told the Ruess family, "We will search for him as though he were our own son."[5]

THE GULCH

A few days before the searchers departed, Gail Bailey came into town from the Escalante Desert with a bridle he had found. The sheepman had a camp fifty miles to the south, and he had gone into nearby Davis Gulch in mid-February to check on grazing conditions. Reaching the bottom, he found a bridle and halter on a makeshift fence running from one side of the narrow gorge to the other. And confined to the upper three miles of canyon were two burros left unattended for about two months, during which time they had eaten most of the available feed. In town he learned they likely belonged to a young artist who had been reported missing. The news he brought helped narrow the search area while raising concerns. If Everett Ruess had failed to retrieve his burros after the lapse of so much time, his chances of still being found alive were slim.

MARCH 1935

A cowboy wrote Christopher Ruess from Escalante on March 1, the day the search for his son was set in motion. Allen Pollock had seen Everett when he passed through in November and said he was last seen fifty miles south of town. Pollock understood the difficulties someone unfamiliar with the terrain would face. And Everett's plans to cross the Colorado River worried him, having himself once floated down the river to Lees Ferry. "The only way that he could cross," the cowboy wrote, "was to swim the river. And that is awful dangerous."[1]

That day a news story updated readers on the search for Dan Thrapp, who was now believed to have drowned while crossing the Colorado somewhere upriver. It then covered the disappearance of Everett Ruess, who was said to be missing in the same region where the scientist had vanished. The artist's family had received no word from him since November 11. "The painter's mother," it reported, "now believes her son is dead, another victim of the wild and desolate region. She fears that he may have fallen over a cliff."[2]

Several days later a bold headline reported that Dan Thrapp had been found and flown back to Salt Lake City. Next to it readers were informed of a posse trailing a man who had murdered two cattlemen in Johns Canyon. Another article, almost an afterthought, mentioned the search for Everett Ruess. It told about the discovery of his burros and Bailey's concern for the missing man. "He is afraid Ruess choked to death, as water holes there are scarce and hard to find, and there are treacherous slides over which he might have fallen."[3]

Newspapermen were having trouble coming to terms with the outbreak of so many searches taking place at the same time. An editorial in the *Salt Lake Tribune* on March 9 expressed a degree of exasperation, perhaps aggravated by the *Deseret News* having scooped them on the Dan Thrapp story. "The rugged mountain ranges of Utah," it began, "have been crossed and recrossed, over ridges and through passes, along icy streams and down snow-bound canyon trails, from border to border, during the past few days, looking for scientists and artists, fugitives from justice and escaped convicts."[4] It then had fun with Dan Thrapp, "an eastern investigator for scientific circles, who had settled himself smugly in a remote corner of the commonwealth to enjoy calm meditation and write results." As for Everett Ruess, it added, he had planned to paint landscapes as long as he found the scenery beautiful and interesting. "That he has not returned to civilization seems to indicate that the charm of Utah scenery is inexhaustible, and that he is still making pictures while a search is being carried on at the request of perturbed relatives.... On errands of succor and expeditions of justice," it continued, "men are combing the hills, camping in the wilds, following snow-covered clues, winding through dangerous trails, looking for fellowmen who, for divergent reasons, have hidden themselves from observation and communication." The editorial suggested the disappearances were self-inflicted and ended with the following: "It remains a strange world, inhabited by strange characters whose actions are a constant worry and surprise to their fellowmen." Several months later the newspaper would sponsor its own expedition in an attempt to solve the mystery of what happened to Everett Ruess.

Leading the initial effort to locate the missing artist was Jennings Allen, supported by Harvey Bailey, the Mormon bishop. They first sent Jack Woolsey and Chester Lay by car to establish a base camp forty miles south of town. Beyond that point the horsemen had to pack their own supplies. The search team rode horseback along the Hole-in-the-Rock trail into the Escalante Desert, a wide-open landscape trenched by canyons. They headed in the same direction taken by Everett when he left town in November. The route took them southeast across sandy benchlands flanked by the Straight Cliffs below Fiftymile Mountain. The farther they went, the wilder and more desolate the country became.

Bundled against the cold in heavy coats and under wide-brim hats, the men rode steadily along. Lean and weather hardened, the volunteers were used to traveling long miles in the saddle and knew how to cover ground without complaint. The trail took them straight into one ravine after another as the country grew rougher by the mile. Shadscale and blackbrush dotted the flats with just enough grass to draw a few cowboys and sheepmen onto the range in winter. Deep-cut gulches began forcing the trail closer to the cliffs as it crossed branches funneling into the Escalante River. The horsemen rode to the sheep camp where Everett was last seen and began the search by checking the canyons just north of Davis Gulch. All of the drainages fed into the Escalante River. They entered Willow and Fiftymile without finding any trace of him and moved on to Davis. In this expanse of desert and hidden canyons, they hoped to find some trace of young Everett and send word of his fate back to his parents.

Everett must have known about the hidden trail into Davis because the descent route can be difficult to locate. Just getting to the trailhead requires navigating a rough sea of sandstone swells and sandy troughs. The searchers dismounted at the top and then descended, leading their horses over ledges and across steep slickrock above a sheer cliff. At this point stockmen had roughed out a narrow treadway to improve the footing. Once on the canyon bottom, the team found the burros reported by Bailey. Some witnesses claimed they were emaciated, while others insisted they were fit, the first of many inconsistencies to hamper later investigators. The searchers noticed a panel of petroglyphs carved in a cliff nearby, and one of them added to it by carving, "Mar. 6, Walter Allen 1935."[5] In January Allen had been on Fiftymile Mountain and discounted the theory that Everett had wandered onto the plateau and gotten lost.

They soon found his camp at the base of a south-facing cliff, which flared overhead to create a protected alcove. He had left behind an empty can of condensed milk, several corn husks, and a few chocolate wrappers scattered about, which sounds more like the work of rodents than the resident artist. And they claimed to have found an impression in the dust showing where his saddle blankets had been rolled up. Years later one of the searchers, Chester Lay, recalled a set of footprints leading north from another camp in a cave on top to an unnamed place matching Cave Point, where they found moccasin tracks and sharpened sticks for roasting meat. With a spring and sheltering cliffs, the Navajo often used it as a camp. Chester saw size-9 tracks he thought belonged to Everett. Other searchers disagreed, and they never reached a consensus.

In Davis the men were able to follow his "zigzag" trail for some distance as it threaded through the compressed meanders of the gulch. They were uncertain where he left the canyon, but did find two Moqui-step routes leading out of it. And a newspaper dangled the possibility of an accidental fall by reporting, "The footprints, the searchers said, led to a cliff and vanished."[6] Jennings Allen noted, "From where the bridle and rope were located they tracked him out of the canyon; he had followed an old Indian trail." This must refer to a Moqui-step route, and just below where the bridle had been left is an ancient foothold route leaving the gorge on the south side. The trackers also said he had climbed "many dangerous cliffs," but they found no evidence of a fall. During the summer on Skeleton Mesa, Everett had become comfortable in a vertical world of cliffs and empty spaces. He had learned to climb the hand- and foothold routes with confidence, and in Davis Gulch he had continued to test his skills. And his luck.

Jennings Allen updated the Ruess family on March 8 when a car was sent into town for more supplies. His message told them of finding Everett's tracks, which indicated he had been exploring the gulch with a particular interest in the ruins and rock art. Next to some "Indian drawings" inside an overhang, they noticed an inscription thought to have been left by Everett.[7] The cliff curved high above the rock-art site, and a waterfall cascaded between pools on the creek bed below. Bold pictographs, painted with white pigments, lined the wall, depicting a dozen or more human figures with patterned bodies and horned headgear. Scattered among them were shields painted with geometric designs, rendered in a style attributed to prehistoric Fremont Indians. Everett added to the panel an enigmatic inscription, "NEMO 1934."

A thorough investigation of the wider area, conducted mostly on horseback, was impossible under the constraints they faced. The search party was too small to cover much of the immense canyon system, and winter conditions prevailed. A blizzard swept in on the sixth day of the search, further reducing the chances of finding Everett alive. And snow kept falling. Meanwhile, John Wetherill told a reporter he believed the artist might be holed up in some canyon on the Kaiparowits or camped in the San Juan River country. The article added, "Ruess is an experienced desert man, according to Wetherill, who believes the artist could take care of himself unless he suffered an accident."[8]

After ten futile days, they called off the search. The horsemen packed up and faced a critical decision. Left in the canyon, the burros might starve, but to remove them would leave Everett stranded if by some chance he returned. The searchers concluded that the camp had been abandoned either by choice or by chance and chose to take the burros. When the horsemen attempted to drive them out of the canyon, the animals locked their legs on a smooth pitch and refused to climb. No one was able to persuade them, so two riders roped the burros and dragged them up the sandstone on their sides. This raised the possibility that Everett had faced the same problem, forcing him to delay his travels or to leave them behind with the expectation of returning.

The searchers took the rescued burros with them as they began the long ride back to town by way of Bailey's sheep camp on the ridge separating Davis from Fiftymile Creek. Chester Lay recalled seeing the pack bags and a pack saddle belonging to Everett in camp. Exactly what items Bailey removed from Davis would be debated in the coming years, with Chester believing he grabbed the bedding and Navajo blankets before Everett was reported missing. Rumors, never substantiated, claimed he also found the 1934 diary. Bailey initially denied removing anything but the bridle and only later admitted to having taken other items. The sheepherders who hosted Everett also admitted to having gone through his outfit. Whether before or after his disappearance, they didn't say.

Late on Friday evening, March 15, the search party entered Escalante and made their report. Having failed to locate the missing artist or find his body, the searchers were puzzled. Death by quicksand or drowning in the river, trapped in deep snows on the Kaiparowits, or wintering over with the Navajo—nothing had been ruled out. Christopher Ruess summarized the findings of the first search, reflecting his own state of mind. "They rather despair of finding him alive," he wrote.[9]

Jennings Allen and the volunteers from Escalante refused to give up. Knowing the agony Everett's parents were experiencing and driven to solve the mystery, they began planning round two. The initial search had not covered the south rim of Davis to their satisfaction, so they would focus on that side, another slickrock wilderness. On March 23 a second search party left town, with each rider trailing a packhorse. They returned empty-handed after two weeks and left few details of the second attempt. Allen now believed Everett must have crossed the river and entered the Navajo country. "He can't be anywhere on this side of the Colorado River alive," he reported to the Ruess family, "because every inch has been searched."[10]

THE SEARCH

The artist entered the sandstone maze and never returned. On his wanderings Everett Ruess had acquired a taste for Spotted Dog, slickrock expanses, and Moqui steps leading high up the canyon walls. Standing alone on the edge of a cliff or walking up a trail, he would sing for the pure joy of it, and he disappeared with his wild enthusiasms unchecked. When he did not return, parties set out from Escalante to find him and failed each time. The searchers made a good-faith effort and could have ended the operation without regrets. Instead, they began preparations for a third attempt.

LATE SPRING 1935

Unable to get help from the state and federal governments, Jennings Allen approached a consortium of businessmen and civic leaders. The Associated Civic Clubs of Southern Utah, representing fifteen counties, agreed to finance a new effort. With the right leadership, they believed, another try would get results using a more systematic approach. Perry Shurtz, described as "being wise in the ways of the grim desert," was put in charge of the all-volunteer search team.[1] A few of the men had been on earlier searches, and most understood the hard work and dangers they faced. Impressed by their selfless determination, Everett's father praised them as "good neighbors following the wilderness code."[2]

Preparations were nearly complete in late May as temperatures in the Escalante Desert began to climb. Nine horsemen would be involved in the search, supported by a heavy wagon to carry supplies. An automobile could not go beyond Fortymile Gulch, but if a wagon could reach Davis Gulch, then no time would be wasted riding back to get resupplied. The association secretary, Ray Carr, planned to accompany the expedition and send regular updates back to the *Salt Lake Telegram*. "The people of Escalante," he wrote, "have literally been on edge with excitement and the anticipation of solving the mystery that has existed for nearly six months."[3] With high spirits and unshakable confidence, they were eager to start.

At daybreak on Friday, May 30, nine "weather-beaten desert riders" left town for the Hole-in-the-Rock country.[4] The citizens of Escalante had made sure they were mounted on the best horses available. Along the way, the searchers talked with sheepman Joe Woolsey and his herder Addlin Lay. Everett Ruess had spent two nights with Lay at his camp in November. The herder, who had participated in the original search, gave the searchers precise directions on finding the descent route into Davis. On the first day the horsemen covered more than forty miles before stopping at Dance Hall Rock, where they met the provision wagon sent out two days earlier. In 1879 the natural amphitheater had been the setting for evening dances held by Mormon pioneers taking a break from their efforts to push a road through the desert. Next morning the search party continued south into increasingly dissected terrain along a trail growing more difficult for the wagon to negotiate.

Saddle horses had to tie on and help pull it straight up the sides of ravines, and when the wagon nearly slipped over a cliff four men jumped on the uphill side to prevent it from toppling over the edge. By staying close to the Straight Cliffs, the trail avoided the worst obstacles, but not all of them. At one point they struggled for an hour and made only two hundred yards. The plan was to camp at Cave Point the second night, but insufficient water forced the party to push on to Soda Seep.

As some of the men set up a base of operations, others searched an intriguing outcrop of red sandstone a mile to the south below Fiftymile Mountain. Weathered into bald knobs and molded cliffs, it was the type of scenery an artist might want to paint. They found numerous places where Everett could have fallen, but no evidence he had been there. That evening around the campfire, Captain Shurtz briefed his team on the key landmarks in the area to prevent anyone else from wandering off and getting lost.

On June 1 the searchers left their horses on top and descended into Davis Gulch. At noon they reached his last known camp and carefully inspected it for any clues. They were operating on the belief that Everett had left his burros here and went on foot to explore the canyon, carrying enough gear to bivouac if necessary. He may have gotten sick or suffered an accident at an outlying camp, preventing him from returning. The men divided into teams and began to scour the canyon, thoroughly working one section before moving on to the next. Red and white flags were used to mark areas already searched to avoid overlooking any spot. This time they would leave nothing to chance.

Because he might have become trapped in a deep pothole or stranded on a ledge, all possibilities had to be checked. They inspected every overhang where he might have camped and every ruin he might have explored. The work was exhausting. "One not familiar with the territory in which the search is being made," ran a news story, "cannot appreciate the hardships endured by members of the party."[5]

Working down canyon, they found the NEMO inscription reported during the first search. They had no idea what it meant but assumed Everett had carved it because he was the only one known to have been in the gulch for the past year. Near a deep cleft at the top of a cliff, they spotted a swarm of blowflies, normally found around a fresh carcass, and a team climbed up to investigate. They used a 150-foot rope to lower several men, stopping only when the slope ended in a sheer drop, plunging into darkness. Unable to see the bottom, they concluded it was an unlikely place for Ruess to have explored, after all. That afternoon they shifted the search to the ridge north of Davis and found it incised by ravines and riddled with deep potholes.

Next morning some men continued to work the ridge, while others headed to the south side of Davis. They followed the Hole-in-the-Rock trail six miles to the notch in the rim of Glen Canyon, where a rough roadway had been blasted down to the Colorado, twelve hundred feet below. The river was overflowing its banks, and they found no recent sign of anyone having used either of the two trails to reach it. Having failed to find any trace of the missing artist, they spent the next two days combing the ridges on both sides of Davis. They were still confident, despite the setbacks, of finding him somewhere in the vicinity.

Hot weather was compounding the difficulties. Water holes had begun to dry up, forcing them to pack extra water with them on the searches, and the horses often had to go without, reducing their efficiency. On Thursday they pushed from first light to last, rechecking the ridgetops and scrambling along brittle rims. A team took their shovels and descended Fiftymile Creek to overhangs where recent rockfall might have buried someone. Digging beneath the rubble, they found nothing. Before returning, one man left a record carved on the cliff face, "E Reus Hunters, June 6, 1935."[6]

That day Clayton Porter stopped to talk with the searchers. He had been herding sheep with Addlin Lay in November when Everett passed through. Porter told them the young artist was intent on reaching Navajo Mountain and asked about the shortest route. When he told them of his plans to cross the river at Hole-in-the-Rock, they suggested he use the bridge at Lees Ferry. To reach it, however, meant abandoning his burros, so it was unlikely he took that route. Before continuing his journey, Everett told them he did not intend to return home until the Fourth of July.

With hope slipping away, the leaders were on the verge of ending the search. And then a discovery on Friday renewed their optimism. A mile above the mouth of Davis Gulch, Frank Barney spotted a prehistoric ruin perched high on a cliff face. Barney, who had participated in the first search, reached the site by a friction climb up the slickrock face, and the others followed. The ruin was a simple one-room masonry structure without a roof, and on the ledge they found a large prehistoric pot placed there recently alongside two grinding stones. Size-9 tracks were all about, and the remains of a campfire indicated Everett had spent the night there. And scratched into the doorstep was another "NEMO 1934."

Ray Carr wired Stella Ruess about the inscription, asking if it had any significance. She immediately responded, saying Everett had been reading a translation of *The Odyssey* by T. E. Lawrence, of Lawrence of Arabia fame. And she added, *nemo* was a Latin word for "nobody." Her response was relayed to the searchers in the field. Christopher followed up with a letter giving the fuller story of how Odysseus had used the name to trick the man-eating Cyclops and escape from his cave. He compared Everett's journey to the epic voyage of Odysseus and told Carr he believed his son had arranged to cross the Colorado with two Navajo "in the Indian canoe at Hole in Rock."[7]

Back in Escalante, the Garfield County sheriff and the county attorney were having doubts about the story Gail Bailey told of finding the burros. His delay in reporting it had raised questions, and the circumstances, said the sheriff, warranted an investigation. The authorities also questioned Quinn Roundy, who had herded sheep at Hole-in-the-Rock beginning December 12, and perhaps earlier. He was certain no one had come his way during the winter, as any travelers would be visible in such wide-open country.

Having been out for more than a week without having solved the mystery, the searchers turned toward home. They had hay to harvest and cattle to move from the winter ranges to the higher elevations for summer. On Sunday, June 10, they were back in Escalante. Ray Carr wrote to Christopher Ruess, informing him that they were unable to finish searching the territory they had wanted to cover. The consensus, he added, was that his son had not crossed the river to Navajo Mountain. And while Carr mentioned preparations for a new search using packhorses, nothing appears to have come of it. He said they would focus on a rugged thirty-square-mile zone, "immediately southeast of the Davis Gulch and the Escalante Creek.... The tracks last found indicated that he had gone in this direction."[8] In the end, they were left with a single word, *NEMO*, and a set of tracks fading away into the unknown.

FORBIDDING CANYON

Red sand trickled across the highway, carried by a wind out of the north as pickups drove past with red Christmas bows fastened to the grills. Beyond Inscription House, the pavement ended, and the road pointed north toward a bulge of blue mountain. The Navajo know it as the Head of Earth Woman, and they describe the red canyons encircling it as her coral necklace.

Navajo Mountain remains the most isolated community on the reservation and the most traditional. On earlier trips I had spent the night in earth-covered hogans and listened to stories told by old men who didn't speak English. Many of the people still relied on raising horses, sheep, and cattle for their livelihood. A Navajo artist, I learned, knew about a rock face worn smooth by the Ancestral Pueblo sliding down it, but he had died in an accident earlier in the year. Thinking his brother might know its location, I turned onto a branch road at the foot of the mountain leading toward the house of Gary Dougi.

No one was home when I arrived, so I spent the afternoon walking among the cliffs, waiting for the pieces to fall into place. Late in the day, Gary returned from cutting firewood. We sat on the tailgate of his pickup as I explained my reason for being there. It helped I knew his brother. He had only a vague memory of the Sliding Rock lying somewhere to the south. But his father, who grew up in that area, might know. We drove over to his house and walked in.

The woodstove was cranking, and the coffee was on. A tapestry of Jesus hung on the wall above an upright loom holding a half-woven saddle blanket. A piñon tree stood in the corner, decorated for Christmas with home-made ornaments and a single present lying underneath. Tom Dougi was a roadman of the Native American Church with a certificate on the wall to prove it. In their ceremonies, they use peyote as a sacrament. His father, who had met Everett Ruess, had frequently traveled beyond the rivers on trading expeditions and had guided Anglo parties into the Kaiparowits country.

Father and son spoke to each other in Navajo. The old man told him the Sliding Rock lay west of Inscription House, where he used to herd sheep. The place I was looking for, he said, was a healing shrine used by the Ancestral Puebloan long ago and where the Navajo used to make offerings. As they prayed, they touched parts of their bodies, starting with the feet and moving upward in the direction of growth. And then they slid down the rock face as part of the ritual. In the past they kept the location secret, he said, but now it did not matter. Tomorrow the roadman would take us there.

The conversation drifted to the sacredness of the land, as it often does when you show an interest in a particular place. "You take a handful of dirt," Gary said, "and bring it inside and put it in a dark corner and nothing happens. But put it outside, give it water and sun, and something will grow from it. We are plants. The earth is our mother. It doesn't belong to us; we belong to the earth. There is power in this place, Naatsis'áán. Where else could I live? Chicago? Nothing would talk to me there."

Gary related a story, new to me, of the Holy Twins, Monster Slayer and Born for Water. He said they were raised at Navajo Mountain, and his father knew where they still lived. Born for Water once floated down the Colorado River, while his brother stayed behind and kept track of him by crystal gazing. His only companion on the trip was a turkey that followed along the bank. When they reached Needles, California, they left the river and planted four kinds of corn from seed tucked away in the turkey's feathers. He said you can still see it—blue, yellow, white, and a dark-colored corn, now turned to stone.

That night I camped at his place on Balanced Rock Mesa, below the ruins of a large Ancestral Puebloan pueblo. The Navajo continued to use the prehistoric catchment, a low stone dam set to catch runoff from the slickrock. Frozen solid, the water had never thawed during the day under the low winter sun. Next morning we drove south to the Sliding Rock, through a country of sand and sagebrush and sandstone, taking two trucks to carry five of the family and me.

With its serpentine gorges and barrier cliffs, the Navajo Mountain country has long provided refuge for bands of Navajo and Paiute Indians.

During the 1860s, Navajo families escaped into these rugged backlands to hide from pursuing soldiers. They eluded capture by covering their trails and keeping the water sources secret. Their descendants take pride in this legacy of stubborn independence. "We never surrendered," said Gary, adding with a smile, "I guess we're still renegades."

We followed a back road, which turned onto a sandy track and ended on the crest of a hill. The old man stepped out, wearing a cowboy hat with a silver waterbird dangling from the crown. He looked toward a series of sandstone fins, angling skyward in the upper reaches of a wash with a linear mark running down the face of the tallest slab. "The Sliding Rock is down there," he said in Navajo. Unable to walk that far, he stayed behind as we dropped downslope to the foot of the rocks.

Potsherds lay scattered in the sand, and the remnants of a few simple walls were tucked under the overhanging ledges. We circled around to the trackway, a set of two grooves and the trace of a third worn into the sandstone. Beginning at a horizontal line pecked on the face, they angled steeply down for about twenty-five feet to a mound of stone rubble. When they were kids, Tom had told us, they would pick up three flat rocks. Holding one in each hand for balance, they stood on the third stone, crouched down, and pushed off. Each run became faster as loose sand caught in the smooth track. Gary's son Leo now chose three rocks from the pile of discards at the bottom of the slide. He climbed to the top and balanced on a flat stone fitting inside the groove. In an instant he was sliding down the face, speed increasing and his eyes locked on the rocks below. Reaching the bottom, the boy stepped off the stone at a run as it hit the mound of rubble, his face set in a serious expression.

On the ride back, Gary began reading the surroundings the way I might scan a book. Each terrain feature was part of a story told in song, and the story line ran through the landscape. As I drove he named places, letting each mesa and butte trigger an association. "Square Butte is the home of Spotted Lightning," he said, moving fast, not pausing for questions.

The four rocks sticking out on that side are the shields. That window in the white rock, they passed evil through the opening against the Twins, taking all the plants and animals from Navajo Mountain and passing them through it. That was when the two were hidden in the Haystack rock. Big Snake went through Red Lake and coiled up where that red mesa is to the north. At Blue Canyon they had the first Yeibichai, and you can still see the people sitting around in the rocks. If you want to be sure to get a good horse, you go up on Middle Mesa and pray at dawn and you'll catch a good one. At Wildcat Peak, the Twins rested four days. The bear and the cougar were traveling with them to protect them.

The Navajo continued, reciting one name after another, and pointed out Tall Mountain, a red butte on a ridge to the east. Navajo Mountain is the head, Gary said, Tall Mountain the heart, and Black Mesa the body. He said the composite form is female, like the Colorado River beyond. At the confluence, now under Lake Powell, the male waters of the San Juan flow on top of the female waters. "They come together," he added, "and form a river called the Long Soul." He motioned far to the south where the Colorado flows into Grand Canyon. Listening to him, I saw the image of a river now running deep below the lake surface.

At one point I asked Gary about his grandfather, who used to travel across the rivers to trade, the Navajo who sang with Everett Ruess before he left town. Gary confirmed that his grandfather had known the trails and had a reputation as a tracker. When filmmaker Dianne Orr interviewed Tom Dougi for her documentary on the missing artist, he told her about the time they met the lone traveler.

The Navajo said he was seven or eight years old when a young Anglo arrived with a pair of burros, leading one, with the pack burro following behind. They were in the canyons south of Navajo Mountain at the time. The stranger arrived when the family had gathered to eat and asked them something they couldn't understand. Nobody spoke English, and they were uncertain what he wanted. The young man drew a line on the ground and walked along it as if he was following a trail. Still not understanding, they fed him while sending for someone who could interpret. Finally, they learned what he needed and gave him directions on where to find the trail out of the canyon. Tom Dougi said his father had cornfields in the canyons leading to the river crossing, and being a strong swimmer he could cross at the right water levels without a boat. Before dams were built upstream, the river could fluctuate wildly. "They know when to go across and when not to go across," he said. "They knew how strong the currents would be." And before crossing his father would pray and make offerings for a safe passage. Tom believed Everett was on his way back to Navajo Mountain when he disappeared. Because the Navajo, Paiute, Mormons, and Anglos were all peaceful then, he did not believe he was killed.

Navajo Mountain has a way of drawing me back to it. I returned on an assignment in early April a couple of years after the Sliding Rock trip. Our group planned to explore slot canyons farther west, spending the first two days by horseback and the rest on foot. We began descending a steep, broken trail and rode through a narrows the Navajo called "Passage through Rock." The first night found us camped in Forbidding Canyon. We sat around the campfire talking long after dark, and one by one most of the others turned in.

Our Navajo guide, Leo Manheimer, was the chapter president of the Navajo Mountain community and worked as an outfitter. He was describing how the men in his family had gone to their traditional hunting territory the previous fall to learn the old methods of hunting. They started with a dawn prayer, and then, working together, the young ones drove the game to the more experienced men, waiting in stands. The hunters would ritually butcher the deer, leaving the antlers, reproductive organs, and often the bones. When he mentioned they had been in Harris Wash, a branch of the Escalante, I got curious.

"Have you ever heard about a young *bilagáana* who disappeared in that area in the 1930s?" I asked.

He looked directly at me, surprised by the question. "Yes," he answered. "My father-in-law told us a story last fall. He said it happened somewhere between where we were camped at Harris Wash and the Colorado River. It's a story only the locals know." Down by the creek, a hobbled horse hopped twice and stopped as if listening.

"Some Navajos met him out there," he told me. "They were on their way to Escalante. One of them decided to take his livestock. He tracked him back to his camp. He killed him with his own ax. He didn't take the animals. He felt guilty and left them there. He buried the body in a crack and covered it with rocks and sand. He hid his tracks and didn't tell anybody about it. He spoke about it for the first time four or five years later at a Squaw Dance."

The dance takes place during the Enemyway, a ceremony used to ritually purify a Navajo who has been exposed to the death of an outsider.

I had planned on returning to Navajo Mountain a couple of weeks after our trip and arranged for Leo to introduce me to his father-in-law. I wanted to interview him about other matters and follow up on the story of the killing. But when I called ahead, Leo said the old man couldn't remember who told the story. His tone had changed, becoming more guarded. "It wasn't my father-in-law," he said. "It must have been one of the other elders." But he was willing to be interviewed, and Leo agreed to interpret.

Ashley Atene was a traditional herbalist who lived in an earth-covered hogan. Inside, logs crisscrossed overhead to form a domed roof, and dried plants rested on the table, while bright drawings from his great-grandchildren hung on the walls. After he talked about his work as a healer and the potential impact on the community of the plan to pave the only road reaching them, I went ahead and asked about the disappearance of the young Anglo. The two men spoke to each other in Navajo at some length, and finally Leo turned to me. "He says he doesn't know anything about that. He thinks he was at boarding school. That was in the 1930s."

The story I heard in Forbidding Canyon roughly fitted the Ruess case. On the other hand, it could also have been the weaving of various incidents into a campfire tale. So I headed to the archives, seeking evidence of a Navajo connection to the missing artist.

As Everett began to understand their culture, I learned, he found himself drawn to the people. He was stirred by their songs and started wearing a turquoise bracelet. By Everett's last season of travels, his father noted how his stride now resembled that of an Indian. He sought out the Navajo in towns he passed through and told a number of people he planned to cross the Colorado River and spend an extended period with them. And at various times after he disappeared, reports surfaced claiming he may have been murdered by a Navajo.

SUMMER 1941

The possibility of Navajo involvement in the disappearance of Everett Ruess was taken seriously during a murder investigation. An unusual number of Enemyway ceremonies, more than two dozen, were taking place in the western reservation in 1941. Reports had filtered in to traders and Indian agents about medicine men using the scalp of a white man in their ritual. The victim was said to have been killed in the 1930s beyond Navajo Mountain, and the circumstances suggested a connection to the missing artist.

The trader at Inscription House, Gladwell Richardson, first learned of the incident when a fugitive Paiute came in the dead of night to get supplies. The Indian told him of a white man "sleeping" in the sand across the Colorado River, and the trader immediately thought of Everett. Richardson pressed him for more details, and the Paiute told him to ask the Navajo about it. Later, a Navajo woman said she had looked down from above, possibly from the rim of a canyon, and saw the body. And then, being coy, she told him she might be lying, and if he wanted to know more, then he should ask the Paiute, since they knew all about it.

The Navajo word normally translated as "scalp" means a remnant of the dead person and can be the hair, bones, and even pieces of clothing. When the medicine man uses the actual scalp, a small piece is cut off to be ritually killed near the end of a ceremony lasting several days. Navajo perform the Enemyway to restore the order essential to life and to counter the confusion and violence resulting from exposure to alien cultures and the death of strangers. Soldiers returning from war have had the sing performed to exorcise the ghosts of slain enemies, and sometimes children returning from boarding school have undergone the ritual purification. Conducted with serious intent, the ceremony also has a social component known as the Squaw Dance.

An investigation began, and the authorities soon tracked down multiple scalps. One of them had belonged to an Anglo killed while traveling alone on the rim of Tsegi Canyon a quarter century before. A trader linked another scalp to an even older incident, the killing of a white man on a sandbar in the San Juan River around 1882. Then the investigators learned of an active case involving John Chief, a fifty-one-year-old Navajo living south of the San Juan River who was respected by his neighbors and the local traders. Earlier, he joined a delegation that traveled by train to Washington, DC, to protest the stock-reduction program that was hurting their people. The delegates had pawned their jewelry to cover expenses.

The Navajo Police Patrol and the Federal Bureau of Investigation (FBI) staked out an Enemyway being held near the Oljeto Trading Post. The scalp of an unidentified white man, said to have been killed by John Chief, was being used. Their suspect rode horseback to the gathering and stopped on the fringes of the fire without dismounting. Striking up a friendly conversation, a range rider fluent in Navajo worked in close and suddenly grabbed the reins. John Chief gave a warning cry, alerting the others to his danger. He kicked his horse in an attempt to escape and struck the special agent with a quirt. The other officers rushed in and dragged him off the horse, making the arrest.

A second suspect was already in custody on a charge of interfering with federal agents who had been sent to enforce the grazing laws. Jack Crank, the thirty-eight-year-old son-in-law of John Chief, had a wife and six children to support in the hard times brought about by the loss of sheep and horses. Joined by other Navajo, Crank had overturned a car with tribal police inside to protest the taking of their animals. The authorities returned at night to make the arrest, grabbing him out of bed at two in the morning. Handcuffed, he was placed in the back of a pickup without clothes and taken to jail.

The police obtained confessions from the suspects, eight different statements admitting to several versions of the crime, confessions the men later claimed were coerced. Jack Crank tried without success to take full blame for the killing. At the end of September, John Chief led the police to the murder scene in the rim country near the junction of Moonlight Creek with the San Juan. He showed them where they had burned and buried the stranger's personal property in the sand and then pointed out the location of the body. The second shovelful uncovered the corpse of a white man still wearing a denim jacket. He had two front teeth made of gold, and his skull had been crushed. The body was tentatively identified as Andy DeLaney, the cowboy Dan Thrapp had met in 1934, who was thought to have drowned. When the authorities learned the killing happened in the summer of 1930, DeLaney was ruled out as the victim.

The trial was held the following year, and a throng of Navajo from the reservation converged on the courthouse in Monticello to see justice done. The presiding judge was F. W. Keller, who earlier had been involved in the Johns Canyon killings as district attorney. That position was now held by Donald Adams, the former county prosecutor who represented the state. In 1935 he had traveled to Texas with the sheriff to interview Clint Palmer and Lucy Garrett. The court appointed Knox Patterson, a top criminal attorney, to represent the defendants.

As dozens of witnesses testified, a more coherent account of the incident emerged. A destitute prospector, about fifty years old and known as Shorty, had wandered into the country north of Oljeto Trading Post, begging food from the trader and the local Navajo families. He was also suspected of having stolen flour, coffee, and tools from a hogan. A more serious crime, when many were struggling to feed their families, was letting his three horses graze in a cornfield until they had destroyed the crop. Jack Crank and John Chief mounted their horses and trailed him north toward the San Juan River. They overtook the prospector at his camp and confronted him about the loss of corn. When they demanded compensation, Shorty drew his gun. Crank grabbed his arms from behind, causing him to shoot wild as Chief struck him in the head with the blunt end of an ax. The prospector fell to the ground, and Crank picked up the ax and gave him a final killing blow. John Chief graphically demonstrated for the jury how he had swung the ax and disposed of the body.

When the case went to the jury, they returned a verdict after only four hours of deliberation. Both men were found guilty of second-degree murder. Judge Keller had little choice but to sentence each defendant to ten years in prison, hoping an appeal would allow them to be released as soon as possible. An editorial in the *San Juan Record* stated that an injustice had been perpetrated and criticized "the seemingly unfair laws which take away the rights of a people who have lived in certain locations in this southwest country for centuries of time."[1] The newspaper believed the men should have been acquitted.

In the months before the trial, Christopher Ruess became convinced his son was the murder victim and wrote a detailed letter to E. R. Fryer, head of the Navajo Agency. The father informed the superintendent that he was opposed on principle to the death penalty and that life imprisonment would be sufficient. He also wanted the killer to locate his son's remains and specifically requested the 1934 diary be turned over to him in case they wanted to publish it. Several months into the investigation, Fryer wrote to update the family on what he had learned. The superintendent told Christopher that he had questioned the defendants about the Ruess case, as had the FBI. "We are convinced," he said, "that these men, murderers by their own admission, had no part in the disappearance of your son."[2] The mystery of Everett's disappearance remained unsolved.

Among the Ghosts

The hunt for Everett Ruess in the Escalante Desert had failed, and his parents were close to abandoning hope. On June 21 they began a two-week journey through the region where their son had traveled, letting the landscape stir memories of their son. For Stella and Christopher, the trip became a pilgrimage. Everyone they encountered knew the details of Everett's disappearance, and they questioned anyone who might have a new lead. In Kayenta John Wetherill dismissed the possibility their son was living with an Indian family. He knew the Navajo people as well as anyone, and after six months he was certain word would have reached him. Everett, he told them, had taken chances no archaeologist took and lost his life.

August 1935

By the end of the trip, they had moved a step closer to accepting his death, and then a letter arrived from Salt Lake City. Once again, Neal Johnson was ready to tell them what they were so desperate to hear. The convicted forger wrote on August 12 to inform them of a major development in his investigation. A white boy, he said, was living with an Indian family in the vicinity of Navajo Mountain. Although no one was sure he was Everett, the person had undergone a tribal wedding ceremony. The *Salt Lake Tribune* was sending him to search for their son. "The orders from the Tribune," he wrote, "is to find him."[1]

Somehow Johnson had convinced the newspaper to finance an expedition, and the editors would send reporter John U. Terrell along to cover the story. Terrell, who had run away from home as a kid to become a cowboy, was a veteran journalist. He worked as a correspondent for United Press, wrote investigative pieces for various newspapers, and the following year would report on Marie Ogden's continuing attempts to raise the dead. To ensure they had an exclusive story, Terrell insisted on secrecy.

In the letter, Johnson told Christopher Ruess that he must keep their plans an absolute secret. "We do not want no one," he wrote, "to know where we are going nor why." And by the way, Johnson added, he was out of pocket for money spent on trinkets and bright cloth as gifts for the Indians, since the newspaper would not cover his personal expenses. He enclosed a blank check to facilitate depositing twenty-five dollars in his account, and once again the father complied. The miner ended the letter by signing his name as usual, "Capt. Neal Johnson." He claimed the rank was earned while flying airplanes for the Mexican Army.

Early on August 13, the journalist and the desert rat headed south from Salt Lake in a Model T Ford. The account of the trip began to appear in the *Tribune* on August 25 with the first of four articles running on the front page of the Sunday paper. At every outpost, Terrell wrote, he questioned the most knowledgeable of the locals, including any Indians, traders, cowboys, or government agents who might have word of the missing artist. In such a wild region, they told him, a stranger would be noticed immediately and even the tracks of an unfamiliar horse scrutinized. If Ruess crossed the river, they would have known it.

As they drove south of Bluff, conditions deteriorated. "The road, only two ruts wandering through deep valleys and across high sage covered mesas," wrote Terrell, "seems uncertain of its destination."[2] And from Monument Pass, the land stretched out in "an endless confusion of red mountains and barren desert." Reaching the trading post at Kayenta, he interviewed John Wetherill, and the trader gave a blunt assessment of the fate of the missing artist. "Dead," he said.

In his reporting, Terrell recounted a dramatic moment when he reached the camp of a Navajo headman that evening. Having forgotten his name, the reporter simply referred to him as Natani, taken from *naat'áannii*, meaning "speaker." His interpreter told the Navajo that the white men had come to find their friend who had disappeared six months before. "Why have you waited so long to look for your friend?" he asked.[3]

More Navajo drifted into the brush shelter as the headman began to chant. His wife covered her face with a blanket and swayed back and forth, entering a trance state. The youngest of three wives, she had a reputation as a skilled trembling-hand diviner. The reporter listened while the rain began to fall and the chanting grew louder. Suddenly, she uncovered her face and raked her fingers through the sand, throwing some on herself and building a mound representing Navajo Mountain. Lines indicating canyons trailed out from it, and she drew others for the San Juan and Colorado Rivers. When the chant ended, the diviner's head fell to her chest.

Terrell reported that the headman then spoke for her. "Go to the forks of the river. He was there. Close by he made a camp. You will find the fire."[4] His wife added that he was no longer there and had gone away. She had seen him talking with two Navajo friends, young men like him. They ate together and sang. "Then there is shadow," Natani continued. "He has gone away. The Navajos have left the place. They are no longer with him. She says they have traveled together. He has given himself to our gods. He has taken us in his arms and wished to come away with us."

The investigators spent two days in Kayenta before continuing to the distant trading post at Navajo Mountain, the end of the road. Using an interpreter, they learned that no Indian had crossed the Colorado River since the previous fall. And they met Dougi, Tom's father, the best tracker in the region, spelling his name as "Dougeye." The reporter learned that he had traveled to Escalante in November with two companions to trade for horses and while there talked with Everett. The artist spoke only a little Navajo, but they were able to carry on a conversation because one of the Navajo traders knew some English. The reporter asked Dougi to be their guide.

The tracker was reluctant to take them to a place haunted by the ghost of a dead man. If they went looking for a body, he feared they might find one. After negotiating a price, the tracker agreed to lead them on one condition—the reporter had to leave the camera behind. Terrell claimed the Indian was afraid of having his soul stolen, so he was never able to provide the editors with photographs to illustrate the story. Before they could start, Dougi had to first round up his horses, so he arranged to meet them in two days. That gave the reporter time to question the locals as they came in to the trading post the next day.

The night before departing, Captain Johnson wrote to Everett's parents. His letter casts doubt on the version later published. Dated August 16, Johnson began on a bleak note. "People here," he wrote, "Including The Indians have no hopes for Everett."[5] The man who had held fast to the belief that the artist was alive now had his doubts. "We have Very Little left to work on that shows he is still alive." Johnson continued to hope the missing artist had gone native and was with an Indian family. He did manage to learn the names of the Navajo who had crossed the rivers last November to trade. Accompanying Dougi were Luke Chief and Charlie Drake. He had left town two days before the artist and passed a party of Navajo traveling north as the three men were preparing to cross the San Juan River. Providing phonetic spellings of their Navajo names and the English translations, Johnson said the men in the second party were Red Shirt, White Hat, and Jene Holgate.

Apprehensive of the upcoming trip, Johnson went on to describe the difficulties he would face. "I am Going down in the morning to Hole in the wall. We will ford the San Juan River also the Colorado. Here I will spend some days. Dougi is Going with me. We are riding two horses and packing 2. Mr. Terrell went to Ka Ba To this morning to check up on a leed we have from there.... The Indian will be with me all the time untill I start down the River." Or he might decide to return with Dougi to Navajo Mountain.

"This is a tough trip I am going on," he continued. "Mr. Terrell will meet me at Lees Ferry. Mr. Ruess and Mrs. Ruess I am doing all in my power I hope you Believe this." Johnson had his appendix removed two months before and worried about the strenuous trip ahead. "Tomorrow I make a 20 mile ride on a horse. The Dr forbid me of making a horse back ride for at least 4 months. For days I will ride a horse. I must, also I will be walking for miles where a horse wont go. I hope I have your Blessings and may God be with me. A quitter never wins and a winner never quits."

The reporter had already left for Kaibeto and planned to meet Johnson later in Lees Ferry, at the head of Marble Canyon. The miner was heading out alone with the Navajo guide in the morning.

In the published story, the three of them reached the San Juan and found the river at flood stage due to recent rains. Dougi knew the danger they faced and told them, "No cross."[6] In a rash move, Terrell insisted they push on, and the next morning he described Johnson plunging into the churning waters and the rest following. "It was a wild scramble," Terrell wrote. "Twice one of the pack horses went under and each time came up coughing. We were wet, chilled, but eagerly went on." Crossing Wilson Mesa, they descended to the fast-flowing Colorado and made another wet crossing. Along the way, Dougi searched for any sign of Everett, concluding he had not forded either river and had not floated downstream on a raft. He was certain of this. Only six men, the two Navajo trading parties, had made the passage since the previous year.

The second night they camped on the north side of the river and headed to Davis Gulch on the third day. In 1928 Clyde Kluckhohn and friends had undertaken a similar pack trip from Navajo Mountain to the Kaiparowits Plateau, following the route later claimed to have been used by the Terrell-Johnson party. And they were led by the same guide, Dougi. Kluckhohn wrote an adventurous account of the expedition in *Beyond the Rainbow*, and he would go on to become one of the best ethnographers of his generation, specializing in studies of the Navajo. He documented the trip with film and still photography, which showed Dougi was not camera shy. Though reluctant to be filmed, he willingly posed for photographs. The twenty-three-year-old Kluckhohn and his party took six days to reach the head of Davis under less trying conditions.

The published account of the Terrell-Johnson pack trips, culminating in a search of Davis Gulch, cannot be relied upon. Contradicting what Johnson wrote, it rests on an improbable time line combined with a vague and inaccurate description of the route. When Terrell reached the Kaibeto trading post, however, the narrative becomes more reliable.

After taking several days to make arrangements, the reporter interviewed Geishi Betah, a leader who knew the business of every Indian who passed through that country. "There are many places there a man might die," he said, referring to the region north of the Colorado.[7] The Navajo began counting on his fingers. "But only one, two, three, four, five where a man might camp. Man camps only at water." He told the reporter that the white boy did not come south of the river, and when the interpreter suggested Indians had killed Ruess, Geishi studied the reporter's expression. "You do not believe that." Terrell told him he had nothing to believe—yet. The Navajo headman then expressed concern that policemen would come to investigate and promised his cooperation. "We want no trouble," he said.

As planned, the reporter met Johnson at Marble Canyon, and together they reviewed what had been learned. They were now certain Everett had never entered the Navajo country, which was the main contribution of the expedition. Terrell concluded his series of articles with three observations. "Everett Ruess was murdered in the vicinity of Davis canyon. His valuable outfit was stolen. He never reached the Colorado river."[8] For him, the only question remaining was whether the killer was a renegade Indian or a white outlaw. His accusation of murder changed the dynamic of the search, forcing the authorities to take action. The hunt for a missing person now became a murder investigation.

Utah authorities requested that the *Salt Lake Tribune* turn over all evidence gathered on the expedition, without waiting for the full account to appear in print. The attorney general immediately called for an intensive investigation into the disappearance and probable murder of Everett Ruess. And he promised to get to the bottom of the case and see justice done, if a crime had been committed. Based on circumstantial evidence, the names of four suspects, three Indians and a white man, were handed over to the attorney general's office. The locals now scaled back their efforts, letting the authorities take the lead.

LATE SUMMER 1935

By designating the incident a murder case, anyone who might have taken some of Everett's gear or personal items became a suspect. If one of the searchers had appropriated a Dutch oven or saddle blanket as compensation for the time and effort invested, he now had to keep it secret. And anything identifiable as having belonged to Everett would have to be destroyed or risk incriminating the person who possessed it.

Publicity surrounding the case put pressure on the federal government to intervene, but the FBI said the evidence was not sufficient to warrant an investigation. The agent in charge thought they first needed to find a body to see if a murder had actually been committed. In early September the Salt Lake newspapers reported that another possibility was being considered. Everett may have accidentally wandered into the hideout of a narcotics ring thought to be operating in the mountains of southern Utah and was shot to silence him. Cattle rustlers were also said to be active in the area, and the region was known as a fugitive hideout.

With claims of murder dominating the news coverage, a prominent rancher traveled to Salt Lake to set the record straight. John Black, representing the citizens of Escalante, called the murder theory "unfounded and fantastic" and believed the accusations were doing an injustice to the people of southern Utah. "No one in that part of the country thinks Everett Ruess was murdered," he said. "Of course, there's not much doubt but that he's dead, but there's no logical reason for believing he was deliberately done away with.... What probably happened is that he stumbled, slipped or fell in some way as to injure himself and it was impossible to get help. He laid there until the drifting sand caused by the frequent windstorms covered his body completely and left no trace. The danger of accidents in that country is very great, because of the ruggedness and loose rocks."[9]

R. H. Wooten, who headed the state bureau of criminal investigation, planned to lead a new search sometime in September. His effort, however, kept getting delayed until the snows forced a postponement, and by spring no funds were available for a state-sponsored search. The agents never turned up enough evidence to file charges, and the case went cold. But suspicions continued, and rumors of murder would keep surfacing for decades, fueled by personal feuds, drunken confessions, and death-bed retractions.

Some have considered a pair of cowboys, Joe Pollock and Keith Riddle, to be prime suspects. When camped in the vicinity of Davis Gulch, they reported hearing a voice shortly after the young artist was known to be missing, which would have been sometime in February. They were unable to locate the source of the sound. When Everett entered the Escalante Desert the previous November, both cowboys were facing charges of cattle rustling and scheduled to be tried in Kanab. The court postponed their case until the next session, leaving open the possibility that they returned to their winter range when Everett was still at Davis.

Pollock eventually served time in prison on a separate charge of cattle rustling. Riders working for the Escalante Cattle Growers Association caught him red-handed in the summer of 1940, having killed a cow belonging to Gail Bailey. Riddle joined the US Marines when World War II broke out. Despite all of the rumors and innuendo, no compelling evidence has linked either of them to the disappearance of Everett Ruess.

FALL 1935

Another incident occurred in September when a young man in search of solitude entered the Escalante Desert and barely made his way out. He took off on foot from Henrieville with the intention of reaching Bluff, 125 cliff-broken miles away. A couple of weeks later, Walt Allen and another cowboy were driving cattle about fifteen miles from Davis Gulch. They spotted a pair of feet sticking out from a clump of sagebrush. Allen, who had been involved in the early searches for Everett, discovered an unidentified man in starving condition unable to speak. He kept lapsing into unconsciousness, and only after they revived him did they learn he had been wandering around lost for many days. The cowboys shared what remained of their food and told him to stay with them for another day until they reached a food cache. But he insisted on following the trail back to Escalante and took off on his own.

Ten days later he staggered into a ranch near town, dazed and exhausted. When the sheriff arrived, he refused to talk, raising suspicions among some that he may have been involved in Everett's disappearance. On the drive to the jail in Panguitch, he opened up and identified himself as George Johnson, a thirty-year-old from Massachusetts. He told the sheriff he had headed into the wilderness because "I just like the hills, like to be alone, and thought it would improve my health."[10] The sheriff estimated Johnson, who ran out of food early on his walkabout, had covered about 200 miles. The Massachusetts man was held in jail until his fingerprints could be cleared through the federal database in Salt Lake.

The last search of 1935 ended as a ghost story. Once again the tenacious Jennings Allen sent a search party out for Everett Ruess. This time it consisted of one individual, T. J. Sparks, a "veteran desert man of Wolf Hole, Arizona."[11] In a news photo he stands next to his mule, looking rather forlorn in a pith helmet and Vandyke beard. His plan was to enter places inaccessible to earlier searchers using a two-hundred-foot rope he carried. Grubstaked by Jennings, Sparks was prepared to remain three months if necessary, and he was confident it wouldn't be necessary. He believed Everett had been murdered and declared he would either find the boy or locate his outfit.

After getting a lift to Fortymile Creek, the desert veteran set out alone down the Hole-in-the-Rock trail. It was a land, as one account described it, filled with danger. "For mile after mile it looms, a silent, yet living, breathing ghost-like land. It is mysterious and unconquerable. Few men have ever penetrated its remote sections."[12] Sparks reached Davis Gulch and descended the trail to the canyon bottom. From the start, he sensed the strangeness of his surroundings, and in his state of mind even the birds sounded different. As night came, the dark cliffs pressed close, and he sat listening.

The man from Wolf Hole began hearing strange voices coming from the rock ledges above. When daylight finally came, he climbed up to investigate and was unable to find any human trace, not a single footprint. Spooked, the desert veteran packed up and left, abandoning his cache of provisions meant to last sixty days. He reached Escalante, to the surprise of many, after having been gone only ten days. With his return, the search for Everett Ruess ended for that year.

THE INSCRIPTION

Navajo Mountain bulged to the southwest, a massive dome edged by strata fractured and upended, while the prow of Fiftymile Point dominated the west. In the northeast quarter stood the Henry Mountains, hazy with distance and as weightless as a mirage. Spreading out around us, the bare rock rolled into swells and sank into sand-trapping hollows. What appeared to be smooth undulations of terrain forced constant detours and scrambles when crossing it on foot. Greg Funseth took the lead, and we tried to pick out the line of least resistance to the rim of Davis Gulch. It was the early fall of 2009.

A couple of weeks before, I received a call from David Roberts, who was writing a book on Everett Ruess. He invited me to meet him in Escalante, where we would be taken to "a secret find." And letting the suspense build, he would only say it had something to do with the lost artist. A good mystery is hard to turn down, so I told him to sign me up. A few days before the trip, the writer divulged the details. Greg had contacted him about having found an unknown NEMO inscription near Davis Gulch. The site must have been missed by previous searchers, and the photos he sent matched the two known NEMO inscriptions. Roberts was convinced the new site was genuine.

"I am exploring southward to the Colorado where no one lives," wrote Everett in his last letter. The final clue to his disappearance was the word *Nemo*, found scratched on both a rock-art panel and on the doorsill of a ruin in Davis. For Everett, the word would have had literary associations, being familiar with Jules Verne's Captain Nemo and the hero of Homer's *Odyssey*, who had called himself Nemo to escape the cave of the Cyclops. Rising lake waters covered the NEMO inscriptions after the building of Glen

NEMO, 1934. An inscription found above Davis Gulch may have been carved by Everett Ruess shortly before he disappeared. Courtesy of Scott Thybony.

Canyon Dam and over time obliterated them. We were now on our way to check what might be the last remaining NEMO inscription.

Relying on friction alone, the three of us angled down a slickrock face toward a sandstone knoll. We entered the main chamber, crowded with breakdown and the matted sticks of a packrat midden, the dust untracked. I scanned the back wall and saw, more than six feet off the ground, an inscription reading "NEMO 1934."

Greg had told us he watched a film about Everett in the summer of 2001 and, intrigued by the story, headed alone to Davis Gulch. Searching for some evidence of the missing artist, he took the trail into the canyon and began exploring. The former climber, who now worked in the information technology field, looked for places that might have caught Everett's attention. After a while he spotted an unusual sandstone knob on the rim. Just the sort of place, he thought, to draw the young artist. Turning back, Greg found a set of Moqui steps leading out of the gulch and climbed them. He worked his way to the knoll and entered the cave. Thinking he might find fragments of Everett's sketchbook, he began by inspecting the floor. When he straightened up, the inscription was right in front of him.

The NEMO, small enough to cover with the palm of a hand, had been cut into the sandstone with a narrow tool rounding to a point, probably the punch on a jackknife. While the lettering resembled the two known inscriptions, I had a few reservations, which surprised David, who had no doubt it was real. Because other NEMOs have been faked, I wanted to take a close look. My initial concern was the fresh appearance of the inscription. But I had seen thousand-year-old pictographs in sheltered locations so unaged they could have been painted the week before. The alcove had protected the NEMO inscription from the weathering of rain and sun, and the sharp edges might argue for its authenticity. Someone going to the trouble of faking it would likely have tried to make it look older. Greg saw the carving years before on his only trip to the site. "The inscription," he said, "doesn't appear to have aged at all."

Another problem was the most obvious one: the site had been missed by search parties for the past seventy-five years. This could have been due to the searchers having concentrated their efforts inside the canyon and in the area north of the gulch. It was never clear how thoroughly they covered this sector. Tucked away in the rolling dunestone terrain, the site could have been overlooked, especially if they kept mainly to their saddles. "This could be the last known word of Everett Ruess," said David as I finished inspecting the carving.

I stooped down to peer through a circular passage in a stone bulkhead leading to the next chamber. Entering the room, I found a domed ceiling and a rounded opening framing Davis Gulch. As much porthole as window, it gave the room a nautical feel, like a ship's cabin. If Everett had made it this far, he would have found himself in a familiar setting, having sailed with Captain Nemo many times while reading his worn copy of *Twenty Thousand Leagues under the Sea*. An old fire ring and a few pieces of firewood indicated someone had camped here long ago. As I checked the interior, Greg sat motionless, staring through the stone portal, taking in the canyon scene below.

After spending a good hour at the site, we worked our way east along the rim. About a mile from the cave was a deep pocket, green with cottonwood, scrub oak, and a mosaic of seep-dependent plants. Water pooled below a rock face, supporting a hanging garden of maidenhair fern and red monkeyflower. And a string of potholes followed a runoff channel below the slickrock oasis. Not far beyond the unmapped spring, we reached the head of a Moqui-step route I had used years earlier. Centuries of rain and grit-charged winds had smoothed the footholds, leaving a sketchy traverse on a steep-angled face where a slip could be fatal. Still, the route was not as dangerous as some of the climbs Everett had pulled off in Tsegi Canyon. The bottom of the step trail began near his base camp, and I was convinced he would have climbed it even without the cave as an inducement. David and Greg returned to explore the rim country, and I continued to the bottom.

A creek flowed through the deep passageway of the canyon, undercutting the cliffs in graceful curves. Gambel oak bordered the stream along with bigtooth maple, willows, and a few giant cottonwoods felled by beaver. The elemental blue of the sky spread overhead, troweled on thick above the lithic reds and dense whites of the rock. The intensity of the colors came as a surprise. After more than a dozen years since my last trip, they had faded from memory faster than the shape of the land. I walked along a terrace to where Everett had made his camp. Tucked under a soaring cliff, it had been set at a south-facing bend in the canyon wall, a good location to catch the sun on a cold fall morning. The searchers had also found an outlying camp down canyon, near the ruin where he carved one of his NEMOs.

Leaving by the horse trail, I circled around the head of the gulch and reached our camp soon after the others had arrived. Greg had a long drive back to Salt Lake, while David and I settled in for a second night on the sandstone barrens. Roberts hauled out the wood he bought in town, and in the evening we sat around the campfire. Our conversation ranged widely, from forensic anthropology to writing, from Navajo Indians to Mormon history, and at one point he talked about an accident he had the previous year.

It happened at his office in Cambridge, Massachusetts, where he often stayed when writing late. He woke up in the middle of the night and, still groggy, mistook a door leading to the basement for the bathroom door next to it. Instead of entering the bathroom, he stepped into a void, falling headfirst. The climber, known for his major ascents in Alaska, nearly died on the basement steps. He remembered waking up and wondering what he was doing lying on the stairs in the dark. His injuries included a fractured skull, broken ribs and vertebrae, and a collapsed lung. At the hospital he contracted a staph infection followed by life-threatening renal failure. A

Navajo, David added, blamed his accident on the Comb Ridge burial. "You've been messing with Everett Ruess's bones," Denny Bellson had told him.

All summer Roberts had been embroiled in a controversy over the fate of Everett Ruess after publishing an article in *National Geographic Adventure*, announcing that the mystery had been solved. The year before, Bellson, a Navajo construction worker from Bluff, had taken Roberts to a burial on Comb Ridge, within view of Monument Valley. The Navajo told him a story, passed down through his family, about the murder of a young white man by Ute Indians sometime in the 1930s. His grandfather had witnessed the incident, watching from above as they chased him up Chinle Wash and battered him to death with rocks. After they left, the Navajo packed the body on his horse and gave it a proper burial high in the cliffs. He told no one about it until 1971, when he was diagnosed with cancer. An Enemyway had to be performed, so he returned to the body and cut a lock of hair to be used in the curing ceremony. His grandson, who heard the story secondhand, believed the victim was Everett Ruess and set out to find the bones. After first leading the sheriff and FBI to a burial that proved to be an Ancestral Puebloan mother and child, he found Comb Ridge Man.

Roberts contacted a tribal archaeologist, who agreed the burial was not Navajo and authorized an excavation. His assessment supported the Ruess theory, while a visit to the site by the sheriff and FBI, with a pair of criminal investigators from the Navajo police, identified it as a Navajo burial. Meanwhile, Roberts gathered a team of anthropologists and geneticists from the University of Colorado at Boulder. An initial DNA test was dismissed as inconclusive due to a degraded sample, while the forensic analysis of the physical remains concluded they were from a male Caucasian, between nineteen and twenty-two years old, and the same height as Ruess. A facial reconstruction, using fragments of bone, was superimposed on a known photograph of the artist, and anthropologist Dennis Van Gerven stated that it was a perfect match.

In what appeared to be conclusive proof, the results of a second DNA test confirmed a match. The investigators announced they had positively identified the remains of Everett Ruess, based on what the scientists called "essentially irrefutable evidence." Case closed. Major media outlets around the country covered the news, sending a shock wave through a surprisingly large community of people with a passionate attachment to the Everett

Ruess story. Emotions were stirred up on both sides of the issue, with true believers facing down the skeptics. Those who still expressed doubts were branded as flat-earthers, while some skeptics were privately accusing Roberts of perpetrating a hoax. It was all getting out of hand.

Over the summer I had talked with David and exchanged messages a number of times. Admitting he was wrong ten years before when he thought cattle rustlers had killed Ruess, he now held to the unshakable belief of having found the burial of Everett Ruess. The way I saw it, he was in a bind. A writer's job is to uncover a story and follow it. He had found a promising lead and pushed it as far as he could. Wanting the story to be true, he minimized the countervailing evidence. To me, nothing made sense about the Comb Ridge burial except the DNA evidence, which I found compelling. But other lines of evidence contradicted it and needed to be addressed.

The oral accounts of the murder didn't fit what I knew about traditional Navajo people. If a Navajo had witnessed the murder of an Anglo on their lands by Ute Indians, I thought, the incident would have been perceived as a threat to their own people and immediately reported to relatives. They would have tracked their former enemies to determine if other crimes had been committed and to learn their intentions. Unless a Navajo was involved, the killing would have been reported to a trader or Indian agent to keep the blame from being placed on them. And a traditional Navajo would not handle the body without some compelling reason. The fear of contagion by the spirit of the dead, which I had seen firsthand in more recent times, was real. Also, the artifact assemblage, the *jishchaa'*, was typical of a historical American Indian burial, most likely Navajo but possibly Ute or Paiute. A large quantity of colored beads and a few turquoise pendants had turned up during the excavation, along with a Navajo-style belt and buttons made from Liberty dimes. No item found with the burial could be linked to Ruess.

Another concern was the location of the burial. The remains were found in an area with other Navajo burials, 125 miles by trail from Everett's last known camp. Having left his burros in Davis Gulch, he would have needed to acquire horses from the Indians and somehow cross the Colorado River and get through the incredibly rough country beyond. Though not permanently inhabited, it was frequented by cowboys, trappers, Indians, and an occasional prospector. No one reported seeing the young artist, despite his family's having sent out inquiries to every rancher and trading post in the area. He would have had to purposely keep clear of others to avoid detection, very uncharacteristic of him. But humans sometimes act out of character.

What could not be explained away was the discrepancy in the teeth. Archaeologist Paul Leatherbury pursued this angle tenaciously. His interest in Everett Ruess was long-standing. I first met him years before, when he worked at the Museum of Northern Arizona and stopped by to tell me about a watercolor sketch, likely done by Everett, he had found in the collections. In early June he called to say he had located the dental records belonging to Everett in the University of Utah archives. The teeth from the burial, shown in photographs, did not match the dental records of the missing artist, which indicated that several fillings and gold-foil work had been done. The same teeth appeared unaltered in the photos. And no dental work had been found on the recovered teeth. The wear pattern on the teeth indicated a high-grit diet typical of someone eating corn ground on a stone metate, not a young Los Angeles artist. He was denied permission to examine the remains in person by Van Gerven, and the anthropologist considered his suggestion to have the teeth X-rayed to be unnecessary. Leatherbury continued to research the issue, getting the opinions of various dentists, who agreed with his assessment. The archaeologist eventually summarized his findings in a detailed forty-page document and circulated it to both skeptics and members of Roberts's team, who dismissed the dental charts as poor record keeping. The family of Everett Ruess took it more seriously.

They were on the verge of having the remains cremated and the ashes scattered over the Pacific Ocean when Utah state archaeologist Kevin Jones went on record questioning the identity of the bones. His standing added weight to the research done by Leatherbury, which the family later credited for their decision to retest the remains and prevent a terrible mistake from occurring. Recognizing their obligation to conduct a definitive test, they contacted one of the top laboratories in the world for analyzing older genetic material. The Armed Forces DNA Identification Laboratory agreed to assist, and everything now rested on the final study.

The results came back soon after our trip to Davis Gulch. The government scientists identified the remains as a Navajo man, not the missing artist, and they were returned to the tribal archaeologist for reburial. The scientists at the University of Colorado accepted the findings and attributed their error to problems with a new technology unsuited for analyzing older DNA.

In a remarkable convergence of mistakes, a team of experts had repeatedly found what they expected to find. The archaeological analysis, the forensic analysis of the skeletal remains, and the genetic analysis had confirmed one another. All were wrong. The bones proved not to be the remains of Everett Ruess, and the mystery of his disappearance was once again unsolved.

A CRACK IN THE RIM

Our trek to the NEMO inscription got me digging in the files when I returned to Flagstaff. The setting reminded me of a story I had heard years before of bones turning up in Davis Gulch sometime during the 1970s. I pulled out my notes from an interview with Roe Barney, who worked for the National Park Service at Lake Powell.

In 1991 I heard a rumor of human remains having been found and blocked out a couple of days to go to Page, Arizona. Dave Pape, the head of interpretation, took an interest in the story and checked the Park Service records and the warehouse where physical remains might have been stored. He was unable to find the bones or any mention of them. I next intercepted Roe Barney when he was coming off the lake. As maintenance foreman he had a job to finish, so I arranged to call him at his home in Escalante a few days later.

His unadorned account came across as credible. Roe told me he was motoring across Lake Powell in a Park Service boat when "a gentleman from California" flagged him down and handed him a sack of human bones.[1] The visitor had just returned from Davis Gulch, where he had been looking for Indian ruins, something he often did. He had left his wife and daughters on the boat and walked up the creek. The Californian spotted a sandstone knoll on top, which appeared to be a good location for a ruin. Finding a way out of the canyon bottom, he headed toward it.

He reached a broad ledge and, looking behind it, saw bones wedged deep within a crack. He "scaled in with a rope" and saw indications of a broken hip and fractured collar bone. Leaving most of the remains in place, he took a few of the bones for identification. He placed them in a sack, along with his name, and turned it over to the ranger. Being curious whether they were prehistoric Indian or more recent, the Californian asked to be notified once they had been studied. "Right away," Roe told me, "I thought about Ruess. I had heard stories about him growing up."

Upon returning to headquarters, then located at Wahweap, he gave the bones to his supervisor, and at that point they disappeared. Rereading the notes, I saw similarities in his description to the knoll with the NEMO inscription.

A year after the trip with Roberts, a friend and I were on foot, taking a direct route to the rim of Davis Gulch. We intended to search the area for any feature matching the Californian's "big ledge with a crack behind it." Knowing it would be hot, Tony Williams and I had packed up our gear the evening before to get an early start. We were on the move at dawn and had the GPS locked in to a cluster of satellites passing overhead. A message on the screen read, "North to Nemo," with an arrow pointing to a waypoint on the rim. Every pothole we passed was dry, and by eight in the morning it was already hot. Reaching the canyon edge, we worked our way above a line of cliffs dropping three hundred feet in sheer planes of Navajo sandstone. Soon the knoll came into view, and we worked down to the cave, sunk deep in shadows this time of day. I relocated the inscription and noticed the "NEMO 1934" showed no sign of having weathered over the past year.

Wanting to take a closer look at the old campsite, I entered the second chamber. A stillness permeated the confined space, and a subdued light filled the interior. An ancient juniper had been dragged in for firewood, and a small ring of stones had been placed against the far wall, containing a scatter of charcoal mixed with sand. From the absence of smoke stains, it appeared to have been used for only a night or two. A flat stone, set on rocks, sat next to it for keeping things off the sand, an arrangement showing the work of an experienced hand. By the cliffside opening, a row of stones had been laid out for leveling the sandy floor wide enough for a single bedroll. The site contained no evidence of prehistoric use, not even a potsherd or chert flake.

The most intriguing feature was a juniper-root stool with a sandstone slab placed on top for a comfortable seat. It wasn't next to the campfire but positioned to take advantage of the dramatic view of Davis Gulch framed by the rock window. It made an ideal perch for someone to sit and sketch the scene below. Everett had mentioned building a stone seat at one of his

The cave. Author Scott Thybony stands in a sandstone chamber overlooking Davis Gulch, searching for clues to the disappearance of the young artist. Courtesy of Anthony Williams.

camps in Canyon de Chelly, and sitting on the juniper roots I was beginning to think of this as his camp. When Tony joined me, he was having similar thoughts. "I'm assuming," he said, "this was his last stop."

We next worked below the cave to the brow of the cliff. Looking upstream, I immediately saw a vertical crack where a section of cliff had separated from the rim. It reached almost to the streambed far below. Pointing this out to Tony, he noticed a wide ledge formed by the top of the spall, fitting the description given by the Californian. I could imagine him walking up the creek in the 1970s in search of ruins. He would have seen any number of sandstone domes rimming the canyon, but only this one had the potential for sheltering a prehistoric site. Then he found a way to reach it, using the Indian foothold route. The two of us ascended a steep rib of sandstone for a better look at where the edge of the cliff had cracked open.

As we began to traverse across the slickrock face above it, I noticed hematite concretions covering the micro ledge we followed. Known as Moqui marbles, they made the footing treacherous. A wrong move could result in an accelerating slide of twenty-five feet, ending with a free fall into the sandstone crevasse. Tony and I had enough experience scrambling on slickrock to know when to back off. Changing course, we angled up the rock to a safer route and climbed down to a ledge with a stunted hackberry tree. We checked it carefully to make sure it would serve as a secure anchor point. Tony had a rope and climbing gear back at the truck, so we returned the next morning.

After he rigged the rope to his satisfaction, I double-checked his work, following standard practice. Soon he was rappelling over the edge and about thirty feet down stopped on top of the slab and unclipped. Empty space fell away on three sides of the landing. Using a flashlight, he took his time inspecting the cleft behind the ledge, which formed a natural trap. He jumared back up the rope and told me, "This has to be it. Everything fits." How far the crack extended he couldn't say, and whether anything was buried in the sand beyond reach couldn't be determined. If this was where the Californian had found the bones, he may have loosened what remained of the skeleton by removing some of them. Falling to the inaccessible floor, they would have washed out during heavy downpours. "Every rainstorm would flush the crack," Tony said, "and drain toward the tight end."

A year later I returned with my own gear and rappelled down to the ledge. Once off rope I worked into the wider section of the crack along a slanting floor. It had a slot-canyon feel to it—perpetual twilight, cliff walls pressing close, a fissure of sky above. The crevice was two feet wide where I entered and sloped downward to a narrow crack. The far end flared open at the top to form a rock funnel and pinched down to only four inches wide. I shone my headlamp to the bottom fifteen feet below and realized any pieces of bone would have been lost in the interstices of the crack system. Backtracking, I climbed onto the spall and studied the slickrock slope above. Anyone taking a slide down the face would hit the ledge I was standing on with enough force to cause major injury, if not death, before jamming deep in the crack.

The more I studied it, the more the entire configuration of terrain and circumstance had a compelling fit. I could see the incident playing out clearly. Distracted by the beauty around him, the explorer's attention may have wandered for a second as he stepped on a loose rock or a thin ledge snapped underfoot. Suddenly, he was in a slide, unable to arrest his fall before going over the edge. In an instant, the rock swallowed him, leaving no trace. I ascended the rope and joined Tony on top.

The slickrock of southern Utah, mostly Navajo sandstone, provides good friction for scrambling until it gets wet. Then the footing becomes slippery, and the thin bedding planes, normally solid, can crumble under weight. When Everett headed south on the Hole-in-the-Rock trail, a three-day rainstorm broke a long drought, increasing the hazards. And he was known to be cliff climbing. The searchers found his tracks leading up a Moqui-step route to the rim. At first they worked on the assumption that he had fallen until they were unable to find a body, and at that point they started piecing together alternate explanations.

Not knowing what happened to Everett Ruess left the field clear for the imagination to run unchecked. At one time or another, people have had him die from thirst while stuck on a ledge or from starvation after breaking a leg. They have had him swallowed by quicksand, buried under rockfall, frozen in the deep snows of winter, drowned in the river, or simply dead by his own hand. They have had him murdered by drug smugglers and cattle rustlers, fundamentalist Mormons and jealous cowboys. They have had renegade Indians fell him with an ax, drown him in a water pocket, and beat him to death with rocks. The earliest theory, and still the most probable, was that he died in a fall. Those who knew him best and understood the risks he took, such as archaeologist Clay Lockett, believed it. And those who knew the dangers of the terrain he explored, such as John Wetherill, believed it.

Whether he slid into the crack near the inscription remains an open question. If not there, then a similar combination of cliff and crevice makes the most sense to me. Caught deep in a sandstone crevasse, the body was never located. The gear he left behind was picked up by sheepherders, cowboys, or searchers and either kept secret or destroyed when the hunt for the missing artist became a murder investigation. After walking the ground, after digging through the archives and sifting the evidence, I came to a straightforward conclusion: Everett Ruess died in a fall.

At one time I was having a conversation about the missing artist with a woman who looked at me with a sad expression, or maybe it was disappointment. "Please don't nail it down," she said. "Leave it a mystery." Having finished my investigations, the mystery remained intact.

The disappearance of Everett Ruess holds a certain fascination, but the essential interest for me centers on the life he created, the aesthetics of his travels. Much like a painting, his story had a way of drawing me into a landscape of the imagination. I could connect with those moments when he was experiencing the Southwest for the first time, letting his enthusiasm expand to fill the big open spaces he crossed. Following his journeys, I could relive the struggles of someone coming to terms with the hard beauty of the canyons and could see his life taking shape in all its bold brushstrokes and saturated colors. And finally, I came to see his life as a work unfinished, a corner of the canvas left blank.

EPILOGUE
Two Lives and a Legend

A document surfaced near the end of my research mentioning the solitary artist, the bone hunter, and the hunt for the woodcutter's daughter. In a letter typed on official stationery, Sheriff Lawrence Palmer wrote to the parents of Everett Ruess. The sheriff was only a few years older than their son and had just returned from a mad chase after the Johns Canyon killer. Writing on March 9, 1935, the lawman tried to reassure them by saying he had located another young man, a "Mr. Thraupp of the Museum."[1] But he had not found any evidence of their missing son. "I just covered all the territory in and around where you reported that your son was going on a Man Hunt connected with the terrible Murder committed in our County last week, and I saw or heard nothing of your son Everett....I will continue to look for Everett, but sincerely hope that you have some word of him before now." For the rest of their lives, the parents waited for a word that never came. The family of Dan Thrapp was more fortunate.

The explorer returned to New York City after emerging from the wilds of Utah only to learn he had lost his job at the American Museum of Natural History. Making a quick pivot, Dan decided to become a journalist. His confidence must have been boosted by having already received a paycheck for writing about his canyon adventures. For the next several months, he pounded on the doors of newspaper offices, trying to land a job. Without experience or credentials, no editor would hire him, so he headed back to college for his degree. He graduated from the prestigious School of Journalism at the University of Missouri in 1938 and began work as a correspondent for the United Press news agency.

He was stationed in Argentina when word of the attack on Pearl Harbor reached him. His decision to enlist in the military wasn't unusual in that time of national crisis, only his novel way of going about it. To board a ship for the States, he took an indirect route, setting out with a friend on a two-month journey. They crossed the Andes by mule and continued by train to Lima, Peru. He joined the US Army as a private and by the end of the war held the rank of captain, having earned four battle stars. As a mule-pack specialist, his job was to provide long-eared transport for a special-operations command operating in Burma and China. At the war's end he resumed his career, reporting from the London bureau of United Press before covering the civil war in Greece. He posted dispatches describing how he came under fire while accompanying Greek soldiers on a raid and wrote a moving account of an execution of guerrilla fighters that he had witnessed. One of his articles began, "This is the kind of war where mules are more important than machinery . . ."[2] His kind of war.

For the last twenty-four years of his career, he served as religion editor of the *Los Angeles Times*. He began without much training in the field, which helped him to be objective, and over time his respect for religion grew strong. And he continued to have a passion for the West, becoming the leading authority on the Apache wars and a biographer of the frontier period. Skeptical of official records, he made a point of studying the terrain firsthand before writing about it. His interest in the wilderness remained strong, and he stayed active in the Sierra Club. Always curious about the lives of others, he rarely talked about himself, and a close friend of his told me he never mentioned his solo travels as a young man. A *New York Times* obituary in 1994 tagged him as "Chronicler of the West."[3]

During one phase of my research, I was going through the archives when a photograph of Dan in his later years caught my attention. Something about him looked familiar, and I realized we had met. I called Winn Bundy at the Singing Wind Bookshop on her ranch in southern Arizona. Years before, she had invited me to talk to a group of historians in Tucson and now confirmed having introduced us. He was sitting with his wife, Janice, who spoke about a journey Dan had taken as a young man through the canyons of Utah. He gave a slight smile when she suggested somebody should write about it, but let her do the talking. At the time I had to focus solely on paying assignments and couldn't let myself get sidetracked. I forgot about the encounter, or so I thought.

When Dan returned to the Utah canyons years after his explorations, the place was no longer the wild country he remembered. "Now it is all roaded up," he said, "and tamed down."[4]

Lucy Garrett lived a year packed with enough violence and tragedy to have scarred a young girl for life. She was held captive by a murderer who manipulated her through lies and threats of violence. Determined to stay alive, she never gave up hope. Lucy not only beat the odds and survived her ordeal, but also managed to pull her life together. After the trial of Clint Palmer, the Texas authorities had to decide what to do with their star witness.

Her closest relatives were barely able to care for their own children during the Depression years. So the best place for her, court officials decided, was the Texas State Training School for Girls in Gainesville. The institution served as a home for delinquent and dependent girls, providing an education in the skills necessary to live independently. The judge, needing a legal justification, found her guilty of having consorted with a known criminal. Lucy served her sentence and returned to live with relatives when she turned eighteen. With a strong will and a craving for knowledge, she was determined to succeed and put herself through business school. In 1941 she married Hermon Sconce, who was serving as a soldier at the time. She loved children but due to medical complications was able to have only one son, Clyde. "She doted on him completely," said her daughter-in-law, Linda Sconce.[5] And Lucy remembered another child. "Even in later years," Linda said, "she talked about cuddling her little baby. She was talking about the baby she lost in Utah."

Detective magazines continued to tell her story, with varying degrees of accuracy and lurid detail, into the 1970s. Her ordeal even appeared in comic-book form with the forensic wizardry of Dr. Looney playing a key role in solving the murder of her father. Living until 1991, she never talked about her year of terror and kept her past a secret.

While waiting in jail for the outcome of his appeal, Clint Palmer tried to convince reporters he was the victim of an unjust fate. His troubles could be traced back to World War I, he claimed, when he was gassed and wounded during the terrible trench warfare in France. His play for sympathy from the press came soon after jailers found six hacksaw blades hidden in his clothing. The court upheld his sentence, and he was transferred to the Texas State Penitentiary at Huntsville. Utah officials had a hold order placed on him, ensuring they would be notified if Palmer was ever paroled. Upon his release, they would have the option to prosecute him for the double murder he had committed in Utah.

During his incarceration, Clint Palmer became a champion bronc rider in the Texas Prison Rodeo. The inmates wore black-and-white-striped uniforms while participating in "the wildest show behind bars." Cowboy Palmer, as he was known, barely survived his first rodeo. Bucked off his horse, he was dragged all around the arena until they could rescue him. Thought to be dead, he stood up a few minutes later and shook himself off. "I feel fine," he told them.[6] Palmer went on to compete in the annual rodeo until he was sixty-five years old, a painful run to contemplate. He also became an accomplished saddle maker and in his last few years saw the light and got religion. Seeking to make amends, he wrote Bill Oliver's son, asking for forgiveness. Harrison, who never returned to Johns Canyon after the shooting, did not respond to the letter.

Palmer often delivered sermons to other inmates, and while in the prison chapel he suffered a heart attack in 1969. He had refused parole over the years, knowing he would have to face justice in Utah and probable execution for the Johns Canyon killings. As they carried him to the prison hospital, his last words were, "Now they can't hang me."[7] A few minutes later he was dead.

At the start I was reluctant to step into the coils of the Everett Ruess story, knowing the difficulty of untangling the facts from a large body of inspired speculation. But he was an integral part of the story, and it was hard not to be intrigued by his disappearance. After he went missing, letters of sympathy streamed into the Ruess home in Los Angeles, along with advice from an assortment of astrologers, crystal-ball gazers, and clairvoyants. Even Marie Ogden from the Home of Truth contacted the family, writing a letter in longhand rather than on her prophetic typewriter. Both friends and strangers offered a range of conjectures and intuitions, declaring the Ruesses' son had purposely disappeared or had suffered amnesia. And for years Everett sightings were reported from Florida to Mexico. The family checked the more reasonable leads, following whatever thread of hope they provided.

After 1935 the Ruess family had little contact with the con artist Neal Johnson. His fate overtook him sometime in the 1940s when his body was found hanging in a mine shaft across the Colorado River, another unsolved murder. And the searches continued. In 1948 river runner Harry Aleson guided Stella Ruess to Davis Gulch, where she climbed to the ruin with the NEMO inscription. A disappearance is a deep loss without the consolation of a funeral, so she used her trek as a way of grieving. That same year Edson Alvey, a summertime cowboy and schoolteacher from Escalante, left his own inscription in an overhang along the Escalante River.

Edson Alvey
In Search of Nemo
June 19, 1948[8]

Throughout the 1950s Alvey looked for the remains of Everett Ruess. He teamed up with cowboy Delane Griffin to again comb the canyons in the vicinity of the last known camp. Delane told me the only place they found any sign of the missing artist was in Davis Gulch, and they concluded he hadn't been there long before he disappeared. Alvey was hired as the guide for a crew of archaeologists surveying the Escalante River country in 1957. Constantly on the lookout for any clues to the disappearance, they made a detailed study of Davis Gulch. Some crew members worked their way into nearby Cottonwood Canyon and found the remains of an old camp in a rock shelter. Covered by rocks as if intentionally hidden, a collection of heavily rusted eating utensils and cooking gear turned up. A box of razors from a Los Angeles drugstore led them to wonder if they had found one of Everett's camps. His parents were never certain the items had belonged to their son, and eventually Stella came to the opinion they were not part of his outfit. What began as a promising lead brought the family no closer to an answer.

Wilderness outfitter Ken Sleight took up the search in the 1960s. He based his guide service out of Escalante for a couple of years and made multiple trips scouring the country where Everett went missing. Some of the wranglers who worked for him had been on the search parties in 1935. "They didn't know what happened to him," Ken told me as we talked at his ranch outside Moab. "They guessed like everybody else. They wondered what the hell happened to the kid."[9] After years of investigation, the outfitter concluded that Everett tried to cross the Colorado River at the foot of Hole-in-the-Rock. The strong, swirling currents made a crossing dangerous, and the cold water compounded the difficulties. "He just overestimated his ability," Ken said. "Sure, I think he drowned. There's no doubt in my mind. It's a good way to close it."

Over the years Everett Ruess took on a literary afterlife in the writings of Wallace Stegner, Edward Abbey, and Jon Krakauer. The wandering artist became transformed into an environmental icon and wilderness legend, with his story retold in film and onstage. At one time his smiling image even appeared on the label of Vagabond Ale, a sign Everett had finally become a celebrity.

During the course of writing the book, I was involved in various searches for persons lost and missing. People still disappear without a trace in this country, and two of them remain missing. A final incident conveys the essential strangeness of it all.

A tent stood empty on the South Rim of the Grand Canyon in a camp where no one had returned for days. Called to investigate, a park ranger looked for signs of trouble and found no evidence of a robbery or violence. Nothing had been disturbed. He radioed dispatch, and soon a ground and air search began for the overdue hiker. As unlikely as it seemed, a man had disappeared without a trace in a national park visited by millions of people each year.

Tracking dogs arrived on the scene and picked up a scent leading to the canyon rim. Having interviewed those closest to the missing man, investigators found no reason to suspect suicide. His routine was to take solo day hikes, making a fall a stronger possibility than a jump. A team flew in below the cliffs and began combing the talus slopes. They soon located the body of an adult male three hundred feet under the rim and assumed it was the target of their search, case closed. But on closer inspection, the physical remains didn't match the missing hiker. The search party had found another victim, a man they didn't know had disappeared.

When Ken Phillips, the head of search and rescue, first told me about this incident, I thought the chances of unintentionally coming upon another body would be next to zero. But Ken shook his head. "That's happened three times," he said. "Three times."[10] They sought one victim only to find another.

In a country where canyons lie sunk within canyons and tiers of cliffs stack one on top of another, the mysteries come layered.

NOTES

PROLOGUE

1. "Well, it's a hell of a long story": Melvin Gaines, interview with the author, Mexican Hat, UT, November 6, 2008.

THE EXPEDITION

Key sources for the excavation of the dinosaur bones at the Baker Ranch include two accounts written by Barnum Brown for *Natural History* in 1935 and Roland Bird's recollections in *Bones for Barnum Brown*. Newspaper coverage was especially thorough in the *New York Times*.

1. "the crummy jail": "Journal of Dan Thrapp," February 1933, Thrapp Collection.
2. "Doggone! The other night I dreamt of Sally": Ibid.
3. "Old Barnum Brown is the big shot": Dan Thrapp to Dorothy Thrapp, August 1933, Thrapp Collection.
4. "A windstorm was carrying plenty of dust": "Journal of Dan Thrapp," June 9, 1934, Thrapp Collection.
5. "I'll be damned": Ibid.

BELOW THE BIGHORNS

1. "It was my job": "Journal of Dan Thrapp," August 9, 1934, Thrapp Collection.
2. "So far have found at least 6": Dan Thrapp to his father, June 14, 1934, Thrapp Collection.
3. "In more than thirty years of fossil-hunting": *New York Times*, July 29, 1934.
4. "Brown is plenty tough": "Journal of Dan Thrapp," August 11, 1934, Thrapp Collection.
5. "I think it will be a valuable experience": Ibid., June 19, 1934.
6. "Hoss!": Interview with Dan Thrapp's sister, Bea Zeeck, May 19, 2009.
7. "Sounds easy": "Journal of Dan Thrapp," August 9, 1934, Thrapp Collection.
8. "She's the best woman rider": Ibid., August 31, 1934.
9. "That's real love": Ibid., September 25, 1934.

WEST OF SOLITUDE

My primary source on Art Murry and the Horsethief Ranch comes from Michael Behrendt's fine book *Horsethief Ranch: An Oral History*.

1. "erroneous and misleading": "Report of the 1925 San Juan Expedition of the National Geographic Society," January 2, 1924, Gary Topping Papers.
2. "Now I have no doubt but Murry": T. S. Brown to Frank Thrapp, May 9, 1935, Thrapp Collection.
3. "He has offered to sell me": "Journal of Dan Thrapp," November 24, 1934, Thrapp Collection.
4. "Lola is going to marry": Ibid.
5. "like traveling on another planet": Edward T. Hall, *West of the Thirties: Discoveries among the Navajo and Hopi*, xxviii.

HORSETHIEF RANCH

All quotes come from Scott Thybony, fieldnotes, "Horsethief Ranch," March 19, 2009.

LABYRINTH, A WAY IN

1. "Ben was apt to shrink the truth": Thrapp to his parents, n.d., but probably September 1931. He also talked about Ben Black in a letter to his parents, August 31, 1931, Thrapp Collection.
2. "Dan didn't bend for anybody": Interview with Bea Zeeck, May 19, 2009.
3. "the edge of the unknown country": *Salt Lake Telegram*, February 28, 1935.
4. "It starts": Note on the back of photograph 467, Thrapp Collection.
5. "Well, I'm on my own again": "Journal of Dan Thrapp," December 10, 1934, Thrapp Collection.
6. "Right now I'm camped on the White Rim": Ibid.

DESOLATION CAMP

1. "There is no straight across": "Journal of Dan Thrapp," December 11, 1934, Thrapp Collection.
2. "Today was a day of trials": Ibid.
3. "There were one or two places": Ibid., December 15, 1934.

WAITING FOR DAYLIGHT

1. "I sure cooked a real feed": "Journal of Dan Thrapp," December 17, 1934, Thrapp Collection.
2. "Only after some very ticklish work": *Deseret News*, March 5, 1935.
3. "They had strayed": "Journal of Dan Thrapp," December 20, 1934, Thrapp Collection.

WINTER CROSSING

1. "It was one miserable night": "Journal of Dan Thrapp," December 20, 1934, Thrapp Collection.
2. "We thought it over": Ibid.
3. "one long, hard pull": Ibid., December 23, 1934.

THE NEEDLES

My primary source for the Canyonlands National Park adventure is fieldnotes, "The Needles," October 25–28, 2001. Of the many available sources on Marie Ogden, the most useful were "The Home of Truth: The Metaphysical World of Marie Ogden," a master's thesis by Stanley Thayne, and Wallace Stegner's account in *Mormon Country*. The events unfolding at the Home of Truth were widely covered at the time, especially in the Utah newspapers.

1. "Those are supposed to be a Moqui family": Interview with Heidi Redd, May 8, 1992.
2. "The days of tribulation are at hand": *Salt Lake Telegram*, October 27, 1936.
3. "It cannot be!": Thayne, "Home of Truth," 67.
4. "She told me the woman wasn't dead": Ibid., 1.
5. "I hope you didn't have to drive far": Thybony, fieldnotes, October 25–28, 2001.

CIRCLING THE BLUES

1. "Ate enough for two men": "Journal of Dan Thrapp," December 27, 1934, Thrapp Collection.
2. "The last two miles": Ibid., December 28, 1934.
3. "I sure hated to turn back": Ibid., December 30, 1934.
4. "He had a real love of the West": Interview with Bea Zeeck, May 19, 2009.
5. "26 miles and I am so stiff": Dan Thrapp to Edgar Nagel, n.d. [1929], Thrapp Collection.
6. "The discovery of new land": Thrapp, "My Visit with Admiral Byrd," n.d., Thrapp Collection.
7. "They had neither of them ever seen": "Journal of Dan Thrapp," January 6, 1935, Thrapp Collection.
8. "An Indian sheepherder stopped to talk": Ibid.
9. "We're not going to let old Posey": John Rogers interview, Duke Indian Oral History Project, 8.
10. "Just as we came through the last grove": "Journal of Dan Thrapp," January 8, 1935, Thrapp Collection.
11. "the most beautiful spring": Ibid., January 8, 1935.
12. "I found enough pieces": Ibid., January 9, 1935.

13. "He was one of the wildest cowmen": DeReese Nielson, "Cattle Industry in Southeastern Utah Project," 16.

14. "Walt and I sure kidded him": "Journal of Dan Thrapp," January 10, 1935, Thrapp Collection.

FAR REACHES

1. "It was so doggone cold": "Journal of Dan Thrapp," January 18, 1935, Thrapp Collection.

2. "the local calaboose": *San Juan Record*, January 3, 1935.

3. "The trail was a hard one": "Journal of Dan Thrapp," January 22, 1935, Thrapp Collection.

4. "Poor Old Bob felt pretty bad": Ibid.

5. "a beautiful piece of country": Ibid., January 25, 1935.

6. "He said he knew this country": Ibid., January 27, 1935.

7. "Just after sunset": Ibid.

THE BACKBONE

My primary sources for this chapter are three sets of fieldnotes: "The Backbone," April 4–7, 2009; "The Chute," May 3–6, 2009; and "Mikes Canyon," June 6–8, 2009.

1. "This has always been hideout country": Interview with Rigby Wright, November 21, 2008.

BACK TRAIL

1. "A five mile walk": "Journal of Dan Thrapp," January 30, 1935, Thrapp Collection.

2. "I don't mind telling you": Ibid.

3. "ran with a smooth, oily movement": Hugh D. Miser, *The San Juan Canyon of Southeastern Utah*, 58.

4. "I was too scared to think": "Journal of Dan Thrapp," January 30, 1935, Thrapp Collection.

5. "Hope those cowpunchers don't kick": Ibid., February 5, 1935.

6. "I shouted myself hoarse at her": Ibid., February 11, 1935.

7. "We didn't know where": Ibid., February 15, 1935.

8. "This is old desperado country": Ibid., February 14, 1935.

9. "That sets kind of hard": Ibid., February 19, 1935.

10. "While we were hunting it": Ibid., February 24, 1935.

BELOW THE COMB

1. "Who's that?": *Journal of Dan Thrapp*, February 27, 1935.

2. "I may have killed her": Ibid.

TRACKINGS

1. "That took us pretty well out of country": Leland Tidwell, "Report of Search for Young Thrapp," n.d. [March 1935], Thrapp Collection.
2. "Murry tryed to talk": T. S. Brown to Frank Thrapp, February 26, 1935, Thrapp Collection.
3. "one chance in a thousand": *Salt Lake Telegram*, February 28, 1935.
4. "Mr. Tidwell thinks the boy alive": T. S. Brown to F. Thrapp, February 23, 1935, Thrapp Collection.
5. "Don't have any fear of foul play": Ibid., February 26, 1935.
6. "Fear Felt Daniel Thrapp May Have Drowned": Associated Press, March 2, 1935.
7. "It was a disagreeable trip": Tidwell, "Report of Search for Young Thrapp."
8. "I and my husband have never known": Mr. and Mrs. Milo Howe to Mr. and Mrs. Thrapp, February 21, 1935, Thrapp Collection.
9. "The boy picked a tough country": A. R. Kleindienst to F. Thrapp, February 25, 1935, Thrapp Collection.
10. "He said he had plenty of food": *Salt Lake Telegram*, March 2, 1935.
11. "keen-eyed Indians": *Salt Lake Telegram*, February 28, 1935.
12. "a tall, rangy lad": *Salt Lake Telegram*, March 1, 1935.
13. "No one is better able": *New York Times*, February 27, 1935.
14. "I am sure Dan did not lose": F. Thrapp to Barnum Brown, February 27, 1935, Thrapp Collection.
15. "We all extend to you our sympathy": B. Brown to F. Thrapp, February 28, 1935, Thrapp Collection.
16. "An airplane roared above": Associated Press, *Ogden Standard-Examiner*, March 2, 1935.
17. "Yes, I've been with a young fellow": *Deseret News*, March 5, 1935.
18. "What's the matter?": Ibid.
19. "Thrapp closed his three months adventure": Ibid.
20. "The old story about water holes": "Journal of Dan Thrapp," March 4, 1935, Thrapp Collection.
21. "We crossed the Wasatch Plateau": Ibid., March 5, 1935.
22. "Gosh, that little washing my hands": *Deseret News*, March 5, 1935.
23. "Today has certainly been": "Journal of Dan Thrapp," March 5, 1935, Thrapp Collection.
24. "Al and Mahlon are talking of leaving": Ibid., March 7, 1935.
25. "They're going to try Palmer": Ibid., March 10, 1935.
26. "Sure felt like a million": Ibid., March 11, 1935.
27. "Brown said there was no money": Ibid., March 27, 1935.
28. "Dan would have made his way back alone": F. Thrapp to T. S. Brown, March 21, 1935, Thrapp Collection.

THE ROADSIDE

1. "He told us that he had fought this rooster": Lucile Garrett, grand jury testimony, March 7, 1935, Utah State Historical Society, Utah State History Research Library and Collections.
2. "Dillard Garrett, at the time he came to my office": *Greenville (TX) Morning Herald*, April 11, 1935.
3. "At first he was terrible mad": Garrett, grand jury testimony, March 7, 1935.
4. "psychosis, with mental deficiency": Psychiatrist D. E. Singleton to warden E. G. Zerbst, November 27, 1933, United States Penitentiary, Leavenworth, KS.

ACROSS THE RED RIVER

1. "Well, if we are going over to the old man's house": Garrett, grand jury testimony, March 7, 1935.
2. "Do you know you are going to see your father?": *Greenville (TX) Morning Herald*, April 12, 1935.

ON THE RUN

1. "I told him that I did not want to stay with him": Garrett, grand jury testimony, March 7, 1935.
2. "This defendant is a notorius character": Gilberto Espinosa, "Parole Report by United States Attorney."
3. "He hurt me terrible": Garrett, grand jury testimony, March 7, 1935.
4. "I wanted to find my daddy": Ibid.
5. "He said in the letter": Ibid.
6. "He told me to never mention my daddy": Ibid.

A GUN WITHIN REACH

1. "I heard one guy shot another": Thybony, fieldnotes, "North Texas by West," May 17–22, 2009.
2. "The people of Peerless, Texas": Ibid.
3. "I stood out there in the middle": W. K. Stratton, *Chasing the Rodeo: On Wild Rides and Big Dreams, Broken Hearts and Broken Bones, and One Man's Search for the West*, 17.
4. "She didn't talk about this": Thybony, fieldnotes, "North Texas by West."

EMPTY QUARTER

1. "She's older than she looks": Ray Hunt, "The Murder of Norris Shumway and Bill Oliver," 9.
2. "such a frail, little frightened girl": William Oliver, "The Life Story of William Edward Oliver, 1858–1935," 21.
3. "He didn't waste words": Ibid., 33.

4. "He was a man that wasn't scared of anybody": Hunt, "Murder of Shumway and Oliver," 11.
5. "Palmer didn't want the girl to be left alone": Ibid., 5.
6. "All he did there in Bluff": Garrett, grand jury testimony, March 7, 1935.
7. "I'm going to have to kill that fellow": Hunt, "Murder of Shumway and Oliver," 8–9.
8. "They got into a feud": Nielson, "Cattle Industry in Southeastern Utah Project," 52.
9. "Me and another old boy": Ernie Pyle, "Rambling Reporter," *Pittsburgh Press*, August 5, 1939.
10. "It haunts me now": Edward T. Hall, *West of the Thirties: Discoveries among the Navajo and Hopi*, 136.
11. "I was pregnant and beginning to get big": Garrett, grand jury testimony, March 7, 1935.
12. "She said one time": Hunt, "Murder of Shumway and Oliver," 6.
13. "Clinton Palmer was sent for": Garrett, grand jury testimony, March 7, 1935.

SKELETON MURDER CASE

1. "A man does not burn his own clothes": W. C. Reneau, "Murdering Casanova of the Cattle Country," pt. 2, 70.

THE SHOOT-OUT

1. "We had quite a large herd": Oliver, "Life Story," 20.
2. "They were bound for the north breaks": *Salt Lake Tribune*, March 4, 1935.
3. "It is hard to pin anything on anyone": Associated Press, *Reading (CA) Eagle*, March 10, 1935.
4. "I asked Goulding to remove his sheep": Oliver, "Life Story," 20.
5. "What do you mean, old man": Garrett, grand jury testimony, March 7, 1935.
6. "No, you son-of-a-bitch": Garrett, deposition, March 14, 1935.
7. "I saw this": Garrett, grand jury testimony, March 7, 1935.
8. "I saw him put a rope to the old man": Ibid.
9. "Clinton told me that he was going ": Ibid.
10. "If Shumway didn't talk": Garrett, deposition, March 14, 1935.

HAUNTED CANYON

1. "They think it's haunted": Thybony, fieldnotes, February 28–March 1, 2009.
2. "After the sun went down": Hunt, "Murder of Shumway and Oliver," 3–4.
3. "He took that girl": Thybony, backnotes, March 1, 2009.
4. "I'm still haunted": Interview with Wright, November 21, 2008.
5. "Rigby is the kind of guy": Interview with Chuck LaRue, November 19, 2008.
6. "There's a hell of a lot of this country": Interview with Wright, November 21, 2008.

THE MANHUNT

1. "Ha'át'ííshą'?": Harry Goulding, "Depositions Regarding the Oliver-Shumway Murders in San Juan Country, Utah in 1934, 1935," March 9, 1935, Utah State Historical Society, Utah State History Research Library and Collections, 4; Robert W. Young and William Morgan, *The Navajo Language: A Grammar and Colloquial Dictionary*, 1994.
2. "the road of flight": John Steinbeck, *Grapes of Wrath*, 118.
3. "I was 25-years old": Lawrence Palmer, "William Oliver & Norris Shumway."
4. "Oliver himself, while an old Indian fighter": *Salt Lake Telegram*, March 7, 1935.
5. "I thought I would go wild with grief": Oliver, "Life Story," 21.
6. "I was afraid someone was going to kill Goulding": Paul Black, "Paul Black's Story (in His Own Hand Writing) of Sheriff Oliver & Norris Shumway Murder," 8.
7. "Six-Guns Blaze": *Albuquerque Journal*, July 7, 1935.
8. "Two-Gun Jimmy": *Salt Lake Tribune*, March 7, 1935, 3.
9. "We checked the gambling joints": Palmer, "Oliver & Shumway."
10. "Utah Slayer Is Captured": *Deseret News*, March 6, 1935.
11. "He was crazy mad": Black, "Paul Black's Story," 8.
12. "Though Deepening Trials": *Salt Lake Tribune*, March 8, 1935.

TO THE SULPHUR RIVER

1. "What are you doing here?": Associated Press, *Lubbock (TX) Morning Avalanche*, April 12, 1935.
2. "The only reason why I hate to trace": *Hopkins County (TX) Echo*, April 19, 1935.
3. "I was supposed to go under the name": *Lubbock (TX) Morning Avalanche*, April 12, 1935.
4. "I kept hammering away at him": Reneau, "Murdering Casanova," pt. 3, 58.
5. "I tried fatherly admonition": Ibid.
6. "If my daddy's been killed": Ibid.
7. "I killed Oliver and Shumway": *Denver Morning News*, March 7, 1935, 1.
8. "I haven't got any hot seat coming": Associated Press, *Lubbock (TX) Morning Avalanche*, March 7, 1935, 11.
9. "I am going to kill Palmer": Ibid.
10. "There was fear of mob violence": Palmer, "Oliver & Shumway."
11. "It was the most brutal murder": Ibid.
12. "Give him all the time he wants, Judge": *Greenville (TX) Morning Herald*, April 13, 1935.
13. "An innocent man gets 99 years": Associated Press, *Dallas Morning News*, April 14, 1935, 9.

Tracks Blown Over

1. "They were off like a shot": W. L. Rusho, *Everett Ruess: "A Vagabond for Beauty," & Wilderness Journals*, 157.
2. "Though not all of my days ": Ibid., 158.
3. "I was sorry, though": Ibid., 160. Philip Fradkin identifies Frances as Frances Schermerhorn in *Everett Ruess: His Short Life, Mysterious Death, and Astonishing Afterlife*.
4. "I am not willing to take anything": Rusho, *Everett Ruess*, 165.
5. "Your stories if polished and published": Ibid., 169.
6. "I have often stayed with the Navajos": Ibid., 170.
7. "his little odd, peculiar ways": Cordelia Dunaway to Stella Ruess, January 28, 1938, Everett Ruess Family Papers.
8. "likeable and intelligent young fellows": Rusho, *Everett Ruess*, 171.
9. "Before me the desert drops sheer away": Ibid., 173.
10. "The perfection of this place": Ibid., 176.

Into the Dream

1. "These days away from the city": Rusho, *Everett Ruess*, 53.
2. "I must pack my short life full": Ibid., 57.
3. "I'll never stop wandering": Ibid., 92.
4. "I think I have seen too much": Ibid., 314.

Skeleton Mesa

1. "WANTED: 10 EXPLORERS": Melinda Elliott, *Great Excavations*, 193.
2. "We had great fun up there": Rusho, *Everett Ruess*, 183.
3. "We were all thrown together": James A. Russell and Russell White, "Report on Field Work with the Rainbow Bridge–Monument Valley Expedition of 1934," 12.
4. "One mystery lies in the fact": Rusho, *Everett Ruess*, 182.
5. "a grizzled young chap": Ibid.
6. "I had an excellent chance": Clay Lockett to Christopher Ruess, February 15, 1939.
7. "up almost sheer sandstone cliffs": Rusho, *Everett Ruess*, 187.
8. "a very precarious way down the face": Gary J. Bergera, *On Desert Trails with Everett Ruess*, 48.
9. "I have seen more wild country": Ibid.
10. "I personally was scared to death": Lockett to C. Ruess, February 15, 1939.
11. "The last night's work": Bergera, *On Desert Trails*, 48.

The Cave

My primary source is fieldnotes, "Skeleton Mesa," 2009.

1. "Without daring, without extreme daring": Eugene Delacroix, *The Journal of Eugene Delacroix*, 1:370.

262 Notes to pages 190–207

LOST MESAS, BLUE MOUNTAINS

1. "sandstone block had fallen and crushed": Rusho, *Everett Ruess*, 184.
2. "I rode up from the desert floor": Ibid.
3. "I'll take you with me": Ferrell Secakuku, "The Snake Story," 53.
4. "swirling water and a strong, whirling wind": Ibid.
5. "My Hopi friends": Rusho, *Everett Ruess*, 186.
6. "In my wanderings this year": Ibid., 188.
7. "Nothing anywhere can rival": Ibid., 76.
8. "I stopped several days at the Grand Canyon": Ibid., 103.
9. "wandering Navajos": Ibid., 195.
10. "They came to town": Interview with Arnold Alvey, September 25, 2009.
11. "a pantheistic hedonist": Rusho, *Everett Ruess*, 196.
12. "He intended to visit": Maurice Cope to C. Ruess, March 21, 1935.
13. "If I had stayed any longer": Rusho, *Everett Ruess*, 195.
14. "what seems like the rim of the world": Ibid., 196.
15. "A large portion of this area": A. H. Thompson, *Exploration of the Colorado River of the West and Its Tributaries*, 137–38.
16. "Billions of them": Interview with Jerry Roundy, September 22, 2009.
17. "As to when I shall visit civilization": Rusho, *Everett Ruess*, 195.
18. "I was standing out there": Interview with Alvey.

UNKNOWN. RETURN TO SENDER

1. "Mr Everett Ruess, Escalante Rim": Stella Ruess to Everett Ruess, December 22, 1934.
2. "Unknown. Return to sender": Ibid., returned on February 2, 1935.
3. "He had been lost for days repeatedly": Mr. and Mrs. Ruess to Mr. Carter, March 18, 1935.
4. "We are worried but not stampeded": C. Ruess to Neal Johnson, February 23, 1935.
5. "We will search for him": Steve Lacy, "Footprints from the Past."

THE GULCH

1. "The only way that he could cross": Allen Pollock to C. Ruess, March 1, 1935.
2. "The painter's mother": *Salt Lake Telegram*, March 1, 1935.
3. "He is afraid Ruess choked to death": *Deseret News*, March 4, 1935.
4. "The rugged mountain ranges of Utah": *Salt Lake Tribune*, March 9, 1935.
5. "Mar. 6, Walter Allen 1935": Thybony, fieldnotes, "Escalante Canyons," September 21–25, 2009.
6. "The footprints, the searchers said": *Salt Lake Tribune*, March 17, 1935.
7. "Indian drawings": W. L. Rusho, ed., *The Mystery of Everett Ruess*, 215.
8. "Ruess is an experienced desert man": *Salt Lake Telegram*, March 9, 1935.

9. "They rather despair of finding him": C. Ruess to Matt Weinstock, March 20, 1935.
10. "He can't be anywhere on this side": Rusho, *Mystery of Ruess*, 217.

THE SEARCH

1. "being wise in the ways of the grim desert": *Salt Lake Telegram*, May 30, 1935.
2. "good neighbors following the wilderness code": C. Ruess to Ray Carr, October 15, 1935.
3. "The people of Escalante": *Salt Lake Tribune*, May 30, 1935.
4. "weather-beaten desert riders": Associated Press, *Arizona Republican*, May 27, 1935.
5. "One not familiar with the territory": *Salt Lake Tribune*, June 2, 1935.
6. "E Reus Hunters, June 6, 1935": Steve Allen, *Utah's Canyon Country Place Names*, 255.
7. "in the Indian canoe at Hole in Rock": C. Ruess to Carr, June 5, 1935.
8. "immediately southeast of the Davis Gulch": Carr to Mr. and Mrs. Ruess, June 14, 1935.

FORBIDDING CANYON

My primary sources for the Navajo Mountain and Forbidding Canyon trips are fieldnotes, "Navajo Mountain," December 17–18, 1996, and "Across the River," April 21 and May 19, 1998. The best coverage of the trial of John Chief and Jack Crank appeared in the *San Juan Record* from Monticello, Utah. See the March 5, May 21, May 28, June 4, August 6, and August 13, 1942, issues.

1. *San Juan Record*, June 4, 1942.
2. "We are convinced that these men": E. R. Fryer to C. Ruess, January 30, 1942.

AMONG THE GHOSTS

1. "The orders from the Tribune": Johnson to C. Ruess, August 12, 1935.
2. "The road, only two ruts wandering": *Salt Lake Tribune*, August 26, 1935.
3. "Why have you waited so long": Ibid.
4. "Go to the forks": *Salt Lake Tribune*, August 27, 1935.
5. "People here Including The Indians": Johnson to Mr. and Mrs. Ruess, August 16, 1935.
6. "No cross": *Salt Lake Tribune*, August 27, 1935.
7. "There are many places": *Salt Lake Tribune*, August 28, 1935.
8. "Everett Ruess was murdered": Ibid.
9. "No one in that part of the country": *Deseret News*, September 5, 1935.
10. "I just like the hills": *Salt Lake Telegram*, October 4, 1935.
11. "veteran desert man of Wolf Hole": *Salt Lake Tribune*, September 30, 1935.
12. "For mile after mile it looms": Ibid.

THE INSCRIPTION

My primary source for this section is fieldnotes, "Escalante Canyons," September 21–25, 2009.

A CRACK IN THE RIM

My primary sources for this section are fieldnotes, "Nemo Cave," September 3–7, 2010; and "Where No One Lives," November 11–14, 2010.

1. "a gentleman from California": Thybony, backnotes, "The Missing Bones," March 5 and April 9, 1991.

EPILOGUE

1. "Mr. Thraupp of the Museium": L. Palmer to Mr. and Mrs. Ruess, March 9, 1935.
2. "This is the kind of war": *Tucson (AZ) Daily Citizen*, February 4, 1948.
3. "Chronicler of the West": *New York Times*, May 4, 1994.
4. "Now it is all roaded up": "Dan L. Thrapp, June 26, 1913–April 29, 1994, Letters & Writings, 1922–1949," Thrapp Collection.
5. "She doted on him completely": Thybony, fieldnotes, "North Texas by West," May 17–22, 2009.
6. "I feel fine": *Lubbock (TX) Avalanche-Journal*, January 19, 1969.
7. "Now they can't hang me": Ibid.
8. "Edson Alvey, In Search of Nemo": "Lake Powell Diary," October 24–31, 1966, Tad Nichols Collection.
9. "They didn't know what happened": Interview with Ken Sleight, March 19, 2009.
10. "That's happened three times": Interview with Ken Phillips, July 8, 2008.

Selected
Bibliography

Archives and Personal Papers

Arizona Historical Society, Library and Archives Division. Tucson.

Black, Paul. "Paul Black's Story (in His Own Hand Writing) of Sheriff Oliver & Norris Shumway Murder." January 24, 1974.

Espinosa, Gilberto. "Parole Report by United States Attorney." October 20, 1931. Prison records of James C. Palmer, United States Penitentiary, Leavenworth, KS.

Nichols, Tad. Tad Nichols Collection, 1931–2000. NAU.MS.332, Northern Arizona University Cline Library, Special Collections. Flagstaff.

Oliver, William. "The Life Story of William Edward Oliver, 1858–1935." Fern O. Shumway with Alvera O. Norman, 1980.

Palmer, Lawrence. "William Oliver & Norris Shumway." Audiotape 7-23-01:339, n.d. San Juan County Historical Commission, Edge of the Cedars State Park Museum, Blanding, UT.

Ruess, Everett. Family Papers. MS 0687. University of Utah Marriott Library, Special Collections. Salt Lake City.

Russell, James A., and Russell White. "Report on Field Work with the Rainbow Bridge–Monument Valley Expedition of 1934." Cline Library, Northern Arizona University, Flagstaff.

Shumway, Helen. Personal papers. Provo, UT.

Singleton, D. E., to E. G. Zerbst. November 27, 1933. Prison records of James C. Palmer, United States Penitentiary, Leavenworth, KS.

Texas Court of Criminal Appeals and Hopkins County District Court. Records. Austin and Sulphur Springs.

Thrapp, Dan. Collection. Haley Memorial Library and History Center. "Dan L. Thrapp, June 26, 1913–April 29, 1994, Letters & Writings, 1922–1949." Midland, TX.

Thybony, Scott. Personal papers, fieldnotes, and back notes. Flagstaff, AZ.

Topping, Gary. Papers. 1824–2004. Mss B 1028. Utah State Historical Society, Salt Lake City.

Utah State Archives. "Governor Blood, Series 20793, Extradition Case Files, James E. Palmer & Johnnie Rae Palmer." Salt Lake City.

Utah State Historical Society, Utah State History Research Library and Collections. "Depositions Regarding the Oliver-Shumway Murders in San Juan Country, Utah in 1934, 1935." MS A6057. Salt Lake City.

ORAL HISTORIES

Hunt, Ray. "The Murder of Norris Shumway and Bill Oliver." Utah State Historical Society and California State University, Fullerton, Oral History Program. Interviewed by Mary Risher and Bill Mapp, July 16, 1971.

Nielson, DeReese. "Cattle Industry in Southeastern Utah Project." Utah State Historical Society and California State University, Fullerton, Oral History Program. Interviewed by Mary Risher and Bill Mapp, July 17, 1971.

Rogers, John. Duke Indian Oral History Project, University of Utah, 1923.

OTHER SOURCES

Allen, Steve. *Utah's Canyon Country Place Names.* Durango, CO: Canyon Country Press, 2012.

Behrendt, Michael. *Horsethief Ranch: An Oral History.* Self-published, 1985.

Bergera, Gary J. *On Desert Trails with Everett Ruess.* Commemorative ed. Salt Lake City: Gibbs-Smith, 2000.

Bird, Roland T. *Bones for Barnum Brown: Adventures of a Dinosaur Hunter.* Fort Worth: Texas Christian University Press, 1985.

Brown, Barnum. "Flying for Dinosaurs." *Natural History* 36, no. 2 (1935): 95–123.

———. "Sinclair Dinosaur Expedition, 1934." *Natural History* 36, no. 1 (1935): 3–15.

Delacroix, Eugene. *The Journal of Eugene Delacroix.* 4th ed. New York: Phaidon Press, 2001.

Elliott, Melinda. *Great Excavations.* Santa Fe, NM: School of American Research Press, 2004.

Fradkin, Philip. *Everett Ruess: His Short Life, Mysterious Death, and Astonishing Afterlife.* Berkeley: University of California Press, 2011.

Hall, Edward T. *West of the Thirties: Discoveries among the Navajo and Hopi.* New York: Doubleday, 1995.

Kluckhohn, Clyde. *Beyond the Rainbow.* Boston: Christopher, 1933.

Lacy, Steve. "Footprints from the Past." *Utah Peace Officer* (Spring 1992).

Miser, Hugh D. *The San Juan Canyon of Southeastern Utah.* Water-Supply Paper 538, United States Geological Survey. Washington, DC: Government Printing Office, 1924.

Reneau, W. C. "Murdering Casanova of the Cattle Country." Pts. 1–3. *Master Detective,* October, November, and December 1936.

Roberts, David. *Finding Everett Ruess.* New York: Broadway Books, 2011.

———. "The Mystery of Everett Ruess Solved." *National Geographic Adventure*, April–May 2009.

Rusho, W. L., ed. *Everett Ruess: A Vagabond for Beauty & Wilderness Journals.* Salt Lake City: Gibbs-Smith, 2002.

———, ed. *The Mystery of Everett Ruess.* Salt Lake City: Gibbs-Smith, 2010.

Secakuku, Ferrell. "The Snake Story." *Plateau* 2, no. 2 (2005–6).

Stegner, Wallace. *Mormon Country.* New York: Bonanza Books, 1942.

Steinbeck, John. *Grapes of Wrath.* 1939. Reprint, New York: Penguin Books, 2006.

Stratton, W. K. *Chasing the Rodeo: On Wild Rides and Big Dreams, Broken Hearts and Broken Bones, and One Man's Search for the West.* New York: Harcourt, 2005.

Thayne, Stanley J. "The Home of Truth: The Metaphysical World of Marie Ogden." Master's thesis, Brigham Young University, 2009.

Thompson, A. H. *Exploration of the Colorado River of the West and Its Tributaries.* Washington, DC: Government Printing Office, 1875.

Young, Robert W., and William Morgan. *The Navajo Language: A Grammar and Colloquial Dictionary.* Rev. ed. Albuquerque: University of New Mexico Press, 1994.

INDEX